SEX, DRUGS, AND FASHION IN 1970s MADRID

FRANCISCO FERNÁNDEZ DE ALBA

Sex, Drugs, and Fashion in 1970s Madrid

UNIVERSITY OF TORONTO PRESS
Toronto Buffalo London

Toronto Buffalo London
utorontopress.com

ISBN 978-1-4875-0148-8 (cloth)
ISBN 978-1-4875-1332-0 (PDF)
ISBN 978-1-4875-1333-7 (EPUB)

Toronto Iberic

Library and Archives Canada Cataloguing in Publication

Title: Sex, drugs, and fashion in 1970s Madrid / Francisco Fernández de Alba.
Names: Fernández de Alba, Francisco, 1969– author.
Description: Series statement: Toronto Iberic series; 50 | Includes bibliographical references and index.
Identifiers: Canadiana (print) 20190213752 | Canadiana (ebook) 20190213787 | ISBN 9781487501488 (hardcover) | ISBN 9781487513320 (PDF) | ISBN 9781487513337 (EPUB)
Subjects: LCSH: Madrid (Spain) – History – 20th century. | LCSH: Madrid (Spain) – Social life and customs – 20th century. | LCSH: Sex – Spain – Madrid – History – 20th century. | LCSH: Sex – Social aspects – Spain – Madrid – 20th century. | LCSH: Drug abuse – Spain – Madrid – History – 20th century. | LCSH: Drug abuse – Social aspects – Spain – Madrid – 20th century. | LCSH: Fashion – Spain – Madrid – History – 20th century. | LCSH: Fashion – Social aspects – Spain – Madrid – 20th century.
Classification: LCC DP362 .F47 2019 | DDC 946/.410827–dc23

This book has been published with the support of Wheaton College.

University of Toronto Press acknowledges the financial assistance to its publishing program of the Canada Council for the Arts and the Ontario Arts Council, an agency of the Government of Ontario.

Canada Council for the Arts
Conseil des Arts du Canada

Funded by the Government of Canada
Financé par le gouvernement du Canada

A mis padres, por creer a largo plazo

Contents

List of Illustrations ix

Acknowledgments xi

Introduction. 1970s Madrid: The Dawn of a New Sensibility 3

1 Madrid: Planning the Democratic City 17

2 Sex: Building Plural Communities 42

3 Drugs: The Burden of Modernity 69

4 Fashion: Democracy Prêt-à-Porter 91

Conclusion. Legacies of the 1970s: The Origins of *la Movida* 116

Notes 123

Works Cited 145

Index 163

Illustrations

1.1 Entrevías Neighbourhood Resettlement Unit, 1969 20
1.2 Flooding in Vallecas Neighbourhood Resettlement Unit, 1971 33
2.1 Gay Pride Day demonstration 62
3.1 "Teresa y Carmen," 1978 79
4.1 Massiel at Eurovision, 1968 96
4.2 *Baja costura*, 1981 114

Acknowledgments

Books are the product of uncountable small moments over the lives of their authors. Only in retrospect might we realize how important these moments were for making them possible. I am grateful to the many people who unwittingly helped me write this book. I was lucky to encounter Antonio Abad, a primary school teacher who recognized my dyslexia, and Ángel Crespo, my teacher in high school who, when lecturing on Mary Shelley's *Frankenstein*, showed me what it means to *really* read a novel. In higher education, I was fortunate to have a supportive group of scholars who taught me how to be in the profession: most notably I want to thank Gail Bulman, Debra Castillo, John Kronik, Joan Ramon Resina, and Alicia Vadillo, who contributed to my education in Syracuse and Cornell. Many friends and colleagues, too numerous to be named, were also important to my intellectual growth. Pedro Pérez del Solar's vast knowledge of *la Movida* helped me reframe my ideas about the period. Montse Pérez-Toribio and Rosi Song deserve special mention for encouraging me to develop the project that became this book. Bob Davidson's stimulating friendship combines high and low, and continues to be a source of creative and critical inspiration. My colleagues in the Hispanic Studies department at Brown provided a vital intellectual home for me. The Kitchen Underground – I could not make it without you – has kept me laughing and well fed over the past decade. Sharing mountains and cold *Mahou* with old friends in Madrid kept this academic expat grounded. *Gracias colegas* for always keeping it real.

Institutions, too, play a role in making books. Many thanks to the Provost Office at Wheaton College (MA) for making this book possible. I would like to thank the library staff at Wheaton and Brown University for their help in the researching of this book. Thanks also to Farleigh Dickinson University Press for allowing us to reproduce sections of chapter 3. Thanks to Covadonga García for searching the archives of the Biblioteca Nacional in Madrid on my behalf. And finally, my deepest thanks go to the anonymous reviewers of this book. They selflessly contribute, together with countless colleagues all over the world, to make scholarship better. Any mistakes, omissions, or erroneous conclusions are my own.

My family has also been instrumental in the creation of this book. In memoriam of José Luis Córdoba and Domingo Córdoba for teaching me what creativity is all about, and to Immaculada Córdoba and Isidro Moreno for opening, always with a witty wisecrack, the doors and windows to the joys of education and of life. The unconditional support of my parents, Ángeles Dolores Córdoba and Paco Fernández de Alba, their patience, and their long-term view resulted in my unpredictably ending up with a PhD. Their endless intellectual curiosity and their thirst for knowledge are an everyday reminder of the power of self-education. I can only hope that I become to my children the ethical model that my parents have been for me. María, Jose, and Marga, my incomparable siblings, make me proud every day, as they exemplify what it means to be dedicated to public service. Once I moved to the United States, Kate Coffey and her extended family took me in as one of their own, putting up with my culture shock and bad accent. Boundlessly intelligent, generous, and compassionate, Kate helped me become a better person, and I am eternally grateful to her.

My children, Kiko and Elías, show me every day the wonderment of growing up as creative and caring boys. Finally, Alizah Holstein, the Jedi of words and images, the anchor of my life, you are my inspiration to become more generous, creative, and awoken to the small beautiful things of the world. Ali, Kiko, and Elías, thank you for the gift of happiness.

SEX, DRUGS, AND FASHION IN 1970s MADRID

Introduction

1970s Madrid: The Dawn of a New Sensibility

When we think of General Francisco Franco's final decade in power, a panoply of images comes to mind: the aging dictator waving from a palace window, demonstrators being beaten by police, and the wrecked car of Prime Minister Admiral Carrero Blanco, who in 1973 was assassinated by ETA. At the same time, we recall black-and-white images of bikinied women on beaches, the sensationalist antics of the famous bullfighter *el Cordobés*, and families proudly posing by their new SEAT 600. Images such as these were ferried into Spanish homes via television sets, those markers of middle-class life that many Spanish families began to acquire during the sixties.[1] Television programs in this period reveal that deep cultural changes were already afoot. They uncover a society that, although still under the firm command of dictatorship, was already taking decisive steps, socially and culturally, toward becoming a modern democracy.

Tele-Club Campo-Pop was a 1970 Televisión Española (TVE) program that illustrates the dissonance between official ideology and a changing cultural reality. This show hosted a music contest for bands originating in towns with fewer than 10,000 inhabitants.[2] Small-town co-ed youngsters sporting long hair and miniskirts were filmed rocking the latest hits of international sensations such as Led Zeppelin and the Animals. Sponsored by the Ministerio de Información y Turismo (the Ministry of Information and Tourism), *Campo-Pop* tried to project a message of modernity and modernization, albeit in a rural Spain still languishing under military dictatorship.[3] In essence, the program was part of Minister Manuel Fraga's gamble on using popular culture and superficial liberalization to re-energize a regime whose claims to power were rapidly eroding. The image of Spain presented in this program, as a modern country free enough to embrace rock music and mini-skirts, was intended to win over a restless emerging middle class that was increasingly choosing Western culture over "national" products and values. *Campo-Pop* reveals the contradictions of Spanish society in the seventies and the tension between popular and official cultures, and illustrates the remarkable speed at which youth culture in Spain adopted foreign trends and fashions.

Another remarkable TVE program was the experimental *Último grito* (*Latest Trend*), produced between 1968 and 1970.[4] Around midnight, the public had a chance to get the latest musical news and listen to international hits while watching video clips that had been made in-house. This show offered the opportunity for viewers to learn about pop art and subcultures (such as hippie and surf communities) in extended feature segments. "Vivimos en la era del comic" ("We live in the age of the comic"), host Judy Stephen said in one program. With disarming candidness, she continued that anybody paying attention would realize that comic books had invaded the city and that people were reading them everywhere. Before fanzines and comics became countercultural mainstays in Barcelona and Madrid, this television program had already declared that graphic narratives defined the historical epoch and urban space.[5] *Último grito* went beyond introducing the latest international trends to the furthest reaches of the Spanish state. By explaining current international countercultural practices and their underground do-it-yourself models, it motivated young Spaniards to be content creators and not just passive consumers. These television offerings evidence how a group of professionals and artists, and a younger public in general, were carving out spaces of free expression and exhibiting a new sensibility toward culture totally alien to that of the Franco regime.

I begin this book with a discussion of Spanish television programs because, despite the critical and commercial interest in everything related to the Spanish transition to democracy, there has been, to date, limited attention to the multi-faceted cultural processes of the Long Transition.[6] To address this lack, this book explores urban planning, narratives of sexual and gender identity, recreational drug use, and fashion design during the seventies. I argue that, during this decade, the material and emotional conditions for the groundbreaking changes of the Transition first began to develop, and that they can be seen in each of these areas.[7] While these themes are not by any means an exhaustive representation of culture in Madrid or Spain in the 1970s, they are fundamental facets of modernity and mass culture that merit deeper examination. The topics this book explores featured prominently in the mass media, which discussed them in a worldwide context as soon as they became internationally conspicuous. Many journalistic reports on

Western underground or changing cultural practices that I will analyse in this book subtly criticized the regime by comparing it with other societies. Mass media stories and images of developed countries laid out possible models for a renewed Spanish society and culture. These images of life abroad that came to inundate the public sphere allowed citizens to imagine an alternative to the ideology pushed by the regime. The early presence of countercultural or underground topics in mainstream media such as *Cuadernos para el Diálogo* (*Notebooks for Dialogue*) or *Triunfo* (*Triumph*), either by way of articles or book reviews, paved the way both for the emergence of alternative lifestyles in Spain and for tolerance of them by the larger population that began to share a common, transnational understanding of what these new cultural trends meant.

The history of the moment goes something like this. During the final two decades of Franco's dictatorship, the government, in an effort to avoid bankruptcy, ensure social order, and preserve the regime, took steps to modernize Spain's economy and infrastructure. Plans were made for an eventual transfer of power, and Juan Carlos I was selected and then groomed to be Franco's successor. The repressive authoritarian regime that governed Spain was unable to fully control its citizens and culture, thus creating a society that in Franco-era minister Rodolfo Martín Villa's appreciation, "se había organizado un poco a su aire, al margen de la situación" ("had organized itself partly on its own criteria, apart from the situation") (41–2). Especially after the easing of censorship laws in 1966, citizens were less isolated from Western culture and politics than one might imagine. Left-leaning books circulated widely, and the citizenry, as I will show, was in touch via mass media with global cultural and political trends. Efforts by the Franco regime to create a dominant official culture had failed, and by the sixties the government found itself unable to curtail or fully control a cultural sector that, despite censorship and fines, operated independently of official lines (Fusi 135). Dissenting journals such as *Cuadernos para el Diálogo* and *Triunfo*, and books on progressive politics were permitted to circulate, as long as they did not challenge the legitimacy of the regime. By the seventies, mainstream Spanish culture was decidedly left leaning (Fusi 138). Those who could afford it travelled abroad for tourism or study. In addition, about 1.5 million people, travelled abroad to find work in other European countries between 1960 and 1973, sending back remittances that funded in part a new-found, albeit modest, Spanish prosperity (Balfour 269; Townson 13). The economic opening, in Tatjana Pavlovic's analysis, "was marked by new social and sexual mores and consumer habits of a society of leisure ... The age of prosperity no longer equated economic gain and sexual pleasure with moral loss" (*Mobile*

15). Encouraged by the regime, a tourist infrastructure sprang up, and foreign vacationers flocked to Spanish seashores. Widely celebrated by mass media, tourism became a mainstay of the Spanish GDP, which created, albeit unintentionally, a collective sense of cultural opening.[8]

Upon Franco's death in 1975, the political transition toward democracy commenced in full. The economy, after decades of autarky, partial implementation of development plans, and tax reforms that favoured the rich, was suffering substantially from the seventies' oil crisis. The apparent success of the regime, attributable to the international economic boom of the sixties, crumbled at the first global recession (Carr and Fusi 59).[9] As democratic institutions and a constitution took form, citizens experienced the myriad economic, social, and political uncertainties of the Transition. In this environment, Spanish youth wholeheartedly adopted and adapted international subcultural forms of visual culture, music, and letters.

Reassessing the Long Transition

Given its social and cultural complexity, the Spanish transition to democracy is one of the most fascinating political phenomena in Western Europe during the second half of the twentieth century. In analysing this process, the focus of scholars has justifiably been on the political, economic, and social consequences of the regime change following Franco's death.[10] This has meant that scholars have often overlooked the final decade of the dictatorship and the popular culture that emerged during that time. Yet it was during the late sixties and early seventies that Franco's regime, after being forced to abandon autarky and to implement neoliberal economic development policies known as *el desarrollismo*, witnessed general economic improvement.[11] The principal outcomes of these policies were an expanding economy, a growing middle class, and a generalized, though modest, new-found sense of affluence.[12] With respect to such changes, Pavlovic notes, "Owning a car, possessing a television set and going on vacation do truly point to profoundly changed modes of transportation, communication, organization of leisure-time, gender relations and so on" (*Mobile* 15). Spanish popular culture was decisively merging with international trends, despite the regime's authoritarian and repressive policies and its wholly traditional Catholic outlook. The results were groundbreaking, as Pavlovic suggests, not only because they affected people's lifestyles but also because they fundamentally changed the collective perception of self and one's relation to the world. In other words, these changes made people aware of the agency they had over their own lives, and their power to contradict, even if in limited ways, the regime's expected behaviours.

During the seventies, Madrid would emerge as one of two countercultural hubs in Spain. In this it overlapped with pioneer Barcelona, a beacon of modernity for the better part of the twentieth century. As *Campo-Pop* made clear, the cultural changes of the seventies were not uniquely urban but rather, thanks to mass media, extended throughout the Spanish state via networks of mutual influence and collective experience. It would be a fiction to maintain that, in a context in which television ownership multiplied exponentially with every passing year, rural areas and mid-sized cities somehow persisted in a state of cultural isolation.[13] While the mutual influence and dialectical tension between the capital and other cities and towns are undeniable, the cultural processes that unfolded during the seventies would be most noticeable in cities like Madrid. The gravitational weight of the largest city in the peninsula, its media conglomeration, the debates about and solutions offered for its poor urban conditions, and the successful emergence of urban social movements and underground culture make Madrid an interesting and relevant case to study.

The newly emerging mentalities and cultural practices in Spain during the seventies that this book explores have sometimes been dismissed as simple imitations of international trends or, worse, as a byproduct of citizens' abandonment of political mobilization for consumer capitalism. This book presents a supplementary narrative of this period, arguing that Madrid's citizens were moving, even before the actual political transition, toward new subjectivities and experiences by conceiving frames of perception that diverged from those imposed by Franco's regime. Residents of Madrid embodied and practised modernity in their everyday lives. They did this, among other ways, by creating associations, occupying public spaces, consuming drugs, and altering the way they dressed – practices that Germán Labrador Méndez has termed "vida expandida" ("expanded life") (*Culpables* 60).

This book's chronological frame runs roughly from the late sixties to the early eighties. This time period is bracketed, at one end, by the 1966 *Ley de prensa* (Press Law), which significantly altered the censorship laws and facilitated the editorial discussion of topics and the release of titles that were previously forbidden, and, at the other end, by the 1982 electoral victory of the Spanish Socialist Party (Partido Socialista Obrero Español, PSOE). Yet the core focus of this book is on the seventies, a decade that has often been overlooked. When examined, the period from 1966 to 1982 yields rich insights about the ways in which Spanish citizens in general, and residents of Madrid in particular, developed cultural mentalities and behaviours distinct from those of the regime well before the dictator's death.[14] This book bridges and complements the recent work of Justin Crumbaugh, Germán Labrador Méndez, Tatjana Pavlovic, and Hamilton Stapell, among others, to map the ways in which a new popular sensibility emerged, in part invigorated by underground and alternative cultural practices, and became central to Madrid's identity.

This changing collective sensibility was undoubtedly shaped by mass media's broadcasting of international underground culture and other mass culture trends. Drawing upon Benjamin Fraser's concept of urban cultural studies, this book illustrates the dynamic tension between "material conditions and cultural imaginaries" in 1970s Madrid (Fraser, *Towards* 20). Mass media played a significant role in presenting opportunities for audiences, readers, and spectators to imagine alternative ways to live and, therefore, to call into question their material conditions. Whether testing acceptable behaviours in public spaces or inspiring new private practices, magazines such as *Cuadernos para el Diálogo* or *Triunfo,* as well as countless books, television programs, and movies, provided examples of a widened menu of alternative moral, political, or cultural ways of life.[15] There is no question that the sudden availability of texts previously forbidden or unavailable fed the rebellious identities that many youth felt or yearned for (Labrador Méndez, *Culpables* 189).

The shift in publication standards had an impact on the wider population as well. These magazines, and mass media more generally, offered a symbolic space for cultural and political resistance to the regime, and became references for university students, intellectuals, and the liberal professions (e.g., doctors, lawyers, architects), as well as for public administrators and the growing middle class (Muñoz Soro 22, 2007). By creating public spaces of "intellectual sociability" free from the official discourse of the regime, these magazines formalized a public sphere where alternative discourses, trends, and ideas were introduced and brought into the mainstream (Muñoz Soro 21, 2007).

This is not to say that mass media were the only decisive factor in democratization. In this evolving cultural environment that was often under a state of exception, or state of emergency, we cannot forget that citizens created, organized, and participated in experimental collective experiences such as parents' associations, neighbourhood associations, and cooperatives of all kinds. Citizens fashioned an alternative public sphere out of a collective desire for improved political, ethical, and material circumstances. In other words, they formed a civic and popular culture that had personal and collective autonomy, democratization, and creativity as its main principles (Labrador Méndez, *Culpables* 201).

Evolving cultural imaginaries, and subsequent changes in material conditions, explain how the capital city of the dictatorship managed to reinvent itself during the Transition as a site of modernity.

A New Sensibility

This book is concerned with the massive "re-structuring of feeling" during the long seventies. Raymond Williams's well-known term articulated a process-based concept of culture as lived experience embodied in material culture, art, perceptions, and values.[16] In my analysis of the final years of Franco's regime, I follow Williams's consideration of the difference between ideology and experience to capture the changing "sensibility of an era," a concept that Susan Sontag described in 1966 as "not only its [an era's] most decisive, but also its most perishable aspect" ("Notes on Camp" n1). More recently, Jo Labanyi has challenged Spanish cultural studies to see cultural texts as practices that go beyond representing and has encouraged critics to explore the material consequences of the affects they generate.[17]

This book responds to Labanyi's challenge by examining the role of mass media in the emergence of a new sensibility – reflected in the civic ownership of Madrid – and the significant transformations that spheres of public and private life underwent during the seventies. These transformations could be seen in urban planning and architecture; neighbourhood associations and the evolving concept of citizenship; alternative gender and sexual identities and their place in public discourse; recreational drug use and its social implications; and the production, distribution, and social relevance of fashion. Despite the long shadow of authoritarian government in this period, Spanish citizens found ways to build a culture alternative to the regime's ideology. Thanks in part to a particular mix of do-it-yourself attitude and the local appropriation and adaptation of international trends, Madrid in the seventies incubated entirely new cultural practices and affects that would come to transform youth culture, social and political life, and art.

Germán Labrador Méndez has detailed in *Culpables por la literatura* (*Guilty by Literature*) the myriad ways in which alternative popular culture and civic organizations, which began to emerge in the sixties, created a parallel Transition that was countercultural, popular, and civic. These associations, athenaeums, communes, and cooperatives were "collective experiments" that developed at the margins of the state and were separated from market capitalism. According to Labrador Méndez, they would be "incomprensibles sin un largo trabajo de la sensibilidad y de la imaginación operado previamente por la literatura" ("inconceivable without the prior long-term work on sensibility and the imagination put into motion by literature") (60). But I would argue further that these collective experiments also relied for their formation on mainstream mass media, which early on reflected the international reach of the counterculture and its impact on Western societies. Labrador Méndez's focus is on the role of literature in linking politics and life for the generations that came of age in the sixties, seventies, and eighties. For them, literature was the way to imagine and construct alternative lives that were morally, ethically, and politically opposed both to Franco's regime and the new democracy that limited citizens' participation and representation (189). But I would argue that, for many citizens, magazines, movies, and other forms of mass media were the main conveyers of the cultural changes already afoot both in Spain and abroad.

The changes I discuss were not distant mirages or underground secrets. National television brought them directly to people's living rooms. While we may find *Campo-Pop*'s humble rock bands endearing, the main conclusion I extract from the video footage of this contest is that 1970s rural Spain smelled of teen spirit. In other words, Spanish youths were, to the extent that their circumstances allowed, embracing sex, drugs, and rock: a catchphrase that first appeared in a 1969 *Life* magazine article that attempted to define the lifestyle of countercultural American youth.[18] This trifecta soon became an ideal that rebellious youngsters aspired to live up to. This was true even in the most remote parts of Spain, where young co-eds quickly adopted some elements of the international counterculture, especially those, such as fashion, that were easy to implement.

Discussing and analysing seventies' culture from an affective point of view, as this book does, is nothing new. The palpable changes in the collective sensibility were central themes of cultural critics at the time. In 1969, Manuel Vázquez Montalbán published his popular series of essays "Crónica sentimental de España" ("Sentimental Chronicle of Spain," CSE) in *Triunfo*.[19] In this five-part series, Vázquez Montalbán produced a critical understanding of Spanish cultural processes in which popular culture, the market, politics, and international trends figured prominently in explaining the changing perceptions that people had about themselves and their reality. "La sentimentalidad colectiva" Vázquez Montalbán wrote, "se identifica con una serie de signos de exteriorización: las canciones, los mitos personales y anecdóticos, las modas, los gustos y la sabiduría convencional ... Todos estos signos exteriores son cultura popular y están configurados por los medios de ¿in?formación [*sic*] de la cultura de masas" ("Collective sentimentality is identified with a number of exterior signs: songs, personal myths and anecdotes, fashions, tastes, and conventional wisdom ... All these exterior signs are popular culture and are configured by the ¿in?formation mass media") (CSE I: 30). Vázquez Montalbán explained the way that people found meaning and resignified commercial folksongs, deriving mostly from Andalusian culture, to give voice to their emotional circumstances and their dissent.[20] Through Vázquez Montalbán's essays, we can trace the moment in which these popular folksongs begin to lose their primacy, ceding place to a new type of music, Anglo-American rock and pop. This switch in taste, and the role youngsters assumed as (re)producers of mass culture, reflects the political and social transformations underway in Spain and is clearly visible in the TVE *Campo-Pop* contest, in which mass media mediates – or, in Vázquez Montalbán's words, "configures" – a new sensibility.

Vázquez Montalbán was not the only intellectual trying to explain the culture of the moment from an emotional point of view. His work on collective ways of feeling resounded powerfully with Susan Sontag's efforts to define and describe the elusive affect of her time.[21] Indeed, the same year that Vázquez Montalbán was unlocking the affective dimensions of Spanish popular culture in his "Crónica sentimental," Sontag's famous essay collection *Against Interpretation* was published in Spanish translation. Reviewing her book in *Triunfo*, Eduardo Rico praised the author for her freshness, humour, and boldness. Rico argued that her non-interpretative vision was healthily cheeky in a cultural environment built on myths, and he described her "Notes on Camp" as a magisterial essay on this aesthetic phenomenon ("Susan Sontag" 54).[22] Sontag's systematic demolishing of cultural myths and her radical aperture of "a new sensibility," Rico overstated, had the result of dissolving the generalized sclerosis of the Spanish critical apparatus (ibid.). Vázquez Montalbán, Sontag, and Rico index and explain the changing collective sensibility or, in other words, the shifting affects that fuel social and cultural change.

The impact of Sontag's "Notes on Camp" would be extensive and rapid enough for Alfredo Amestoy, the host of the TVE *Campo-Pop* contest, to suggest renaming his program "Campo-Camp." The concept also featured prominently in the introduction of *Nueve novísimos poetas españoles* (*Nine Very New Spanish Poets*) (1970), a work that had a profound impact on the peninsular cultural environment, as it represented a radical aesthetic and political break with the cultural order of the moment.[23] I bring up these details to emphasize how widely the concept of "camp" was circulating at the turn of the decade. To recognize that camp was one of the main cultural notions of the day is to grasp the emergence of new ways of conceptualizing politics, art, and lifestyles in the city.

That the appraisal of Sontag's work in *Triunfo* appeared alongside a review of Henri Lefevbre's *Right to the City* by Alonso de los Ríos is no coincidence. Their publication was the sign of a cultural environment brimming with fundamental changes in the structure of feeling, one that would quickly take root in Madrid. While Sontag's radical approach to hermeneutics supposedly shook the conservative heart of the Spanish cultural establishment, Lefebvre's book contributed greatly to redressing the relationship between the people and their built environment. Madrid, as we will see, would come to embody Lefebvre's ideals expressed perfectly by the following quote: "The right to the city manifests itself as a superior form of rights: right to freedom, to individualization in socialization, to habitat and to inhabit. The right to the oeuvre, to participation and appropriation (clearly distinct from the right to property) are implied in the right to the city" (Lefebvre, *Writings* 173–4). Residents of Madrid got ready in the seventies to reclaim their city from neglectful municipal governments and speculators.

Organization of This Book

The evolution of the civic ownership of Madrid is discussed in Chapter 1, "Madrid: Planning the Democratic City." In that chapter, I examine the public debates on urban planning that simmered during the seventies and that allowed the new city government, dominated by socialists and communists, to enact a sophisticated urban plan when it took power in 1979. Municipal issues were one area in which Franco's regime allowed a modicum of dissent and criticism. Under the guise of quotidian necessity rather than politics, urban planners and neighbourhood associations worked to solve Madrid's major contemporary issues: infrastructure and housing. These issues were contemplated extensively in magazines such as *Cuadernos para el Diálogo* and *Triunfo*, where architects such as Antonio Fernández Alba put forward a view of the city that went beyond modernist urban concepts. Books by Henri Lefebvre, such as *Right to the City* (1968) and *The Urban Revolution* (1970), wielded great influence on the way that the public saw Madrid and its future. The influence was noticeable in *Madrid para la democracia: la propuesta de los comunistas* (*Madrid for Democracy: The Communists' Proposal*) (1977), a book coordinated by Manuel Castells and Ramón Tamames, among others. This volume constituted the Communist Party's comprehensive urban plan for Madrid, and was researched and developed in collaboration with neighbourhood associations. The urban political logic of the moment dictated that, if the city was the reflection of the class structure, to change the city was to change the status quo. Thus, the urban planning debates that took place beginning in the seventies radically changed residents' attitudes toward their city and foreshadowed its new democratic and pluralistic identity. No longer Franco's city, Madrid would become an open cultural public space where citizens had the right to inhabit, to participate, and to create.

Chapter 2, "Sex: Building Plural Communities," explores the conflict that emerged in the seventies between two fundamentally opposed notions of the body that would end up creating a new collective sensibility toward sex and gender. One of those views was pushed by feminism and sexual liberation, while the other, although necessarily dependent on the first, commodified women's bodies and monetized Spaniards' sexual repression. Not unlike other Western countries, Spain saw the emergence of an industry that purposely used the discourse of freedom and liberation to profit from the objectification of women's bodies. Step by step, first with "sexy comedies" and later with *el destape* (the uncovering), Spanish movies would uncover women's bodies, reifying the male gaze in a society that hoped to become modern and liberated from the cultural weight of Franco's regime.

Critics on the right saw these movies as immoral and as a reflection of a corrupt society that was losing its traditional values, while progressive critics saw them not as the product of new freedoms but, rather, as a consequence of capitalism. A 1975 article in *Triunfo* by José Vanaclocha condenses the position of film critics on the left. Analysing the evolution of eroticism and moral values in Spanish films, Vanaclocha determined that "las razones económicas vencieron, una vez más, una moral puritana y trasnochada" ("Pecuniary reasons won out, once more, over worn-out puritan values") (23). Critics recognized the progressive commodification of sex in Spanish films for what it was, and condemned its simplistic profit-making premises. Yet these movies were not made in a vacuum. They were responding both to capitalistic practices and to a broader cultural environment, which explains their evolution toward topics and aesthetics that had previously been taboo in Spanish cinema.

Beginning in the mid-sixties, there were open discussions in the public sphere about feminism, sexuality, and gender. These focused, with varying degrees of success and with differing motivations, on the topics of the women's movement, gay rights, and sexual liberation underway in Western countries. A 1965 special issue of *Cuadernos para el Diálogo*, "La mujer" ("Woman"), was a pioneer publication that reflected the rekindling of Spanish feminism and the publication's concern with women's rights. Later, magazines such as *Triunfo* offered informative and critical reflections of women's role in society, reporting as well on the sexual liberation movement both in Western countries and even in the Soviet Union. Concurrently, movies such as *No desearás al vecino del quinto* (*You Shall Not Covet Your Fifth Floor Neighbour*) (Ramón Fernández, 1970) and *Mi querida señorita* (*My Dear Lady*) (Jaime Armiñán, 1972) offered early representations of homosexuals and transgender characters.

Topics related to sex and gender, regardless of their treatment, saturated the public sphere in 1970s Madrid. Responsible for changes in the perceptions about sex and gender were magazines, which pushed a progressive view on women and LGBT rights, and the media industry, including publishers of books such as Eduardo Mendicutti's novel *Una mala noche la tiene cualquiera* (*Anybody Can Have a Bad Night*) (1982), that cashed in on the public's interest in these topics. Finally, the chapter examines Eduardo Mendicutti's novel *Una mala noche la tiene cualquiera* (*Anybody Can Have a Bad Night*) (1982), and argues that, as a result of the wider cultural changes of this period, changing ideas around sex and gender became fundamental for imagining the possibility of a pluralistic democratic community occupying urban public space.

Chapter 3, "Drugs: The Burden of Modernity," examines the origins of the heroin epidemic that would decimate some boroughs of Madrid during the eighties. The chapter argues that the growth in heroin use resulted from a perfect storm caused by a sense of modest affluence, a contradictory mass-media discourse on drugs, and changes in substance-abuse culture that identified the drug with modernity. Spanish mass media had covered increased use of drugs, and especially heroin, in the United States starting in the sixties by publishing translations of articles and reportage provided by news agencies. The media in Spain would adopt the same tone – alarmist and moralistic, but with some degree of fascination – as the first Spanish heroin-users gained their attention. This set up a pattern of confirmation bias among the general population, which perceived heroin use to be widespread and related to worsening public safety. Pharmaceuticals, legally obtained over the counter in some cases until the mid-eighties, greatly contributed to the drug epidemic, as did the government, which overlooked repeated warnings that specialists had issued as early as 1972. I argue that the abuse of heroin by so many during these years was, rather than an act of escapism, an identity-making act of status-seeking rebellion.

Like heroin, fashion helped the public to tailor an alternative sense of identity. Chapter 4, "Fashion: Democracy Prêt-à-porter," explains the success of Spanish fashion designers in the eighties by examining the evolution of *alta costura* (haute couture), new shopping habits, and clothing as a form of self-expression. *Alta costura* was, from the sixties onward, on the front burner of Spanish mass media and governmental policy. This chapter traces the evolution of the Spanish fashion industry by examining newsreels, articles in *Triunfo,* and early examples of fashion studies in Spain. Supported by Franco's government, *alta costura* was used to promote Spain internationally and to provide the domestic textile industry with clients. Spanish *alta costura* evolved in response to trends set in Paris but never successfully adapted to the new sensibility arising in the mid-sixties, with its emphasis on youth culture and prêt-à-porter. Occupying the gap between *alta costura* and its cheaper, industrially mass-produced copies (*alta confección*) found in department stores, a group of young designers introduced a renewed aesthetic and emotional approach to clothing. Far from the traditional centres of fashion such as Paris or Milan, Madrid's cultural evolution offered the perfect background for clothes embodying the new collective sentiment of openness, freedom, and cosmopolitanism. The designers who emerged in the seventies became the dealers of modernity for a public anxious to abandon the regime's tired palette of army green, fascist blue, and police grey.

In the conclusion, "Legacies of the 1970s: The Origins of *la Movida,*" I offer a modest proposal for the study of *la Movida* that emerges from the ground the preceding chapters cover. The conclusion connects the cultural changes of the seventies with the underground beginnings of what would come to be labelled *la Movida.* The continuities between the the cultural practices developing throughout the seventies and *la Movida* explain how an alternative underground cultural movement came in short time to occupy the cultural epicentre of the city. Underground, clean of any reference or connection to Franco's regime, and seemingly free of any inferiority complex, an active alternative cultural sphere thrived during the seventies in Madrid. In the collective search for fresh, modern culture devoid of any relation to the past – that is, culture that would make people feel different and that would speak to their present and future – mass media, politicians, and citizens at large found something unapologetically modern, cosmopolitan, free, and fun in those who had embraced countercultural practices. Eduardo Haro Ibars explained in his *Triunfo* column "Cultura a la contra" ("Counter Culture") (1979) the radical emancipatory drive of *la nueva ola* (new wave), the term by which *la Movida* was first known: "La nueva ola no tiene una estética definida, ni tampoco – menos – una ética: ambos son valores que pertenecen a una generación y a un estado de cosas anteriores: [*sic*] sus padres, e incluso sus hermanos mayores, han definido lo que es bueno y malo, lo bonito y lo feo. Y ellos no quieren cambiar una definición por otra, sino simplemente abolir las diferencias" (60). ("The new wave has no defined aesthetics, nor – even less – an ethic: both are values that belong to another generation and to a previous state of affairs: their fathers, even their older brothers, have defined what is good or bad, what is beautiful or ugly. And they don't want to substitute one definition for another, but rather, to simply abolish those differences.")

Haro Ibars's definition matches Susan Sontag's thesis 34 of her "Notes on Camp."[24] Sontag's famous essay provides a list of master tropes and practices that *la Movida* would employ. Among others, *la Movida* embraced the appropriation of local and international culture with a total lack of regard for the status of the objects or discourses it redeployed and "a vision of the world in terms of style." Nothing like that had existed either in the official culture of Franco's regime or in the cultural mainstream dominated by the opposition to the regime. The appropriation and mixing of international trends and local culture, one of *la Movida*'s central strategies, would be practised to perfection over the course of the seventies.

The seventies were years of transformation that engendered a democratic understanding of urban space and its relation to the citizen, the public emergence of alternative sexual subjectivities, the evolution of substance-abuse culture, and the importance of fashion design and consumption in identity building. These changes were stimulated decisively by the parallel emergence of a civil society and mass media in search of improved material and ethical lives that would match the democratic aspirations of most Spanish citizens.

A quick note on sources: the corrective interpretation of 1970s Madrid that I attempt to delineate in this book can be formulated thanks to digitalized archives (TVE, *Triunfo*, Filmoteca Nacional), YouTube, and the vast trove of images now available online. Readers are invited to locate visual references in this book, and of course many more, on the Web.

Chapter One

Madrid: Planning the Democratic City

Three short paragraphs into his first speech as mayor of Madrid in 1979, Enrique Tierno Galván decisively weighed in on one of the hottest debates regarding the future of the city. What he focused on in this speech was not finances or safety, as one might expect, but rather, new principles of urbanism that aimed to align the city's built environment with the needs of its residents.[1] Tierno's speech laid out the main elements of the program that his team, then in control of Madrid's municipal government, would carry out over the course of the eighties. He began by finding common ground across the political spectrum to work to benefit the citizens of Madrid through peace, order, and culture as well as to better organize the city (Tierno 6). Taken at face value, this declaration of intentions seems little more than a political cliché, yet, for a city like Madrid that, in that moment, was just beginning to emerge from decades of Francoist repression, speculation, and neglect, Tierno's focus on the citizen experience represented a completely new approach to city governance.

City Hall's commitment to making Madrid livable and putting its residents at the centre of municipal policy represented a radical change from previous municipal administrations. It would also have clear consequences in fostering the Madrid known today as "el Madrid de la Movida," when, during the 1980s, the city gained the reputation, both locally and internationally, as a multicultural hotbed of creativity. But this cultural flowering did not appear *ex nihilo*. Madrid would be shaped throughout the seventies by a paradigm shift in architecture and urban planning, the activism of combative neighbourhood associations, and a municipal election that put the left and its governing program into City Hall. This fun-loving, liberated Madrid emerged both from the intense debates about city planning and architecture taking place in print media during the seventies, and from the activism of new urban social actors such as neighbourhood associations. Thanks to a public sphere that made urbanism a recurrent topic, residents of Madrid were able to start imagining what their city could look like in a democratic state. Also fundamental was the profound change in outlook required to imagine an alternative Madrid, one in which citizens would have a right to inhabit, to appropriate, and to participate creatively in their city. Paraphrasing Kevin Lynch, this shift in outlook made it possible for citizens of Madrid to remake en masse the mental map of their own city.

Benjamin Fraser has argued that the material conditions of urbanization evolve hand-in-hand with the development of an urbanized cultural imaginary (*Towards* 23). In this dialectical process, material conditions and imaginaries evolve in a process of reciprocal influence. Ideas about cities, he concludes, shape city plans, "which physically shape cities, which in turn engender ideas about cities" (ibid.). In 1970s Madrid, this feedback loop was not limited to urban planners and architects. Ideas related to a new Madrid were highly influenced by the civil society developing in Spain. Neighbourhood associations (NAs) and other urban social movements (USMs) such as community radio stations, alternative schools, and cooperatives, as well as many other types of associations, shared a strong anti-authoritarian spirit and dared to dream of and implement alternative ways of living in the city. The radical ideas for 1970s Madrid that I will examine in this book were the consequence of a long-term process that involved the reciprocal influence and stimulus of a wide variety of organizations, institutions, and professionals. Democratic political and cultural practices in the *barrios* (boroughs), for example, alongside innovative ways of theorizing urban spaces and cities, transformed Madrid's material conditions and nudged the city toward a new imaginary.

Seeking broader support, Tierno needed to soothe the fears of Madrid's conservative sectors by pushing a pragmatic municipal program committed to construction instead of destruction (6).[2] But here, Tierno was using double-speak. On the one hand, he was clearly addressing those who feared the radical municipal policies that might emerge from the coalition between the Partido Socialista Obrero Español (PSOE, the Spanish Socialist Workers Party) and the Partido Comunista de España (PCE, the Spanish Communist Party). On the other hand, he was referring to Madrid's built environment and siding with the voices that had been denouncing the destruction of the city's architectural heritage. To be specific, the demolition of significant structures like the Pelota Court in Recoletos in 1973, the Olavide market in 1974, and the Gesa gas station in 1976 had generated a great deal of complaint.[3] Architects such as Antonio Fernández Alba and Leopoldo Uría, and journalists Victor Márquez Reviriego and Santiago Amón, among others, lamented in articles from 1974 onward that Madrid's municipal government had no interest in protecting the city's architectural heritage and had abandoned it to speculators who had no qualms about destroying historical structures to make space for lucrative residential or commercial buildings.[4]

Another issue that Tierno needed to address was the ghost of the Spanish Civil War and its consequences. He did so by talking about the way in which social conflict and class differences are expressed in urban space (6–7). Decades of mixed modernist, Falange, and neoliberal policies had enticed the working class to Madrid, only to then push them to the city outskirts to be segregated and better controlled.[5] Migrants attracted to Madrid for its economic activity had settled in peripheral areas where speculation and shoddy construction deals had created boroughs without infrastructure, schools, or municipal services. In the Madrid of the seventies, fragmented residential areas surrounded the urban core. In most cases, these formerly rural areas were developed ad hoc. They were often noncontiguous, separated from one another by agricultural land, shantytowns, or vacant lots. They had no parks, playgrounds, schools, hospitals, sports facilities, or cultural services. Their streets were unpaved, and public transportation options were limited or non-existent. The language Tierno used to evoke the architectural consequences of the Civil War and the dictatorship was soon replaced by his stated hope for an inclusive city that could respect its past while working toward a fair and equitable future through the thoughtful organization of public space and the civic functions that would take place in it (7).[6]

The "Right to the City" Enters the Public Sphere

It is not surprising that Tierno, a professor with doctorates in law and philosophy, would be concerned with the preservation of the city's architectural heritage. Neither should it be surprising that, given his socialist ideology, he was concerned about class struggle and the living conditions of the working class. However, the specific language that he used emerged directly out of the debate about architecture and urbanism that had simmered in Spanish journals and magazines throughout the seventies. Tierno was clearly influenced in his language and positions on the urban environment by authors such as Henri Lefebvre, whose *Right to the City* (1968) and *The Urban Revolution* (1970) were popular books at the time.[7] Although I cannot confirm that Tierno read

1.1 Poblado de absorción de Entrevías (Entrevías Neighbourhood Resettlement Unit), 1969. Hastily and cheaply built resettlement units offered housing to immigrants to halt the growth of shantytowns in the south of Madrid.

these books, I am certain that he knew of the French author and his work through contemporary intellectual and political discourse.[8]

I have no doubt that Tierno had knowledge of *Madrid para la democracia: la propuesta de los comunistas* (*Madrid for Democracy: The Communists' Proposal*) (1977), the book the Communist Party published ahead of the 1979 municipal elections.[9] Co-authored by Manuel Castells and Ramón Tamames, with Eduardo Leira, Ignacio Quintana, Emilio Ramón, Julian Rebollo, and many others, this book was the Communist Party's comprehensive urban plan for Madrid.[10] A Marxist analysis of the city, it hinted at how the built environment reflected labour relations and the state of capitalism. But this was not a dogmatic document. It was, rather, a comprehensive analysis and blueprint for the development of the city and its democratic institutions, drawn from the latest knowledge and theories about the city, and written by pedigreed intellectuals such as Castells and Tamames. It did not use theoretical language or hypothetical proposals because it was grounded in the work and demands of neighbourhood associations, which had been struggling since the mid-sixties to improve living conditions in Madrid.[11] Many of their petitions would eventually be implemented, transforming Madrid into the modern city it aspired to be.

This programmatic book, as we will see later in this chapter, was an outgrowth of public and intellectual interest in city issues, urbanism, and architecture that took root in the seventies. Debates among city planners, lawyers, economists, sociologists, engineers, and architects spilled from the professional journals into political and cultural journals like *Cuadernos para el Diálogo*, *Triunfo*, and even women's fashion magazines such as *Telva*.[12] Most articles reflected on four main issues: the role of architecture in contemporary society (ethics); architecture and building construction (technique); urban problems and their solutions (theory); and the relationships between art, architecture, and industrial design (aesthetics). Unsurprisingly, the debates expressed significant concerns about the education of architects, perhaps because, during the seventies and eighties, Madrid's School of Architecture was locked in an ongoing struggle to change its authoritarian administrative structures, antiquated curriculum, and hierarchical academic culture.[13] These recurring themes were not only about pedagogical technicalities or aesthetic positions; they were also about the role of the architect and urban planner in democratic Spain. Those advocating a new role for the architect in society sought to reposition these professionals as an important voice in the general culture by re-imagining the role of the architect from technical practitioner to positive contributor to the physical environment of the city, and therefore to the larger society and culture. It could be said that they envisioned architects as a class of cultural agents unto themselves.[14]

These concerns about the role of the architect were not restricted to the left. In 1968, the pro-government professional journal *Hogar y Arquitectura* (*Home and Architecture*) proclaimed on its front cover: "In Search of a New Meaning for the Word Architect."[15] Even conservative journals wanted to partake in the international debates on architecture, which had been brought about in part by the student revolts in France.[16] So important was architecture that, in Madrid during the seventies, there were no fewer than six professional journals dedicated to the topic.[17] Just as remarkable as the number of specialist journals proliferating in this period is that generalist magazines also displayed strong interest in architecture and urban planning. Professional debates spilled into mass media, thereby educating citizens about the material conditions of cities, including speculation and fraud cases, while also providing a space for public debate on new urban theories and imaginaries for the future of cities.

Victor Márquez Reviriego, for instance, published an extended essay in 1968 in *Triunfo* entitled "La ciudad en el espacio" ("The City in Space"). This was a full-colour feature highlighting the ideas of the Barcelona-based *Taller de Arquitectura*, the collective workshop project of Ricardo Bofill, Jose Agustín Goytisolo, and Carlos Ruiz de la Prada, among others. The task of the *Taller* was to imagine a utopian city made to human needs and measure. Almost a living organism, the city was presented as an object of collective creation in constant evolution (43). The article also challenged the fundamental principles of urban planning, which, until that point, had held that the working classes be pushed to the periphery, separated from the city centre and other working-class suburbs by highways and green zones.

Márquez Reviriego argued that the solution to urban problems would not be found in regional planning and the creation of new satellite suburbs, but rather by remodelling urban centres and building working-class boroughs in the heart of the city (41). These were the kind of radical ideas that had been repressed following the Spanish Civil War. Consequently, reintegrating the working class into the city centre resonated powerfully against the fascist understanding of the crowd and the working class.[18] Márquez Reviriego and the *Taller de Arquitectura*'s call for the working class to occupy the city centre would be answered during the Transition, as people from the *barrios* appropriated the city by taking to the streets to participate in downtown political, civic, and cultural life.[19]

These articles and essays on urban themes provided a public way to imagine and discuss alternative, equitable, and democratic ways of living in the cities of Francoist Spain. In 1970, the influential *Cuadernos para el Diálogo* published "Urbanismo y sociedad en España" ("Urbanism and Society in Spain"), a comprehensive special issue in which the urban question was methodically discussed.[20] As a technical publication showcasing the most important voices in urbanism, the special issue was a direct critique of the regime. For instance, the editorial attributed public interest in architecture and urbanism to the urban consequences of the dictatorship by describing the situation in cities as incoherent, lacking, and dramatic, as large numbers of inmigrants came to Madrid to find their housing options limited to shanty towns or hurriedly built resettlement units (3). It continued by describing the "right to the city" as a basic social demand and a national priority (3). An unattributed quotation of Henri Lefebvre's *Right to the City* followed, leaving no doubts about the position of the magazine vis-à-vis urban processes and their relationship to democracy. The editorial ended by lamenting the difficulty of bringing together urban planning and democracy in a city space created from "una sociedad invalidada en sus supuestos más básicos" ("a society invalidated in its most basic principles") (3). In other words, the introduction to the special issue was a form of public resistance against the regime. Its major contribution was to elucidate the total incompatibility between the Franco dictatorship and contemporary democratic urban practices.

Even though municipal management had been the only area where criticism of the government had been permitted in Francoist Spain, the editors of the special issue tried to reduce the political implications of their and their co-authors' withering criticism of the political situation, urban plans, and municipal management by disingenuously stating that these were polemical technical issues "con ligeras connotaciones políticas" ("with slight political connotations") (4). Yet most essays made direct references to democracy, public participation, and the inability or unwillingness of public administrations to manage the city. They could hardly hide the radical premise of this special issue: that citizens have a right to their city. As Lefebvre's quotation underscored, the journal issue advanced the idea that the right to democratic participation had to be achieved first at the local level – that is, in the city and its neighbourhoods.

In practical terms, this premise moved the idea of "rights" from an abstract ideal to urban action. It empowered neighbours to believe that, at the very least, they had a say in any modification or preservation of their shared habitat. Flipping the formula that urban space reflects societal labour relations, this special issue operated from the idea that to change the city was to modify the social and the political environments. The city was thus not a final reflection of the social, but rather a product of citizens' work – something that materialized through association, participation, and the appropriation of urban space (Lefebvre, *Writings* 173–4). "Owning" the city – that is, actively tackling its problems and proposing solutions – was yet another step toward recovering citizen rights in Franco's Spain. This special issue would go far in helping readers seize their city by providing the technical tools for understanding Madrid's problems and envisioning possible solutions. Putting emphasis on the collective aspect of the right to the city, *Cuadernos* provided with a space where readers sensed being part of a larger, and concerned, public sphere working toward improving their city.

With that task in mind, this special issue of *Cuadernos* went on to create informed public opinion about Madrid's future. The section dealing with urban challenges included articles concentrating on demography

(J. Díez Nicolás); private property (J. Elizalde); social issues in the peripheral boroughs (A.R. López de Lucio); the construction of new boroughs and resettlement units (E. Mangada and C. Ferrán); public transport and traffic (F.G. García Rosales); corruption (M. Gaviria); urban psychopathologies (C. Castillo del Pino); and publicity (P. Altares). The theoretical section presented articles on urban theory (M. Solá-Morales); sociology (A. Rodríguez-Bachiller); economics (J. Oria); public transportation as a nonprofit service (A. Iglesias, E. Leira, D. Quero, J. Solana, V. Velez); cybernetics (J.A. Soláns Huquet); class struggle (A. Rodríguez-Bachiller, J. Solana, A. Iglesias, E. Leira, D. Quero); and an appraisal of Madrid's *ciudad universitaria* (university complex) by J.L. Aranguren. The technical section contained essays on management, Barcelona as a model of development, the role of tourism in urbanism, and the laws regulating urban land and its possible development. Two remarkable examples from this section are Rafael Moneo's appraisal of Madrid's urban development from the 1940s to the 1960s, and a co-authored essay that discussed models for citizen participation in urban planning (Bringas, Fernández, Rodríguez-Bachiller, and Ruiz de Elvira).[21]

I list these essays to underscore how comprehensive and technical the special issue was, and how diverse the set of authors. For scholars, this issue constitutes an intellectual map illustrating the intricate web of professionals working toward a democratic future. As early as 1970, the authors put forth a specific set of measures that they proposed to create a progressive, democratic, and functional city in which citizens would be the primary concern of urban planning. Aside from educating readers and infusing the public sphere with a concern for urbanism, the issue helped people realize that a significant number of professionals had concrete plans for their city, ideas for solutions to their problems, and an apparent willingness to work toward creating an improved urban experience. Readers could perceive that the professional elites writing in this issue opposed the regime and its policies. In short, the special issue was a virtual and theoretical rehearsal for a projected future in which a new political and cultural regime would reign in their city.

The Architect as a Socially Conscious Cultural Agent

Looking at the list of collaborators writing for the special issue of *Cuadernos*, it is hard to miss the large number of architects. These professionals would become one of the groups that would spearhead urban change in Madrid. Antonio Fernández Alba, one of the authors in the special issue, would become one of the most vocal and productive polemicists of the seventies. It is easy to find his byline in multiple publications; he authored articles whose content ranged from technical issues to direct complaints about the speculation then rampant in Madrid. Starting in 1971, Fernández Alba's essays in *Triunfo* were double-page illustrated features that occupied a central position in the magazine. His articles illuminate the concerns that were driving progressive architects at the time, mainly, their role in the thoughtful recovery of the city as a place to live. Fernández Alba challenged, in the strongest terms, Madrid city planning, which he saw as driven by speculation and the complicity of architects in the capitalist system.

In an early article titled "Arquitectura y ciudad" ("Architecture and City") (1971), Fernández Alba introduced the concept of Madrid as an "anti-city." Planned according to premises of urbanism that dated to the 1940s, Madrid would fully implement these premises in the sixties (34). This planning was a reflection of the concept of the city that emerged from the 1943 Athens Charter.[22] City leaders and authorities saw this postwar urban concept as appropriate for coping with the need to house the large numbers of immigrants moving to Madrid. The charter's modernist utopian ideals of the radial or functional city included the need for strong laws and effective local governments to support the zoning process through management and the strict execution of urban planning, which would keep opposing interests in balance.

That Madrid at that time had a municipal government crippled by the conflicting agendas of several ideological "families" such as *Falangistas* and conservatives, meant that the city's growth plan looked modernist on paper but was in reality vulnerable to unchecked and unregulated private interests. As a result of speculation, the city limits were extended toward its rural outer limits by simply ignoring the need to account for and build infrastructure, thereby rendering any urban plan obsolete within a few years (Fernández Alba, "Arquitectura" 35). The anti-city that Madrid was, Fernández Alba concluded, had not emerged from collaboration between politicians, architects, engineers, and ideology, but from a system of unrestrained private property in which the collective public interest was secondary to money making (ibid.).[23] The source of Madrid's ailments, he argued, was greed, capitalism, and a municipal government that enabled speculative practices.

Witnessing "unos afanes de lucro históricamente inigualables" ("historically unmatched greed") and a municipal government unwilling or unable to enforce urban planning led Fernández Alba to the conclusion that Madrid was out of control ("Arquitectura" 31). He noted, for instance, that economic interests profited from special interventions that further fragmented the city by zoning specific urban sectors and ignoring the global concept of what a city is (ibid.). He acknowledged that private economic interests and poor execution of urban plans were matters of concern everywhere, including in cities with long democratic histories and strong systems of municipal government. But the toxic combination of private interests and poor public enforcement of the law, he observed, was more acute in a city like Madrid because of the dictatorship. Under that system, he argued, the unelected and unchecked municipal machinery of the dictatorship had worked for decades to enrich a few at the expense of everyone else.

Under the dictatorship, these economic interests were not restricted to the development of new metropolitan areas, but extended even to the renewal of old city centres, where spaces disappeared into the hands of developers and historic structures were demolished to create more profitable ones. For Fernández Alba, the seemingly indiscriminate growth of towers and shopping malls was not only a symptom of a city government that had neither the power nor the interest to control and execute zoning, but also the confirmation of the death of Madrid and its devolution into an anti-city ("Arquitectura" 35). Without mentioning the role of architects in this process, he concluded that the end of cities had come at the hands of developers and the powerful economic interests behind urban housing. Emerging from his article is an image of a lifeless Madrid, an anti-city controlled by economic interests that operated with total disregard for the city's history and the needs and interests of its citizens. Within a decade, however, that image of Madrid would change radically as citizens took over public spaces and made their voices heard in urban planning. But, for the moment, Fernández Alba had raised the level of consciousness about the links between architecture, urban planning, and the capitalist systems that reduced cities to little more than machines of economic speculation and profit making.

Bourgeois society traditionally assumes that the architect is a specialist in building techniques or urbanism. Fernández Alba agreed with this premise, but argued that, in addition to their technical responsibilities, architects' social function was to affirm the status and power of the bourgeoisie. He described architects as separate from society, in some cases as artists, but, in others, as financiers or land developers complicit with the system ("De la arquitectura" 32). Following the collapse of the modernist movement, the architect faced a crisis that was not technical in nature but, rather, political, cultural, and ethical. Because the function of architects in contemporary society had not yet been clearly redefined, Fernández Alba predicted that they would remain a superfluous elite (ibid.). He responded to the changing role of the architect with a direct plea: he asked his colleagues to disassociate themselves from economic interests. If they wanted to have a positive cultural impact, he argued, architects should not partake in a system that seeks to profit from social control through the built environment.

Fernández Alba's articles in *Triunfo*, as well as many shorter pieces in newspapers such as *El País*, would help to solidify the image of a Madrid crushed by capitalism, a city in the hands of speculators with the complicity of politicians and professional elites. But these pieces also contained a glimmer of hope that architects would want to play a constructive role in developing the city by using their training and status to improve living conditions. This hope would be realized when architects began collaborating with neighbourhood associations and seeking citizen input to develop a master plan for Madrid.

Fernández Alba was not the only person discussing urbanism in *Triunfo*. The magazine provided, as had *Cuadernos*, an educative space for readers to learn from debates or exposés about poor conditions in Madrid. For instance, a 1971 debate between Luis Racionero and Antonio Miranda Mata pitted two opposing views about urbanism. Racionero articulated the view that architects were not to blame, since it was not their responsibility, after all, when their designs were not executed to their specifications ("La vivienda" 15).[24] Miranda Mata argued that buildings and spaces should communicate both their social function and the affects (desires, emotions, and vital experiences) of those who create them and use them ("Arquitectura" 36). Miranda Mata's organic humanist understanding of design, deeply influenced by Louis Kahn, went head-to-head with Racionero's technical approach to problem solving for Madrid. In other lengthy pieces, like Fernando Lara's 1974 "Vallecas: Las víctimas del urbanismo oficial" ("Vallecas: Victim of Official Urbanism"), *Triunfo* would present the current conditions of those living in depressed and abandoned areas of the city, raising consciousness about the pressing problems of many residents.

Urban Social Movements

Public debate on urbanism and the continuous stream of scandalous news about urban speculation and fraudulent construction deals had a measurable effect on Madrid residents. This was noticeable in the 1981 survey "Actitudes de la población madrileña respecto al planteamiento urbanístico municipal" ("Madrid Residents' Attitudes toward Municipal Urban Planning"), conducted by Jose Luis de Zárraga and commissioned by Madrid City Hall. Residents' perceptions matched those that architects such as Fernández Alba and others had been putting forward in print media. They saw their city as a chaotic, dense agglomeration. They noted traffic problems and the lack of resources (schools, hospitals, cultural centres), and associated the evident physical decay of Madrid with its less tangible social decline. Most of those polled, distrustful of municipal institutions, wanted localized, specific goals for the upcoming urban plan because they did not believe that the ideas and principles proposed by any plan would be implemented (Ezquiaga 96; *Recuperar Madrid* 79). Not surprisingly, the people of Madrid, after decades of corrupt dictatorship and speculation, did not trust municipal institutions to keep their best interests in mind.

The rock group Leño summarized the feelings of many in its popular 1978 song "Este Madrid" ("This Madrid"). The chorus, "Es una mierda este Madrid que ni las ratas pueden vivir" ("This Madrid is crap where not even rats can live"), encapsulated the mood of the *barrios*. Madrid had reached the tipping point, and its citizens, led by their neighbourhood associations, were no longer willing to accept their circumstances. As a consequence of poor urban conditions and the lack of an effective municipal response, NAs had grown in number and strength throughout the early seventies, reaching their full operational effectiveness by the end of the decade.[25] They were cross-class, cross-age groups that counted on the collaboration of architects, lawyers, and other professionals. Once they had harnessed their social power, they would lead one of the most effective phases of the urban social movement in Spain.[26]

Manuel Castells first coined the term "urban social movement" in his book *The Urban Question* (1972),[27] using it to refer to neighbourhood associations, consumer organizations, associations of housewives, women's groups, youth clubs, pensioner clubs, ecological organizations, shopkeepers' groups, hiking and other sports clubs, and even historical preservation societies. Castells argued that, while cities' built environments tend to reproduce labour relations and existing hierarchical structures, urban social movements (USMs) could transform the social structure of urban systems. In other words, USMs had the potential to alter capitalist relations of property and the system of authority. The caveat, according to Castells, was that the success of USMs depended on awareness and cooperation: they needed to focus on contributing to the class struggle in the city and on coordinating with other political movements ("Theoretical" 151).[28] Much like the special issue of *Cuadernos*, Castells's book saw the potential, in this case by way of USMs, to reshape capitalist society and, by extension, the city.

Castells's experience in co-authoring and coordinating the many social agents contributing to *Madrid para la democracia*, would impel him in *The City and the Grassroots* (1983) to refine the definition and scope of USMs as "urban-orientated mobilizations that influence structural social change and transform the urban meanings" (305). He then further redefined them as focused on demands for collective consumption, cultural identity, and territorial self-management.[29] Other characteristics of the USMs were their peripheral and reluctant relations with government institutions and political parties, and their commitment to being "an urban social movement" rather than a single class or ethnic movement with larger regional or national aspirations (*The City* 322). Some of the USMs' success has been attributed to their use of the media, professionals, and political parties, while remaining autonomous from them (Mayer 205). I would add other key characteristics as well. USMs were open, inclusive, and focused on specific local demands, while weaving networks of solidarity based on common interest in working toward a better Madrid.

Still, Castells did not think of USMs as revolutionary movements. He acknowledged that, although they could transform "urban meanings" (*The City* 329), they would not be able to transform society. The hope was that USMs would undermine the capitalist status quo of urban life, creating in its place a city organized on the basis of collective consumption, local cultural identity, and decentralized participatory democracy (319–20). This "alternative city" that Castells proposed in *The City and the Grassroots* is precisely the type of city the neighbourhood associations were fighting for in Madrid (326). The ideas that would shape this alternative city and the demands of the NAs – ideas that were diametrically opposed to the Madrid that Fernández Alba had described as the anti-city – would be at the core of *Madrid para la democracia* and eventually of the new urban plan for 1980s Madrid.

The Communists Reimagine Madrid

Madrid para la democracia reads more like an expert report of actionable items than a political platform. Like the special issue of *Cuadernos* discussed above, *Madrid para la democracia* was developed through the participation of a sizeable number of people in different working groups. Its editors – Castells, Leira, and Tamames – were academics with extensive research and publishing experience, which gave it the necessary imprimatur of legitimacy. In this section, I will describe *Madrid para la democracia* in detail because many of its proposals, successfully implemented during the eighties and nineties, shaped the city that Madrid is today. Listing the book chapters will provide a wide perspective on the many changes the city underwent during the Transition. The influence of this document, furthermore, continues to be felt even today, as some of its most ambitious proposals – closing the city centre to traffic and creating a downtown pedestrian area, for example – are just now, in the 2010s, being implemented.

Despite naming Madrid "the capital of capital," *Madrid para la democracia* did not assume an overtly anti-capitalist stance. It did not, for example, call for expropriations or the abolition of private property, and it broadly contemplated the role of the private sector in partnership with the municipal government. Instead, it pushed the optimistic and simple message that better living in Madrid was possible (15, 24). *Madrid para la democracia* offered a program for governing, as well as a platform for the demands made by the USMs and the NAs. An exercise in clarity, the introductory chapter is titled "Conclusiones" and it summarized each chapter of the book and its conclusions. Anyone familiar with writing and publishing styles in Spain will recognize how highly unusual this type of structure is. The effect was that the introduction offered a list of talking points that were developed and justified in subsequent chapters. Thanks to this strategy, all readers had in their hands an executive summary and a road map to imagining a new Madrid.

The book progressed from a history of Madrid and its urban and economic development in chapter 1 to a presentation of the problems the city had inherited under Franco's regime in chapter 2. Chapter 3 explained the need to develop democratic institutions and, more importantly, argued for a legal framework that would grant cities autonomy from the central government in important matters like taxes. Chapter 4 discussed the citizen movement in Madrid, the organization of NAs, and their principal demands. Chapter 5 listed twelve action items that the Communist Party thought necessary for improving a democratic Madrid. Some were technical or legal, like decentralizing municipal government and giving City Hall the legal power to raise taxes, or using *Cajas de Ahorros* (credit unions) to fund social projects in the city. For the most part, all the action points had to do with quality of life and centred on citizens' needs and experiences.

These proposals demonstrated a balance between the historic city centre and the neglected boroughs at the city's edge – a balance that reveals the egalitarian ethos behind the work. Eradicating the slums and the crumbling resettlement units of the peripheral *barrios* by building social housing in collaboration with the private sector was the first, and most urgent, item on the list. The second measure was the recovery of Madrid's historical centre by decongesting traffic and discouraging speculation. To achieve this goal, it was proposed that government buildings be moved to the periphery, that high taxes be imposed on new commercial buildings, and that private vehicular traffic in the city centre be strictly limited. Transforming the city centre, especially those sections with tourist attractions, into a pedestrian area was the third item.

A walkable, traffic-free downtown required the parallel expansion of bus and commuter train lines, as well as the creation of free public parking areas outside the city centre near metro stations. *Madrid para la democracia* proposed other actions dedicated to improving the living conditions in central urban neighbourhoods. Among these were municipal support to rehabilitate traditional housing (*corralas*) in Madrid and the allocation of services for collective consumption such as hospitals and schools in the city centre. Another important aspect for the improvement of the centre was the recovery of playgrounds and parks, as well as collaborations with private entities to open public cultural and leisure spaces such as the Cuartel del Conde Duque, the Plaza de las Descalzas Reales, or the gardens of the Liria Palace.

To conclude this section on the recovery of the city centre, I would point out how *Madrid para la democracia* took notice of the ways in which community building had to be developed downtown with the support of city government. This process was intended to encourage local cultural identity, something elusive in a city of immigrants like Madrid. For that reason, the book took the unexpected view that small businesses (taverns, shops, artisans, theatres) were centres of local culture and community. The argument was that creating local commercial and cultural life in the centre, in addition to the measures already mentioned above, would help prevent the formation of an empty and lifeless city centre that functioned merely as a stage for tourists. Focused on the resident experience, *Madrid para la democracia* envisioned a vibrant city centre, not merely a tourist set, but an active urban space where people would enjoy the benefits of city living.

The remaining ideas presented in *Madrid para la democracia* concerned Madrid's metropolitan area, and included environmental proposals such as legal protection for the nearby Sierra de Guadarrama, the creation of new parks and playgrounds, a commitment to the upkeep of these public spaces and to the fight against pollution. Other proposals considered utilities and food-distribution systems. For instance, one discussed Madrid's water supply system and proposed a new central market for the wholesale distribution of foodstuffs, since the traditional markets in the centre (Legazpi for fruits and vegetables, Matadero de Arganzuela for meats, and Puerta de Toledo's fish market) were overwhelmed and antiquated and contributed greatly to traffic congestion. By 1982, Madrid would establish its new central distribution market (Mercamadrid) in the southeast of the city; the new location's easy access to the M-40 would in turn free up the old market structures to become the influential multimedia cultural spaces that they are today.

Madrid para la democracia granted public transportation its own section in the book, proposing something very similar to the city's current public transportation system. To be specific, it recommended coordinating all means of public transportation, declaring all public transit a public service without the expectation of profit, raising investments in infrastructure and line development, and controlling price with one ticket for all means of transportation and discounts for pensioners, the disabled, and young people. The book is limited, however, in that it contemplated the need to encourage citizens to walk and it did not consider bicycles at all as an alternative form of transportation.

Clearly, *Madrid para la democracia* proposed an ambitious and comprehensive program. More than a set of competing political views and proposals on urban development, the document illustrated the many areas in which Madrid had been completely neglected. For instance, the book called for the construction of wastewater treatment plants. By the end of 1977, City Hall and the Ministry of Public Works and Urbanism had finally adopted a *Plan de Saneamiento Integral* (Comprehensive Sanitation Plan).[30] Madrid would get its first residual water treatment plant in 1983. Up to that point, Madrid's wastewater had been collected and discharged into the Manzanares River with minimal treatment, multiplying the river's flow by a factor of sixteen. As the Manzanares was a tributary of the Jarama and, in turn, of the Tajo River, the raw sewage dumped into it not only stank but also contaminated the entire downriver basin, making any activity connected to the river impossible. The same happened to smaller watercourses such as Valdebebas in Vicálvaro, where a collecting pipe dumped raw sewage into a small local stream. The *Plan de Saneamiento Integral de Madrid* would be fully implemented by Madrid's new socialist and communist government. This plan first targeted suburban areas lacking infrastructure, the same areas that suffered from the most polluted rivers and streams. These boroughs (Carabanchel, Hortaleza, San Blas, Vallecas, Vicalvaro, Villaverde) also flooded regularly during heavy rains. They would become a main focus of the new *Plan General de Ordenación Urbana de Madrid* (General Plan for the Urban Order of Madrid), which was in development from 1980 to 1985 and implemented thereafter.[31]

From Theory to Practice

Every twenty years since the 1920s, Madrid has produced a *Plan General* to regulate its growth. Serendipity dictated, then, that the party winning the 1979 municipal election would have the power to greatly influence that plan. Under Franco, the evolution of urban planning in

1.2 Inundaciones barrio de la UVA de Vallecas (Flooding in Vallecas Neighbourhood Resettlement Unit), 1971. The resettlement units' lack of infrastructure, and their poor connection to Madrid's grid, often led to flooding in heavy rain and consequent blackouts.

Madrid had moved from imagining a city that would reflect *falangista* ideals in the Plan Bidagor (*Plan General de Ordenación de Madrid*, 1946) to the disorderly expansion of the city of the 1964 *Plan General del Área Metropolitana de Madrid*. While the Plan Bidagor had focused on rebuilding imperial appearances, the 1964 plan, launched in the middle of the *desarrollismo* (development) frenzy, became instead the strategic plan of speculators and developers (Ezquiaga 93). By the seventies, as Fernández Alba complained, Madrid had no viable regulating plan directing its growth. The conflicting needs of the city and the Franco government had quickly rendered Madrid's master plan obsolete. Encouraging economic forecasts and a modernist theoretical model of the city had resulted in a 1964 plan that, while good in technical terms, had been fundamentally unrealistic (Terán, "Crecimiento" 161). The need to condense Madrid to control its growth had encouraged a model that emphasized the development of the metropolitan region by planning for commercial and cultural centres outside of the city, relocating heavy industry out of the city centre, and building the necessary transportation network. The plan failed to consider that, without the collaboration of Franco's government, there could be no implementation of such ideas. In fact, the central government did not build the planned infrastructure, which undermined the contraction of the city that the plan tried to achieve, making traffic, pollution, and the everyday life of the residents of Madrid worse. Denounced in both *Cuadernos* and *Triunfo*, the plan had been completely abandoned by 1970. The municipal government was proven incapable of implementing its own regulations, and a mentality of *fait accompli* took over the city.

Although created to address this deplorable situation, the 1964 Comisión de Planeamiento y Coordinación (Commission of Planning and Coordination, COPLACO) did little to ameliorate the top-down planning process that ignored the lived realities of residents. COPLACO, under the authority of the Ministry of Housing and later the Ministry of Public Works and Urbanism, was put in charge of managing the urban development of Madrid's metropolitan area. Yet not a single city representative served on this commission. It was immediately discredited, not merely because of its direct connection to Franco's government or its total lack of local representatives, but also because it had been designed solely as a planning organization, completely separate from the entity that would execute the plan. The commission lacked, therefore, any actual power to control the implementation of its own plans.[32] Franco's death eleven years later would bring many changes to the country – among them, a new way of conducting urban planning.

COPLACO's research, however, would serve as another foundational element for the 1985 *Plan General*. Since the failure of the 1964 plan, COPLACO had been working on basic research and analysis to offer a new view of the urban situation for the purpose of making a new plan. The change in urban theory we explored earlier in this chapter, the reorganization of Madrid's School of Architecture, and the creation of new departments or work groups that took urbanism as the centre of their concerns, greatly influenced the urban planning of Madrid. For instance, in 1977 the Departamento de Urbanismo y Organización del Territorio (Department of Urbanism and Organization of the Territory) was founded in Madrid's School of Architecture. The same year, the Centro de Estudios Urbanos, Municipales y Territoriales (Centre for Urban, Municipal, and Territorial Studies, CEUMT), which had originated in 1972 in Barcelona's Centro de Estudios Urbanos (Urban Studies Centre), was reorganized to include other cities like Madrid. Organizations like the CEUMT were true think tanks that would produce white papers, books, and lectures that, in turn, would influence the plans for regulating the development of Spanish cities during the Transition and after. Not only did they help professionalize those in charge of developing cities and planning city growth, they were also interdisciplinary organizations that brought together professional and urban activists to foster popular participation in city planning.

At the end of the seventies, the professionals of COPLACO went into the streets and boroughs to diagnose the real situation. Their conclusions would be used as the point of departure for a set of proposals to improve Madrid. From that work emerged the *Planes de Acción Inmediata* (Immediate Action Plans, PAIs) that would, in some areas, precede the main operations of the 1985 *Plan General*. COPLACO's PAIs were, no doubt, a response to the neighbourhood associations whose relentless actions forcefully articulated the demands and needs of city residents. Reaching their most active period, the tenacious urban activism of the NAs and other USMs was starting to pay off. COPLACO's new attitude and actions came too late, however, and were too strongly identified with both the former right-wing central government and the first democratic centre-right government of Unión de Centro Democrático. Tierno's new municipal government soon broke away from COPLACO and took over the organization of Madrid by developing its own new master plan (Sáinz 125).

The 1985 *Plan General de Ordenación Urbana de Madrid* was founded on a completely different precept than its predecessors. Eduardo Leira (co-editor of the *Cuadernos* special issue and *Madrid para la democracia*) and Eduardo Mangada (contributor to the *Cuadernos* special issue) were designated co-directors of the new plan. Starting from the "right to the city" principle that we have already explored, the new plan sought first and foremost to respond to the real needs of the neighbourhoods and to collaborate with them to better achieve the city's goals (Terán, "Crecimiento" 162–5). According to Carlos Fernández Salgado, at a technical level the plan avoided the zoning concept that had ruled urban planning up to that point, and it tried to work with the citizens at the smallest unit: the street (30). But the central goal of the plan was to implement what had been argued for the previous ten years: the residents' right to the city in the most comprehensive way. The right to fully inhabit and alter the city was to be implemented, both at the grassroots level with the input of social actors and citizens, and from the top to shape priorities and to provide a totalizing vision. This was obviously a completely new practice after decades of hierarchic, opaque, ideological, and abstract planning. In idealistic fashion, the plan sought to engage every social actor at every level of society in Madrid and to provide for channels and spaces of communication.

The plan managers understood that the only way to build credibility for the plan and get buy-in from the neighbourhoods in the process was by communicating with residents and requesting their input. To that end, a massive campaign called *Recuperar Madrid* (Recover Madrid) advertised that the plan was in progress and called for informative assemblies and consultative meetings in the boroughs. For the sake of transparency and feedback, the preliminary plan was eventually presented in 1982 at a public exhibition that was first housed in city hall and later in the Cuartel del Conde Duque. Entitled "50 ideas para recuperar Madrid" ("50 Ideas for Recovering Madrid"), it encouraged residents to imagine different scenarios for Madrid and to comment on them. The massive distribution of an eponymous book that, akin to *Cuadernos'* special issue and *Madrid para la democracia*, comprehensively presented the history and problems of Madrid as well as the central tenets of the 1985 *Plan General*, offered education, information, and transparency to city residents.

Although they had been consulted, the citizens' movement and the NAs nevertheless complained that they had no formal authority in the process and that actual decision-making power lay elsewhere. Francisca Sauquillo, leader of a Vallecas neighbourhood association, complained in *El País* that City Hall had not truly implemented the citizens' will but rather had only pretended to be listening (qtd. in Fernández Salgado 43). The desire for radical popular participation and direct participatory democracy in urban planning collided with the professional, budgetary, and legal structures that limit urban planning. Yet it can be said that the effort to engage citizens, USMs, and other social agents was unprecedented, and to this day remains essentially unmatched. As a consequence of this effort, construction soon began on 39,000 new housing units to resettle people who had been living either in slums or poor quality housing built during Franco's regime. As Fernando de Terán described it, this was a "social debt" that had to be paid before anything else could happen (*Madrid* 290). Fundamentally democratic and egalitarian, the plan sought to improve Madrid as a whole instead of focusing only on the historic city centre and on a few star projects of signature architecture. Instead, medium-size projects sprang up throughout the city, replacing entire slums and dilapidated housing units with new housing in districts like Puente de Vallecas (Palomeras, Pozo del Tío Raimundo, Entrevías) or Usera (Orcasitas, San Fermín), to name a few, among others like Pueblo de Vallecas, or Carabanchel. Public transportation was greatly improved, local roads were finished and highways such as the M-40 completed, and new parks (Tierno Galván) and many new resource centres (for sports and culture) and schools were created.

The *Plan General*, of course, was not perfect and its fate would change over the years.[33] The PSOE victory in the national elections of 1982 and its successive victory in the Madrid municipal elections the following year meant that communist influence in the city would wane. While the earlier version of the 1985 *Plan General* was a direct reflection of *Madrid para la democracia*, later versions, especially after 1983, would diminish the most radical aspects of the plan. On paper, however, the goals for the *Plan General* continued to be clearly progressive, ambitious, and idealistic.[34] For instance, it remained committed to fighting class segregation and stopping the gentrification of the centre, just as Tierno had delineated in his inaugural speech, as well as protecting Madrid's architectural heritage, limiting private vehicle access to the city centre, implementing measures to combat pollution and protect the environment, and committing to the creation of more public space and the preservation of public ownership. As Fernández Salgado reminds us, urban plans are theoretical and political, and they need to adapt to the economic system and to the law. This was especially true in Madrid when City Hall confronted the difficult reality of financing ambitious urban operations.[35] Yet even if some of its goals were never realized, the *Plan General* achieved something perhaps even more important for Madrid: it gave citizens the sense that they were the collective proprietors of their own city, and that they, and their opinions, mattered.

Madrid, Beacon of Modernity

The feeling that something big was happening in Madrid was clear, both locally and to those watching from afar. For instance, *Arquitecturas Bis* in 1978 published a monographic issue on Madrid. It included a piece by Rafael Moneo in which he highlighted twenty-eight architects working in the city, and another by Antón Capitel explaining the architectural history of Madrid and its recent trends. A few years later, in 1983, *International Architect* would feature Madrid in a special issue that included a guide, curated by Haig Beck, to emblematic buildings. Susan Larson explained the burgeoning interest this way: "Cuando el resto del mundo estaba fascinado con los cambios políticos y sociales en España en los ochenta, los arquitectos del mundo descubrieron en España nada más que un capítulo olvidado en la historia de la arquitectura moderna misma" ("When the rest of the world was fascinated, during the eighties, with Spanish political and social changes, international architects discovered in Spain nothing more than a forgotten chapter in the history of modern architecture") (*"La Luna"* 320). Journals and architects echoed the same sentiment: Madrid had plenty of interesting architecture and was worth a visit.

Local architects and professors, such as Antón Capitel, began to frame and situate Madrid's architecture in a broader context. Since the debate was seemingly settled about what to do with Madrid, it was time to assess its most recent past. In his 1978 piece in *Arquitecturas Bis,* Capitel pondered whether there was a "school of Madrid," while Juan Miguel Hernández León, in *International Architect,* argued against that idea. These two journals reflected the wider academic debate about how we ought to think about and understand post–Civil War architecture. This debate is clearly illustrated by the exchange between Carlos Sambricio and Tomás Llorens and Helio Piñón in *Arquitecturas Bis.* Llorens and Piñón had celebrated in an essay what they saw as a contemporary reappraisal of post–Civil War architecture. This reappraisal, they claimed, was a vindication not only of the regime's architects and style, but also of the regime itself (12). In a devastating response, Sambricio chastised Llorens and Piñón for their simplistic professional, aesthetic, and technical approach to architecture, which overlooked political and social context, professional genealogies, and the history of any given project (25). Sambricio concluded that post–Civil War architecture should be viewed, not as a celebration of the achievements of the Franco regime, but as an object of study for cultural historians (26–7). That architects turned to evaluate buildings of the previous three decades is an indication of how much they felt immersed in a new historical period.

For many, Madrid by the mid-eighties had grown into an all-consuming passion. Susan Larson has explained in detail how the typical Spanish *tertulias* (salon-like informal gatherings for discussing literature, art, and/or current events) brought together visual artists, authors, musicians, and architects around issues concerning the city ("Architecture" 192–3).[36] In addition, established publications reflected the collective interest in Madrid. *La Revista de Occidente* (*Journal of the West*), for instance, ran a special issue in 1983 devoted entirely to Madrid. It contained a few institutional pieces by Joaquín Leguina and Enrique Tierno Galván, while the remaining short essays contemplated the city's history (including urban plans), its popular and high culture, the ecology of its surroundings, and its economic patterns. One year after *Recuperar Madrid* had been published and distributed, cultural and political institutions continued to foster an environment in which residents could perceive their ownership of their city.

While special issues in respectable journals such as *La Revista de Occidente* were useful in educating Madrid residents and connecting them to the city's history and culture, other magazines approached the city's built environment in a less academic fashion. Between 1984 and 1985, Manolo Blanco wrote a section in *La Luna de Madrid* (*Madrid Moon*) entitled "Mis horrores favoritos" ("My Favourite Horrors") in which he poked fun at buildings in the city. In this context, it is not surprising that *La Luna*, a magazine driven by "la obsesión total de todos los colaboradores con el espacio urbano donde vivían" ("the absolute obsession of collaborators with the urban space they inhabited") (Larson, "*La Luna*" 311), would offer its readers the opportunity to own a piece of Madrid: some issues would include detachable cut-out models of the city's most emblematic buildings, like Puerta del Sol or Plaza Mayor, so readers could cut out, build, and collect their favourite places in Madrid.[37] The process encouraging a sense of appropriation and ownership of the city by its residents had been completed, and had been turned into a fetishistic ideal: not only could residents of Madrid occupy public spaces in the city centre, but they could also own them in symbolic form, collect them, and proudly display them in their homes as trophies of a re-appropriated and democratic Madrid.

This new way of imagining the city and its inhabitants is clearly evinced in Tierno's 1979 inaugural speech. Toward its end, Tierno changed his focus from urban space and the built environment of Madrid to its citizens:

> Los madrileños constituyen un pueblo joven, de los jóvenes que son jóvenes y de los viejos que son jóvenes y esta juventud se define sobre todo por el deseo de saber, por esa manifiesta curiosidad por la cultura, por la necesidad de estar en contacto con la innovación intelectual y la innovación expresiva, teatral, de otro carácter literario, cinematográfico ... y, al mismo tiempo, alegría, una alegría que nunca ha estado ajena al municipio de Madrid ni a los madrileños, cuya alegría se ha ido angostando, porque la estructura urbana, desordenada y a veces caótica, conlleva consigo una tristeza que seca hasta la sonrisa. (8)
>
> (*Madrileños* are a young people, youngsters who are young and elderly who are young, and this youth is defined above all by the desire for knowledge, by its manifest curiosity about culture, by the need to be in contact with intellectual innovation and innovations in expression, with theatre, literature, or film ... and, at the same time, happiness, a happiness never lost to Madrid and the *Madrileños* whose happiness has been reduced by an unorganized and sometimes chaotic urban structure that produces a sadness that can dry up even a smile.)

In his address, Tierno relates Madrid's built environment to the mood of its citizens, who are young and happy, but who feel oppressed by negative urban circumstances. Curtailed up to that point by Madrid's unorganized and chaotic urban structure, happiness would reign as soon as Madrid improved as a city. In addition to joy, Tierno identifies youthfulness as the main characteristic of residents of Madrid. In doing so, he presents a mirror in which residents, independent of age, can identify with his definition of youth: the desire to know, to be curious about culture, and to be on the cutting edge of intellectual and artistic innovation. Hard to reject, Tierno's vision for the new Madrid is one in which the urban environment and its structures are tightly bound to the physical and cultural well-being of its citizens. To live in Madrid no longer implied local birth or speaking like a *Zarzuela* operetta character; in Tierno's new definition, anyone could be from Madrid, as long as they had the right sensibility.[38] Like a fountain of eternal youth, all one really needed to belong in Madrid was a desire for knowledge and to be in touch with the new.

Tierno's forward-looking formulation, articulated in his 1979 speech, emerged from a long evolution that had taken place both in the mass media and in Madrid society. The Madrid residents described in his speech were those who since the late sixties had been driving Madrid's changing sensibility: they were, on the whole, young, anti-Franco, and obsessed with culture. They embodied a new sense of personal enjoyment, morality, and politics, and they engaged in countercultural practices that overstepped the limits that had been set by both the Franco regime and the leftish parties of the resistance. During the seventies, these youngsters would be indissolubly connected to other changes in Madrid culture that we explore in this book.

In this chapter, I have presented the professional debates in print media about urban architecture and urban planning in Madrid. I have tied the emergence of NAs and other USMs to changes in municipal urban policy, and I have drawn a direct connection between *Madrid para la democracia* and the 1985 *Plan General de Ordenación Urbana de Madrid.* All this is to support my argument that the massive urban changes that Madrid would experience during the eighties were primed during the seventies both by the debates on urban planning and architecture in the media and by the activism of the NAs. The change of consciousness toward Madrid was buttressed, as I have shown, by other important matters informing the architectural and urban planning debates in Madrid: some were paradigmatic, in reference to the role of the architect, while others were technical, economic, political, and social. This renewed sense of the city was the consequence of at least three coinciding crises: first, that of the role of the architect; second, the waning of modernists' urban planning models and the emergence of neo-Marxist interpretations of urban space; and third, the seventies' housing crisis that had resulted from the massive migration of workers to the cities during the fifties and sixties, the subsequent establishment of large shantytowns, and the inadequate response of both municipal and central governments.

Driven by the "right to the city" ideal, urban experiments in Madrid during the seventies were not simply physical. Public awareness of urbanism's changing trends and the emergence of USMs that had carved out a space for protest and resistance during the Long Transition are but a few of the reasons for the changing face of Madrid. Membership in USMs and participation in city planning through collaborations with professionals became important means for improving the city. Behind these changes was a growing sense of entitlement to the city. In other words, residents of Madrid were increasingly possessed of a new collective consciousness, an awareness of their personal and collective ownership of their lives and the material conditions that surrounded them.

Chapter Two

Sex: Building Plural Communities

When it comes to the body, two famous photos illustrate the changes occurring during the Long Transition. In one photo, a man and a woman, both naked, stand atop the Daoiz and Velarde monument in a Malasaña square. Taken in May 1977 during this popular borough's *fiestas,* the photo shows the couple being cheered on by a group of youngsters clapping and raising their fists into the air. In the other photo, taken at the February 1978 gala of the newspaper *Pueblo,* Enrique Tierno Galván, soon-to-be mayor of Madrid, awards a prize to actor Susana Estrada, whose silk jacket has come open, revealing her naked right breast. In this black-and-white picture, her white skin shines in contrast with the smiling middle-aged men in dark suits around her. The first photo tells a story of freedom and spontaneous protest in a public space, liberated bodies standing on the shoulders of heroes.[1] This photo would soon be echoed by others taken at the first gay pride demonstration in Barcelona's Rambla on 26 June 1977. The actions in Malasaña and the Rambla would both end with police violently dispersing the demonstrators. The photo of Tierno and Estrada, however, represents *el destape,* the for-profit explosion of graphic nudity in mass media that began in the mid-seventies. This was the other side of the liberation coin. Leaving behind the dictatorship's moralistic views of sexuality and gender, Madrid would witness the growth of three parallel movements: feminism, the sexual revolution, and the fight for LGBT emancipation. Depicted in movies as the site for immigrants' new lives, Madrid was also the location where new sexual desires and gender behaviours would be exploited and monetized.

Heeding Jorge Pérez's call for a contextualized examination of *el destape,* this chapter seeks to present the wider cultural environment in which alternative views on sex and gender began to percolate through mass media to reach the general population, contradicting those long enforced by the regime. *El destape* has become one of the fundamental concepts for interpreting the Transition, with the body as the "battleground" on which both conservative and progressive critics waged their cultural war (Marí, "El umbral" 257; Pérez 93). The phenomenon of *el destape*, simultaneous proof of both sexual repression and liberation in Spain, is more complicated than it seems to appear. As I will show, it emerged in a public sphere that had been saturated in the previous decade with magazine articles about the emancipatory trifecta of women's liberation, the sexual revolution, and LGBT rights in other Western countries.

Print media reported, with varied degrees of success and with different motivations, on the international challenges to patriarchy and traditional morals, as well as on alternative gender roles and sexualities. Magazines such as *Cuadernos para el Diálogo* would approach the topic academically, by publishing a best-selling special issue on the topic of women. *Triunfo*, on the other hand, tended to be more sensationalist, discussing topics such as sexual desire, pornography, and feminism. Renowned intellectuals published books on similar themes, such as *Sexualidad y represion* (*Sexuality and Repression*) (Carlos Castilla del Pino, 1971) and *Erotismo y liberación de la mujer* (*Eroticism and Women's Liberation*) (José Luis López Aranguren, 1972). Although Madrid was still under the rule of Franco, its public sphere in the 1970s was steeped in every aspect of sex and women's rights, including many film "comedies" that were quickly produced to cash in on Spanish interest in these topics. Not unlike in other Western countries, an entire industry developed that purposely conflated sexual liberation and women's rights with lucrative "erotic" films and magazines.

After Franco's death, the politicization and commodification of the body was evident. Actors such as Susana Estrada, Nadiuska, and Victoria Abril claimed to use their bodies and nudity for the political purpose of free expression in general, and of gaining rights for women in particular.[2] Regardless of how these actors felt about their political role in a liberated Spain, leftist film critics categorically deplored the proliferation of female nudity. As we will see, these critics complained of such films' poor quality and the dull erotic roles that celebrities played in them. While conservative critics decried the films as immoral, their leftist counterparts saw them as exploitative and profit seeking. I read the progressive critics' reactions as an indication of the influence of sexual liberation and feminist discourses and how they were beginning to change the collective sensibility toward sex and gender.

I also examine the ubiquitous presence of essays in the mass media on sex and gender issues for more than ten years and how they contributed to breaking the hold of the regime's Catholic morality over the public and to generating a collective sense of tolerance of other forms of being in the world. Transgender issues, for instance, were one of the early LGBT topics that mainstream magazines and commercial movies treated extensively in the early seventies.[3] After Franco's death, the central position that sexual liberation and women's rights occupied in journals, magazines, and films gradually gave way to a focus on homosexuality. Homoeroticism, cross-dressing, and other forms of gender bending moved from the underground to become recognized and embraced as bona fide countercultural practices. By the early eighties, as scholars have convincingly established, a culture that defied traditional views on sex and gender became pivotal for the creation of the pluralistic community of *la Movida* and the larger sense of openness and tolerance in Madrid.[4]

In what follows, I will examine the sex and gender topics represented in mass media. From feminism to sexual liberation, I will also explore *comedia sexy* and *destape* movies, and illustrate the evolution that allowed transgender characters to personify the Transition (Robbins, "An Introduction" 35; Fouz-Hernández and Martínez-Expósito 143). This chapter will end with a reading of Eduardo Mendicutti's novel *Una mala noche la tiene cualquiera* (*Anybody Can Have a Bad Night*) (1982) in the cultural environment of the long seventies to assess the extent to which sex and gender were fundamental to the period's profound changes in collective sensibility.

Sex: The Condition of Femininity

Beginning in the mid-sixties, women's associations began to form all over Spain. In 1965, for instance, the Movimiento de Mujeres Democráticas (Democratic Women's Movement) separated from the Communist Party, while other women sought to infiltrate and control the originally pro-Franco Asociación de Amas de Casa (Housewives' Association), to push a progressive agenda focused on women's rights. Also during the sixties, feminist pioneer Lidia Falcón published books such as *Los derechos civiles de la mujer* (*Women's Civil Rights*) (1963), *Los derechos laborales de la mujer* (*Women's Labour Rights*) (1964), and *Mujer y sociedad* (*Woman and Society*) (1969). Influential journals and magazines such as *Cuadernos para el Diálogo* and *Triunfo* charted the development of the feminist movement by regularly publishing articles that updated readers on the state of the movement and its principal organizations. *Cuadernos para el Diálogo*, for instance, published a groundbreaking special issue in 1965 entitled "La mujer" ("Woman") and many other pieces on women such as "Las españolas no somos diferentes" ("We Spanish Women Are No Different") by Carmen Nogués (1968) and "La emancipación de la mujer: ¿conquista o alienación?" ("Women's Emancipation: Conquest or Alienation?") by Carmen Mestre (1971). According to Javier Muñoz Soro, this issue was so popular that by 1970, "La mujer" had been reprinted four times (*Cuadernos* 192).[5] The frequency with which feminist essays appeared in print media and the yearly reprinting of "La mujer" make clear that women's issues were of great concern and interest to the public.

"La mujer" is significant because it brought together a plethora of women's views and voices discussing legal and ethical positions on divorce, abortion, socio-economic roles, and women's emancipation from patriarchal rule. Philosopher Amalia Arana, along with representatives of Mujeres de Acción Católica (Women of Catholic Action) and the Unión Mundial de Organizaciones Femeninas Católicas (the International Union of Catholic Feminine Associations), writers such as Carmen Martín Gaite and Maria Aurèlia Capmany, journalist Pilar Narvión, and law students such as Cristina Almeida and Manuela Carmena, all contributed to "La mujer." With this special edition, *Cuadernos* bestowed on women's issues the imprimatur of the highbrow, deliberative journal it sought to be. It was the first salvo informing mainstream Spanish readers that women's lives and aptitudes would no longer be socially constrained, as the regime would have had it, to marriage, home, and children.

Feminism was the topic *du jour*. The public sphere – whether in magazines or books – was brimming with discussions of women's issues. Even commercial movies such as *Pero ... ¡en qué país vivimos!* (*But ... What Country Are We Living In!*) (José Luis Sáenz de Heredia, 1967) showcased feminist ideals. The movie pitted Concha Velasco and Manolo Escobar in a musical battle of the sexes that presented in strong terms, albeit with a patriarchal resolution, feminist arguments for women's liberation from *machista* rule. In order to promote two commercial products, Rodolfo Sicilia (Alfredo Landa) devises a survey and contest between pop singer Bárbara (Concha Velasco), endorsing whiskey, and Spanish folk singer Antonio (Manolo Escobar) promoting brandy. Although they were both already celebrities, Bárbara is motivated by the large amount of money offered for the promotion; by contrast, Antonio refuses the idea on principle, but then, charmed by Bárbara, he finally accepts. After a battle-of-the-bands concert that culminates with Bárbara singing a pop feminist version of the classic *pasodoble* "La morena de mi copla," a massive brawl, and a stop at the police station, the two singers spend the night together.

This movie, a commercial comedy after all, depicts marketing techniques directed at capturing the growing purchasing power of a public interested in fashion, music, and other new habits of consumption such as whiskey drinking. Consumer options, however, go beyond competing products in this movie, and practically represent an ontological choice: Concha Velasco or Manolo Escobar, whiskey or brandy, international or domestic culture, pop or Spanish folk music, feminism or machismo. The simple but effective device of two opposing sides captures the tension in Spanish culture at a moment in which cultural changes were quickly gaining momentum. Without question, the movie sides with tradition and does not miss any opportunity to deride Bárbara, her music, her behaviour, and her feminist ideas. While some might interpret this film as a reaffirmation of machismo, I prefer to see it as an indication of how relevant a topic feminism was at that moment – important enough for a movie to ridicule it and to finally subsume it into a traditional marriage.

At first sight, this movie seems to glorify Antonio's calm taming of the feminist celebrity shrew. With self-assured masculinity, Antonio trolls Bárbara, uttering sentences that encapsulate the traditional image of the domestic woman, delivered with deadpan candidness: "Si una mujer no reza y no cose me parece que no es mujer" ("If a woman does not pray or sew, I don't think she is a woman"). The happy ending, with Bárbara suggesting intercourse and predicting their wedding, proposes metonymically that, despite the palpable tensions in a changing Spain, whiskey and brandy, modernity and tradition, women and men, can get along if only they submit to the gratifying and familiar ways of tradition.

Nonetheless, this movie provided a platform for feminist ideals. Bárbara, as a character, embodies gender equality, assertiveness, self-assuredness, and entrepreneurship. Throughout much of the movie, she is defiant of patriarchal society and male-dominated show business; she achieves her personal and professional goals and thus provides the audience with a model of how an emancipated modern woman might look and sound. In the movie's climax, she takes to the stage with a feminist version of "La morena de mi copla," singing "tirano, déspota, opresor" ("tyrant, despot, oppressors").[6] Bárbara's new lyrics elucidate the ways in which patriarchal society makes women the caretakers of their husbands: "El español que se casa, en lugar de compañera, quiere tener en su casa asistenta y cocinera" ("The married Spanish man, instead of a partner, wants a cleaner and cook at home"). She vocalizes, in no uncertain terms, what many women feel and suffer in patriarchal society. To be sure, the movie's ending reinforces and affirms the heteronormative Catholic order, but, even so, Bárbara displays a clear sense of power and agency. In the end, the shrewd shrew gets what she wants.

Triunfo would soon take up the theme, publishing essays such as "Feminismo contra liberación" ("Feminism vs. Liberation") by Eduardo Rico (1968), "La última ofensiva del feminismo" ("Feminism's Last Offensive") by Romano Giachetti (1970), and the anonymously authored editorial "Racismo y antifeminismo" ("Racism and Anti-Feminism") (1970). Even if they were well-meaning allies, men, fortunately, did not write all of *Triunfo*'s essays on feminism. In 1970, Maria Aurèlia Capmany published "Feminidad o el sexo como condición específica" ("Femininity or Sex as Particular Condition"), an essay whose subject, linking capitalism, society, and sexuality with women's gender roles, remains au courant. Capmany's essay is a relevant example of a rigorous article that, avoiding academic jargon and written in a style for an educated general audience, provides readers with a framework and vocabulary for discussing women's roles.

Capmany begins by narrating how whenever she was invited to a roundtable on women's issues, she had to share the stage with a male OB-GYN, a male psychiatrist, and a Catholic priest (37). Bringing medicine and religion to bear on women's issues was to her an indication that, when it came to women, sexual morality and procreation were still society's main concern. The close relationship between women and sexuality explained why women's sex was not only biological but also a marker of social differentiation with predetermined social roles. Citing Ortega y Gasset and Hegel, Capmany pointed out that men had been able to free themselves from being identified purely with their sex, and therefore were able to realize themselves in multiple social roles (37). Women were a species, while men were individuals, she explained in Hegelian terms. She continued with an analysis of classic Iberian literature to demonstrate how the construction of the "women-sex" identity ran parallel to women's social function in a developing bourgeoisie. In works from Calderón to Moratín, women, "enajenada de cualquier responsabilidad, ... se convierte en pura motivación de tensiones masculinas" ("alienated from any responsibility, ... become the pure motivation for masculine anxieties") (38). Literary women had been nothing but abstract objects or repository of desires, while real women were attached to the social roles assigned to their sex.

In the second part of the essay, Capmany's inquiry into the conditions experienced by contemporary Spanish women sets forth a corrective view of 1970s Spanish culture that I find illuminating. In contrast to the widespread belief that sex remained a taboo subject until the arrival of democracy, Capmany reports that sex education was actually disseminated ubiquitously prior to 1970. She explains that women had access to substantial information about sex from a wide array of literature at press kiosks, much of which was sold in profusely illustrated bound issues (39). She also noted that women knew that they could be equal partners in sexual relations (39). Finally, she commented on the beneficial effect that the expansion of sex education from rich to poor schools, motivated in part by the reprinting of books such as Wilhelm Reich's *The Sexual Revolution* (1936), had had in changing cultural values attached to sex (39). Capmany's 1970 testimony offers the contrasting view that sex education was readily available in schools and at kiosks in the 1960s, a decade traditionally presented as sexually repressed and backward. Just as we saw in *Pero ... ¡en qué país vivimos!*, it is clear that modern and traditional behaviours coexisted and overlapped in 1970s Spain.

But sex education alone was not enough to liberate women. In contemporary capitalism, Capmany explained, Spanish women could discover their sexuality only in the narrow space between catcalls on the street and advertising images and slogans (39). The consequence was not sexual satisfaction but, rather, self-fetishizing, where women were asked to exhibit themselves, by way of consumption, to the satisfaction of a phallocentric society (39). For Capmany, this meant that the changes happening at the time, what she termed the "re-organization of women's roles in society," were not attributable to women's wants but rather to the new needs of capitalism (39–40). Liberating on the surface, consumption was to Capmany just another form of social coercion: "La mujer sigue existiendo como sexualidad. El sexo no es un dato biológico sino social, y la mujer, en el área del neo-capitalismo, permanece irremisiblemente en su condición específica de hembra" ("Women exist as sexuality. Sex is not a biological fact but a social one, and women, in the sphere of neo-capitalism, continue irremissibly in their specific condition of being female") (40). Thus, even in advanced societies, women were relevant only as long as they fulfilled the roles expected of them. And among these, in the midst of massive cultural changes, consumption had taken a dominant position.

Capmany's essay appeared in a special issue of *Triunfo* entitled "El erotismo y España" ("Eroticism and Spain") (1970). As important as I consider her essay to be, analyses such as Capmany's were watered down by virtue of being framed within the broader issue of eroticism, and constituted an example of the confused conflation of sexual liberation and feminism. Elsewhere in "El erotismo y España", Camilo José Cela explored the semantic field of the word *puta* (whore) in *Don Quijote;* Gonzalo Torrente Ballester lamented that the current emphasis on eroticism was simply a by-product of consumption, lacking a new liberating sentiment; and Luis Carandell offered one of his most puzzling and hilarious "Celtiberian Show" columns on the topic of sex.

While Capmany's essay in *Triunfo* undoubtedly enjoyed a wide audience, the surrounding pieces diffused her poignant critique of a capitalist and male-dominated society that continued to discipline women into a specific social function, including, by the early 1970s, through the smooth methods of marketing.

This special issue is, in fact, another example of the incongruities of a changing time. Eduardo Haro Tecglen's piece "Cómo se fabrica a una española" ("How a Spanish Woman Is Made") was interrupted by a two-page spread detailing a state-of-the-art washing machine factory that had been inaugurated by the ministers of labour and industry. "European dimension" and "world class," ran the headline. "El futuro ha comenzado" ("The future has begun") stated one of the subtitles, while the photos of government officials and executives showed not a single woman in sight. The irony of a special feature on washing machines punctuating an article detailing how women are shaped by society cannot be lost on the reader. While Capmany and others engaged in cutting-edge theoretical discussions of sex and gender, government officials saw a future in which women's liberation meant simply the automation of what they saw as feminine chores.

Market capitalism was at the heart of all of these changes. Clearly noted in the special issue's anonymous editorial, liberties in Spain, including sexual freedom, were to be chalked up to a society firmly run by consumption, since "las tendencias socioculturales en una sociedad de consumo moderna ... no concuerdan con la austeridad de una sociedad represiva en materias sexuales" ("The sociocultural trends of modern consumer societies ... do not match with the austerity of a sexually repressive society") (24). Just as *Pero ... ¡en qué país vivimos!* had done, the editorial presented a Spanish society in tension between those who preferred traditional morals and rejected consumption, and those who embraced consumption and exhibited alternative morals. The editorial tied together consumption and the new sexual order emerging in Spain. While it criticized the sublimation of eroticism to consumption, it could not avoid creating connections between modernity, democracy, and new sexual behaviours and attitudes with a market economy driven by consumption.

Sex Sells

Gender and feminism were persistent topics in print media, and, from the late sixties until the mid-seventies, they shared headlines with the sexual revolution. Much more than mere general discussions of eroticism or sexual liberation, these were often groundbreaking explorations of sex that would educate Spanish society and contribute to moving it away from traditional views on sexuality. While Capmany presented a theoretical framework for feminism and reported the scientific and pedagogical side of sex education available in kiosks and schools, other articles provided readers with a catalogue of new sexual practices one might imitate or aspire to.

Triunfo reported on sex and gender in an international context. For instance, Juan Aldebarán examined the sexual revolution, including the legalization of homosexuality, in England in "El sexo y los ingleses" ("Sex and the English") (1967), while Henri Gardi's essay "El fin de los sexos" ("The End of the Sexes") (1968) discussed Marshall McLuhan's theories including sex, drug use, and pornography. *Triunfo* also published an anonymous book review of Vance Packard's *Sex Wilderness* (1968), entitled "Sexo salvaje o domesticado" ("Savage or Domesticated Sex") (1969). Translations from the *Washington Post*'s syndicated columnist Art Buchwald warned about sex being used to promote consumption, and encouraged schools to develop sex education programs ("La educación sexual en la televisión" 8; "La educación sexual: pros" 6). Sexual liberation in other countries was explored in a two-part series from 1969 entitled "Sexo y U.R.S.S." ("Sex and the Soviet Union"), and an article by Jean-Francis Held, "Sexo Über Alles" ("Sex above Everything") (1970) that paraphrased a *Der Spiegel* essay detailing the material culture generated by the sexual revolution in Germany.[7] Held's article included a list of magazines and sex shops that catered to, for example, homosexual, polysexual, sado-masochistic, and fetishistic sex. This constant drip of articles describing the international shift in sexual morality encouraged Spanish readers to create their own version of a sexual revolution and to ask how it might manifest under a far-right Catholic dictatorship.

In his article "Un consumo erótico racionado" ("A Restricted Erotic Consumption") (1969), Jesús García de Dueñas complained that Spain's embrace of eroticism was prudish at best, limited to the exposed back of actor Analía Gadé or Carmen Sevilla's opaque lingerie. He criticized the movies of Manuel Summers for reinforcing sexual repression and Spaniards' unhealthy attitude toward what he saw as normal human sexual behaviour (11). There was little resultant opening of minds in society, the critic concluded, because more flesh on the screen did not address present problems of Spanish women and men (11). This thematic critique, while formally correct, did not address the fact that, by 1970, sex had in many ways been released from its Catholic confines; it was now prominently displayed on screens, the covers of magazines and books, and by extension, in highly visible kiosks and bookstores.

The changing mores of Western societies that the mass media was reporting in detail to Spanish readers were quickly seized upon in service of mass consumption and profit making. Like in a burlesque show, the process of that seizure happened one daring step at a time.[8]

That sexual liberation quickly became a means to serve the ends of profit seekers is evidenced by popular films that explored issues of gender and sexuality, which had hitherto been a major taboo. *No desearás al vecino del quinto* (*You Shall Not Covet Your Fifth Floor Neighbour*) (Ramón Fernández, 1970), one of the earliest examples of what has come to be known as *comedia sexy*, clearly demonstrates this shift in Spanish culture. *No desearás* was for nearly three decades the highest-grossing Spanish film.[9] The film relates the picaresque professional, social, and sexual adventures of Pedro and Antón. Pedro, a young OB-GYN from Toledo and arguably too handsome for his profession, struggles to find female clients for his practice, as suspicious men prohibit female family members from seeing him. In Madrid, serendipity leads him to meet his effeminate neighbour Antón, a *modisto* (fashion designer) and, apparently, a prowling Don Juan on the side. Married with five children, Antón pretends in his atelier to be an effeminate homosexual in order to attract female clients, and has been extremely successful in retaining Toledo's best clientele. Once a month, however, Antón escapes to Madrid to release pent-up sexual energy. During his escapades, he transforms into a playboy looking for female, and preferably foreign, casual sex partners. When Antón and Pedro decide to have a wild week in Madrid, the movie plays to all the typical culturally adapted screwball comedy conventions of misunderstandings and false assumptions.

Since *No desearás* relies on stereotypical misogynistic and homophobic jokes, it is easy for modern viewers to dismiss. But as Justin Crumbaugh has convincingly showed in *Destination Dictatorship*, *No desearás*, when taken in context, also documents the fantasies, fears, and desires projected on Spanish society in the seventies. The movie introduces, for the first time in Spanish film history, an effeminate, supposedly homosexual character (Martínez-Expósito, "Visibility" 12).[10] This character is not unproblematic. In the most clumsy of ways, the effeminate performance of the character is ridiculed, an excuse for cheap laughs.[11] While it might be tempting to view the presence of a "homosexual" character in a leading role as a victory over Franco's censorship, this representation was actually state approved. The film mocked homosexuality and effeminacy, while at the same time elevating its hyper-sexualized, hyper-masculine alter ego. A crude joke, Antón the *modisto* exists only to affirm the *macho ibérico* Antón whose energetic masculinity allows him to play the roles of a leading fashion designer, husband, and father of five, as well as to conduct his adulterous affairs in Madrid. And yet, as Barry Jordan and Alfredo Martínez-Expósito have demonstrated in their analyses, there is so much more in *No desearás*. They have noted how the film simultaneously reaffirms and subverts traditional mores (Martínez-Expósito, "The *Desarrollismo*" 74).[12] I would additionally argue that the movie not only works on an axis of moralistic masculinities but also plays to the *desarrollismo* and entrepreneurial logic of the late Franco regime.

Antón's successful career as *modisto*, a profession traditionally associated in Spanish popular culture with homosexual men, cannot be attributed exclusively to his performance of effeminacy. Couturiers do not build successful businesses on their sexuality, but rather on delivering clothes that respond to clients' tastes and desires, as well as on staying abreast of constantly shifting social and cultural trends.[13] *No desearás* echoes Capmany's essay on sex as a female condition, in that it inadvertently proposes that being skilled at women's fashion, a profession based on creativity and technical skills, has little to do with sexual preference or gender expression. Instead of fighting society's traditional ideas about gender roles and appropriate careers for men, Antón uses popular belief to his own professional and financial advantage. Becoming a message for *desarrollismo*, the movie encourages entrepreneurial Spaniards like Antón to overcome any obstacle in the pursuit of professional success. The message of the movie seems to be that capital accumulation trumps moral codes no longer useful to the modern capitalist reality.

Alberto Mira has warned critics not to take apparently transgressive homosexual characters as definitive proof of a modernizing Spain (435). A subversive interpretation of *No desearás* can nevertheless be coaxed out of the film by reading against the grain of the movie's very traditional, face-value intentions. *No desearás* exemplifies homophobia and patriarchal control over female bodies and sexuality, yet it also responds to the curiosity of a society coming to terms with changing views of gender and sexuality (Jordan 168–70). The movie's conclusion, in which Pedro pretends to be an effeminate gay man in order to prosper in his medical practice, and Antón and Pedro come under the watchful eye of their wives, is perplexing at best and cannot erase the transgressions the protagonists have made against the moral order of the regime. As Tatjana Pavlovic has perceptively noted, the *macho ibérico*'s normative masculinity in the *comedia sexy* cannot be rescued after the devastating series of humiliations it endures, even after the exaltation of traditional values at the films' conclusions (*Despotic* 82). The over-the-top virility and exaggerated patriotism mocked in these films render the masculine character a model to be avoided rather than emulated. We should nevertheless be aware of Crumbaugh's suggestion that, despite the comic and subversive potential of the *comedia sexy*, these movies were a release valve that, while parenthetically overturning normative values, ended up reinforcing them: "By lampooning the macho Ibérico's defiance of official ideology, by parodying his puerile rebelliousness, the representation of transgression may easily serve to neutralize subversiveness" (109–10). We must surely recognize that this movie reproduces the patriarchal and *machista* fantasies of freely available female casual sex partners, as well as easily identifiable, effeminate gay men to victimize. We should also acknowledge Crumbaugh's disquieting conclusion that the actual cruel joke of these movies is that the *comedia sexy* "opened up an illusory space of subjective autonomy" by which Francoist ideology was able to engage Spaniards through ironic distance, thereby ensuring a better alignment of the spectators with the regime (110). And yet, once ironic distance and laughter have demonstrated the emptiness of authority, there is no telling how spectators might respond to it.

I am sceptical of construing spectators' reactions through the lens of a collective and sophisticated althusserian interpellation by which moviegoers would automatically and laughingly fall into ideological closeness with the regime. Although I agree with Crumbaugh that spectators may have perceived how ridiculous and cumbersome it was to rebel against the "natural" way of things, I also believe that spectators may have found their own meanings in these movies – in some cases by identifying with and validating Antón's sexual promiscuity, while in others by sympathizing with the concern family members feel for Pedro when they suspect he is a homosexual. There is also a potential emancipatory reading of the film, in foregrounding the possibility of a same-sex relationship between Antón and Pedro (Jordan 182; Martínez-Expósito, "Visibility" 15). These personal interpretations could be seen as a form of *disidentification*. This is the process, conceived by José Esteban Muñoz, by which minority populations construct identities through the rejection, appropriation, and resignification of normative models of social behaviour including those portrayed in mass media or film (4). Jo Labanyi has also argued that, due to censorship, "Spanish audiences were adept at the art of re-signification" or, in other words, the creation of affects and meanings different from those suggested or intended by conventional film plots ("Race" 216).

Because no cultural product operates in a vacuum, it is important to reiterate that *No desearás* was a part of a larger mass media exploration of similar issues. Spain, even under military dictatorship, was not immune to the influences of women's rights, sexual liberation, and homosexual emancipation movements. The feminist movement and the news of the Stonewall riots in the United States must be also considered as part of the social environment in which this movie was received.[14] I am not claiming that liberation was a goal of the film – quite the contrary – but we have to account for the possibility that the inclusion of non-normative sexual topics in such a blatant way had unintended consequences, such as foregrounding the possibility of being flamboyantly effeminate and professionally successful, or having a same-sex relationship in the anonymity of modern Madrid. *No desearás* was an "ideologically exploitative film" that nevertheless opened up the range of themes that movies could explore and that helped normalize public discussions of gender and sexuality (Martínez-Expósito, "Visibility" 15–17). Even if the intention of the film was to affirm a specific type of traditional masculinity and to mock certain socially deviant behaviours, there is no escaping that sex – including female desire – is central to this comedy. *No desearás* clearly presents both heteronormative and same-sex sexual desire, not as a suggested possibility but, rather, as a joyous certainty, allowing viewers to consider and even confirm the existence in Madrid of lifestyles alternative to those models provided by the regime.

Two years after *No desearás*, another movie, *Mi querida señorita* (*My Dear Lady*) (Jaime Armiñán, 1972), would create a new benchmark in the changing collective sensibility toward gender and sexuality.[15] José Luis López Vázquez gives perhaps one of his best and most nuanced performances playing Adela Castro, a forty-three-year-old, single, upper-class *señorita* from a provincial town who drives a SEAT 600. With a fawning suitor around, Adela seeks the advice of her church's young priest. Adela confesses that she shaves and that she fears men. The priest encourages her to visit a specialist doctor to get some medical advice. The doctor determines that Adela needs a radical gender change because she is not a woman. After the surgery, Adela, now Juan, escapes the clinic before finishing the transition process and acquiring his new identification documents. He moves to Madrid, and we follow his struggles to find a job, build a life, and have a "normal" sexual and emotional relationship. Eventually, Juan meets and courts Isabelita, Adela's former maid, who had also moved to Madrid. He has assumed that she is unaware of his transition and, in the final scene, after the couple has sex for the first time, Juan announces that one day he will reveal a secret to Isabelita. She reponds, "¡Qué me va a contar a mi, señorita!" ("I know well, señorita!"), just as she previously had done when working for Adela. After the initial surprise, Juan and Isabelita embrace and kiss. The apparently happy ending suggests that Isabelita knew all along that Juan was Adela, and that she had already been attracted to her boss when working for her.

Mi querida señorita treats the complex aspects of sex and gender in a more nuanced and humane way than *No desearás*. In doing so, it elucidates the social construction of gender and the problematic repercussions of transitioning, such as fear of judgment, reprisals, and the difficulty of finding a job without documents or education. It is consistent with *No desearás*, however, in showing the characters' desperate need to find a job and make a living in Spain's neo-capitalistic economy. The movie also introduced a cast of characters that were compassionate, supportive, and professional. The doctor, the priest, and even Adela's former suitor – all male voices of authority – don't openly judge, provide useful advice, and support Adela/Juan throughout the transition. Marvin D'Lugo has nevertheless noted that the plot functions as "una parodia grotesca de la ideología cultural del franquismo" ("a grotesque parody of Francoism's cultural ideology") (70). The movie also presents other social issues such as intergenerational conflict and gender bias through Juan's struggles to become a modern urban man in Madrid. He is kicked out of the boarding house he lives in when his conservative landlady discovers that he has female clothing in his luggage, which suggests to her that he is a transvestite, something unacceptable "in a decent household." While we might find fault today with the movie's patriarchal premises and heteronormative conclusion, *Mi querida señorita*'s role in exploring gender dynamics and bringing transgender issues to the public sphere under Franco's rule should not be undervalued: it introduced, for the first time in commercial Spanish film, a thoughtful reflection on bodies and the social construction of gender.[16]

As we have seen, topics related to sexuality and gender were already present in print media before these movies appeared. Some were provocative pieces that sought to titillate, while others were informative articles about feminism or sexual liberation. There were also state-of-the-art essays such as "Los tránsfugas del sexo" ("Sex Renegades") (1969) that thoroughly discussed transgender people and issues. "Los tránsfugas del sexo" was an extended article written by New York City–based freelance Italian journalist Mauro Calamandrei discussing the Johns Hopkins Gender Identity Clinic in the United States. This touchstone article preceded and framed *Mi querida señorita* and the fame of Bibiana Fernández (Bibí Ándersen), the highest-profile Spanish person to transition. She became known for her work in Barcelona's cabarets in the early seventies, for the movie *Cambio de sexo* (*Sex Change*) (Vicente Aranda, 1977), and, in the late eighties, for becoming "chica Almodóvar" (Almodóvar's girl).[17] Her fame, however, needs to be understood as emerging in a public sphere that for a decade had regularly seen articles grappling with gender-related issues through a wider international lens.

"Los tránsfugas del sexo" began with the case study that gave rise to the Johns Hopkins Gender Identity Clinic and explained its status as a pro-bono multidisciplinary centre. Listing other research centres such as those at the University of Minnesota and the University of California, Calamandrei explained that doctors at that time were performing about 1,500 surgeries each year in cities around the world, including Casablanca, Copenhagen, Tokyo, Mexico City, and Rome (39). The goal of the clinic was not to convince transgender individuals to live with the gender assigned at birth, but rather to improve surgery as well as to understand sexual and gender identity issues before and after clinical procedures (39). As to who searched out this surgery, one doctor declared that there was no one type, listing among his patients high-end administrative assistants, shopkeepers, and petit-bourgeois women (42). To reinforce this point, Calamandrei recounted one case featured in a 1967 *Esquire* magazine issue that narrated the story of a US Silver Star war veteran, vice-president of the Veterans of Foreign Wars, who in 1958 travelled to the Netherlands for reassignment surgery.[18] The article internationalized and normalized the matter. It avoided any reference to morality or victimization. Refraining from easy tearjerker stories, it modelled how to treat transgenderism from a scientific and academic point of view.

Toward the end of his article, Calamandrei quoted at length one doctor who articulated a modern understanding of sex and gender: "El hecho es que la identidad sexual es una realidad extremadamente compleja y plástica. El sexo es un dato biológico, pero el género es social" ("The fact is that sexual identity is an extremely complex and plastic reality. Sex is a biological fact, but gender is social") (42). Following an explanation of genes, chromosomes, and hormones, the doctor concluded: "Pero además de estos datos biológicos y fisiológicos, está el comportamiento que se aprende por una serie de indicaciones de la sociedad y de la cultura y por un intricado sistema extraordinariamente refinado de recompensas y castigos que experimentamos desde que nacemos" ("But in addition to these biological and physiological facts, there is behaviour learned through a number of signs from society and culture, and from an intricate but sophisticated system of rewards and punishments that we experience from the day we are born") (42). This article, published in one of Madrid's most widely circulated magazines, introduced into the mainstream a modern and scientific perspective on transgender issues.

In reading this 1969 article, it is hard not to conclude that it was influential in shaping the authoritative doctor in *Cambio de sexo*, or similarly, the priest of *Mi querida señorita*, who recognizes that it is not he, but science that might have something to say about the transgender body. The effects of "Los tránsfugas del sexo" went beyond bringing transgender bodies into the public realm and providing information for screenwriters. First and foremost, it made transgender issues internationally relevant by listing several prestigious academic institutions that were working on the cutting edge of both medical and social research.[19] Second, it provided critical language for separating gender from sex and illustrating the social aspects of gender. Finally, it normalized gender dysphoria by highlighting international discussions of the topic and by highlighting the number of surgeries performed. It portrayed reassignment surgery as a legitimate medical procedure, and a bona fide subject of investigation in some of the world's leading universities.

The topic of transitioning and alternative sexualities would become a persistent theme in movies in the second half of the seventies, especially after Franco's death and the end of official censorship in 1977. Film critic Diego Galán reviewed two highly hyped movies: *Me siento extraña* (*I Feel Weird*) (Enrique Martí Maqueda, 1977) and *El transsexual* (*The Transsexual*) (José Jara, 1977). Galán accused both films of being products of opportunism and official moralism, stating that there was nothing modern about them. He ridiculed the first kiss shared by Barbara Rey and Rocío Durcal in *Me siento extraña*, a commercial film dealing directly with lesbian love and sex, and determined that *El transsexual*, which starred Ágatha Lys, was nothing but a reactionary film made by people who thought Spanish movies should be "productos para idiotas" ("products for idiots") (66). Galán saw no merit or redeeming quality in *Me siento extraña*, and he pointed out how purposely prudish, clumsily constructed, and poorly acted both of these movies were. The low production values of the films were, for the critic, another indication that they had been intended to cash in on audiences' morbid curiosity about female celebrity sex scenes and nothing else. Audiences predisposed by other sympathetic and informed mass media products seemed to agree with Galán.

In 1977, *Me siento extraña* and *Cambio de sexo* each had somewhat under a million viewers each, while *El transsexual* had fewer than half a million.[20] These numbers fall far from the more than four million spectators who went to see *No desearás* in 1970, or the two and a half million who saw María José Cantudo's full frontal scene in *La trastienda* (*The Backroom*, Jorge Grau) in 1975. This precipitous drop in audience over seven years is an indication of a society quickly changing in taste and sensibility, and is attributable to several factors. Some reasons for the audience's declining interest were the lifting of censorship, the decreasing social stigma of sex, a growing selection of television programming, and competing "foreign films that included big-budget Hollywood movies as well as soft-core porn, which drew Spanish spectators away from domestic product" (Kinder 130). By the time of their release, these *destape* movies were already outdated, as more sophisticated depictions of sex had already, in the early seventies, broken into the international mainstream.

The deluge of books, articles, and movies on sex, gender, and feminism that I have been discussing had already to a degree expanded Spaniards' perspectives on sexual mores. Yet there were still films that created scandal, such as that which ultimately came to represent the collective weight of Spanish sexual repression: *Last Tango in Paris* (Bernardo Bertolucci, 1972). Even though it had been banned in Spain, Fernando Lara reviewed *Last Tango* in a February 1973 article in *Triunfo*. It was a very positive assessment rife with spoilers. With Lara's thorough description, even those who could not go to France to watch the forbidden film could now talk about it in scandalizing detail. Vazquéz Montalbán, writing in *Triunfo* the following month, described the now-familiar scene of Spanish citizens crossing the border to Perpignan to get a glimpse of the film. The most relevant part of Vazquéz Montalbán's oft-quoted article is for the most part ignored and yet it is fundamental for understanding the cultural changes that were taking place. He noted that, instead of being shocked, Spanish audiences were by and large unperturbed by the film ("El penúltimo" 47). Furthermore, he reported that a notable segment of the spectators did not understand why the arty film had been censored. The responses charted by Montalbán evidence the growing normalization of sex in Spanish society and culture by the early seventies. Sophisticated audiences recognized the let-down of *Last Tango*'s marketing hype, while Franco's censors ultimately only enhanced its mythical status.

Last Tango was not the only film that gained attention in articles and reviews for its explicit sex scenes. Román Gubern and Ramón Chao, for example, reviewed the new pornographic films appearing both in the United States and Europe. Gubern, for instance, discussed the Paris debut of *Emmanuelle* (Just Jaeckin, 1974). A porn movie with high production values, he explained, it pretended to have an elegant touch by mixing sex with the mystique of Southeast Asia. In an argument that echoed Maria Aurèlia Capmany's early article, Gubern concluded that *Emmanuelle* was simply another example of bourgeois hypocrisy, reflecting a society that now placed on women the burden of making themselves desirable and a commodification that women could acquire through the consumption of clothes and vacations to Southeast Asia ("Industria" 46). Gubern's critical review shared space with Ramón Chao's "En las pantallas francesas: erotismo a go-gó" ("On French Screens: Plenty of Eroticism") (1974). Chao wrote a commentary on the availability in French cinemas of mainstream porn movies such as *Deep Throat* (Gerard Damiano, 1972), *Behind the Green Door* (Artie and Jim Mitchell, 1972), *Immoral Tales* (Walerian Borowczyk, 1973), and *Emmanuelle*.[21] His article functioned both as an index of French sexual liberation and as a vehicle for making Spanish audiences aware of these films. Even though these movies were forbidden in Spain, Spaniards now had a pornographic canon at their disposal to discuss, thanks to these movie reviews, and Spaniards could feel part of a larger cultural conversation.

Surrounded by boundary-pushing international films, and with Spanish censorship on the retreat, audiences' interest in Spanish erotic films and *comedia sexy* dropped exponentially after Franco's death. The genre was exhausted and could no longer claim to be daring, as Spaniards had progressively wider access to uncensored international films and plenty of pornography in print. We also need to consider the wider cultural and intellectual environment; the lack of interest in these films can be partially understood as a rejection of the way in which sex and gender was presented to a more sophisticated audience that had been exposed to feminism and sexual liberation theory.

The film reviews of Galán and Gubern are two examples of a shifting collective sensibility that had moved away from the objectified commercial use of female bodies. By the mid-seventies, Román Gubern, in "En defensa del erotismo" ("In Defense of Eroticism"), declared *el destape* culturally passé. In this devastating commentary, he labelled *el destape* as anachronistic, since the taboos about nudity and its representation had fallen long before (50). Passé and anachronistic as *el destape* may have been, it continued to be the operative logic of some mass media pieces for a few more years because it had its own commercial logic, one that worked hand in hand with Spanish celebrity culture.[22] To be sure, *el destape* was the product of a hypocritical, sexually repressed Catholic culture, wrapped in a discourse of boundary-pushing free expression that fulfilled a craving for "sexy" films on the part of a public seeking shortcuts to sexual liberation. *El destape* was first fuelled by a desire to cash in on free expression through the cynical use of feminism and sexual liberation, and it survived for so long because there was an industry ready to profit from the morbid curiosity that nude celebrities generate. With *Last Tango* and *Emmanuelle* as the new norm, *el destape* continued to offer the cheap thrills of the next local celebrity posing naked. From the bare back of Analía Gadé to Barbara Rey and Rocío Durcal's lesbian sex scenes, not to speak of countless *Interviú* front covers, the evolution of *el destape,* based on the objectification and commodification of female bodies, can be easily traced through its business model.

Sex Changes

Low revenues and increased competition from abroad did not stop producers from making movies that explored sexuality and gender. *Asignatura pendiente* (*Failed Course*) (Jose Luis Garci, 1977), *Los placeres ocultos* (*Hidden Pleasures*) (Eloy de la Iglesia, 1977), and *El diputado* (*The Representative*) (Eloy de la Iglesia, 1978) are a few examples. Filmmakers such as Vicente Aranda continued to push the boundaries of thematic and visual representation. His *Cambio de sexo* (1977) featured transgender star Bibi Ándersen (Bibiana Fernández) and Victoria Abril in the main roles.[23] The film, defined by Marsha Kinder as "subversive melodrama," further made sex a political issue and explored the traumatic process of coming of age and aligning sex and gender in post-Franco Spain (128).[24] José María (Victoria Abril) is an effeminate adolescent boy who is bullied in school. His very traditional *machista* father believes that José María needs to "man up" and takes him to a cabaret show in Barcelona, where they watch the performance of a transitioning Bibi, and then to a prostitute for what turns out to be an unconsummated experience. After that night, José María realizes that he should really be María José. The movie follows the struggles of María José as she escapes to Barcelona to become a woman, makes a living and falls in love. The movie clearly sets forth the violent pressures and threats of patriarchal society for non-normative people, but it also demonstrates that María José enjoys a solid support network. Her landlady, unlike in *Mi querida señorita,* is supportive and maternal, and Bibi becomes María José cicerone, especially after María José castrates herself with a razor blade. The movie, despite some dramatic moments, has a happy ending: Bibi gets a successful reassignment operation, and María José becomes a cabaret star. Still, the conclusion of the movie is a throwback to heteronormativity, as the owner of the cabaret wants to marry María José only after she has surgery. Fulfilment, the movie seems to suggest, is found through a *sui generis* version of the fairy tale.

The movie is groundbreaking not only in its depiction of male genitalia but also in its casting of a trans actor playing herself in one of the main roles. Fouz-Hernández and Martínez-Expósito have explained its uniqueness this way:

> Bibí's character in the film was not only nonfictional, because she played herself, but it was also an eminently pedagogic role; in the story she becomes the guide and mentor of a younger transgender who, like most of the audience, is utterly confused by the conflict between his body and his feelings. In other words, from very early in her career, Bibí Andersen [*sic*] became a source of information about the intrinsically mysterious nature of sex and sex change for a largely ignorant, albeit eager to learn, Spanish audience. (143)

Though I agree with the general terms of this assessment, we should hesitate to attribute such a generalized confusion to the audience. After having mapped in this chapter the media landscape of the previous decade, it is difficult to determine whether spectators were really confused, or whether they had been educated to some degree by years of exposure to articles and books about new ways of considering sex and gender. While confusion certainly existed about non-normative practices, categories, and naming, there is no mistaking the political intentions of *Cambio de sexo* in denouncing homophobia and machismo and in the normalization of transitioning. This being the case, we can reasonably assume that some audience members were seeking validation of their beliefs and the knowledge they had gained over time. The fact that movies such as *Asignatura pendiente, Los placeres ocultos*, and *El diputado* were successful in attracting the attention of the public is a clear indication of audiences' developed taste for truthful and socially relevant representations of a wider palette of experiences.[25]

With feminism and sexual liberation firmly established as cultural entities, plus transgender bodies and themes sharing a central location in the public sphere, homosexuality took over front covers as the next social boundary to cross. From 1977 on, overwhelming numbers of works dealing with homosexuality received attention in the media. First, notices of congresses, meetings, and books appeared. Later, opinion pieces would push for the legalization and normalization of homosexuality. The first gay pride march in Barcelona was quickly picked up in the media, and the way it was covered can help us perceive the webs of solidarity weaving through the Long Transition.

Julia Luzán wrote an illuminating report in *Triunfo* called "La homosexualidad quiere salir del 'Ghetto'" ("Homosexuality Wants to Leave Its 'Ghetto'"). Illustrated with a photo of the gay pride march, Luzán's article summarizes a roundtable in Barcelona in which representatives of gay liberation fronts and feminists from multiple associations discussed a host of issues ranging from sexual liberation to relations between gay and lesbian organizations.[26] The piece is interesting

2.1 Spain's first documented Gay Pride Day demonstration in Barcelona. Manifestación gay, Barcelona, 1977 © Colita.

because it presented to the public the spectrum of positions within feminist and gay liberation fronts and their politics of solidarity. Other pieces in *Triunfo* also evidence the clear relationship between LGBT liberation and leftish politics, including several pieces by Eduardo Haro Ibars.[27] Documentaries and films such as *Ocaña, retrato intermitente* (*Ocaña, Intermittent Portrait*) (Ventura Pons, 1978) and *Un hombre llamado Flor de Otoño* (*A Man Called Autumn Flower*) (Pedro Olea, 1978) further contributed to the normalization in mass media of what for many decades had been taboo.

By the end of the seventies and into the eighties, what had first been social and medical issues became political ones. Transitioning bodies, changing gender roles, alternative sexualities, and leftish politics found expression on the front covers, screens, and streets of Madrid, creating a distinct sense of a wider community whose political demands were emerging during the Long Transition. Fouz-Hernández and Martínez-Expósito have proposed that non-heterosexual normativity is the best category to describe the social and political transformations happening in Spain (143).[28] They argue, more specifically, that during the seventies, "the transvestite and in particular, the transsexual was the epitome of political change" (143). The parallel between political and transgender bodies is too obvious to overlook, as both were in a state of transition. Politics and the transgender body is something explored in particular depth in the novel *Una mala noche la tiene cualquiera* (1982), which I will discuss in the next section.[29]

Narrating Transitions

Eduardo Mendicutti's *Una mala noche la tiene cualquiera* (*Anybody Can Have a Bad Night*) takes place the night of the failed coup d'état of 23 February 1981, when, during a plenary session in the Spanish Congress, a group of Guardia Civil (paramilitary police) kidnapped the congressional representatives. The objective of the coup was to derail the process of democratization in Spain. It ended when King Juan Carlos I appeared on television after midnight dressed in the full regalia of commander-in-chief, stated his support for the democratic process, and commanded the surrender of all rebel military forces.

Una mala noche is a first-person monologue delivered by a transgender cabaret star (la Madelón) as she waits for her roommate (la Begum), who is also transgender, to return home. In her narration, la Madelón blames the hormones she takes for the overwhelming monologue that the novel is, and for its oscillations in tone that jump from heartfelt sentimentality to political commentary.[30] The pace of the actual historical event and the whims of the narrator advance the narration. Exposed to la Madelón's verbal barrage, the reader is funnelled through that night, as it was experienced by some, in a narrative style – free associative and oral – that produces a sort of closeness with the reader, who is pulled into a space of intimacy and confession. The novel brilliantly reproduces a verbal monologue and effectively links its themes to produce a narrative with all the characteristics of the postmodern novelistic style: reflexivity, parody, irony, and the mixing of high and low cultural elements with an emphasis on visual popular culture.[31]

Critical appreciation of *Una mala noche* has grown over the years. Gema Pérez Sánchez has noted that the novel "provides an excellent fictionalized account of the real consequences a queer person could have endured" (388–9), while also noting that it presents an innovative and fresh historical account of events in contemporary Spain focused on gender and sexuality. Jill Robbins has gone further, framing transgender issues as central to the Transition: "The performance of a simulated femininity has been used insistently as a trope for the new identities of post-Franco Spain" (Robbins, "An Introduction" 35).

Critics have celebrated the use of la Madelón to narrate this pivotal moment of recent Spanish history, yet, although her participation is subversive, it is often also seen as frivolous, and, in the end, is not taken seriously. Others critics still have focused on the concept of drag. Patrick Garlinger, for instance, is critical of the simplistic approach to the main figure of la Madelón:

> The use of drag as a metaphor to re-conceptualize Spanish national identity tends to understand the transvestite in binary terms: before Franco/after Franco, old/new, modern/postmodern, authentic/artificial. In [several contemporary] critics' writings, the drag metaphor appears, on the one hand, as liberation – a border crossing that signifies agency and newly constructed identities – or, on the other, as a mere masquerade that cloaks an underlying identity. As a result, the postmodern transvestite represents alternatively a celebration of a Spain finally breaking free of its repressive past ... or a deceptive sign of superficial changes behind which hides a fundamentally unchanged Spain. ("Dragging" 365)

Pérez-Sánchez supports Garlinger's reading as reflecting two currents of criticism about contemporary Spanish culture: those who see a culture in progressive transformation toward a more liberal future and those who see, in those very same changes, the demise of the possibility of a radically changed society. Garlinger concludes that the novel is politically ambiguous, just as the identity of the main character is somewhat undefined ("Dragging" 372). But to think of the novel as ambiguous or vague is to misconstrue the larger cultural landscape in which contradiction and ambiguity were primary tropes.

During the Long Transition, politics were expressed not only through ways we could recognize as directly political – that is, active opposition to Francoism and militancy in leftish political parties. The emerging emancipatory discourses that I have discussed in this chapter played a pivotal role in challenging and eventually changing many moral and social codes of the regime. Leading these shifting collective sensibilities was a set of new actors that overtook the political, social, and cultural scene, bringing along new forms of coming together and of agency. Feminists, cross-dressers, gays and lesbians, and transgender people were but a few of those who, fuelled by theories put forth in print media, formed the pluralistic political community that came together around leftish ideals and grew over the course of the seventies. *Una mala noche* represents this irruption into the public space, going beyond the trespassing of gender boundaries to become a political novel. Critics such as José Colmeiro see in la Madelón's gender performance a political act because, enacted from the margins, it unveils the heteronormative system ("Plumas" 600). In this view, the camp performance, while subversive, does not fully enter the political, remaining at its edges, chipping away at its foundations with irony and double entendre. La Madelón's most radical political act, I would argue, is not cross-dressing or transitioning, but breaking into and owning the public space in which the political takes place.

This claiming of the political sphere is central to the novel from early in the narrative, when la Madelón votes in Madrid in the first democratic elections of June 1977: "Me presenté en mi mesa electoral, la que me correspondía, a media mañana, cuando hay más barullo, hecha un brazo de mar, que fue una sensación, y eché la papeleta del Partido Comunista y lo dije en voz alta: 'yo voto comunista.' Fue divino ... Qué satisfacción" ("I showed up at my polling station, mid-morning, when there is more movement, dressed to the nines – it was a sensation – and I put in the Communist Party ballot and said out loud: 'I vote communist.' It was divine ... What satisfaction") (19). This scene is layered with meanings and affects that cannot be easily parsed. Deliberately scandalous, la Madelón does not shy away from the fact that her official national ID lists Manuel Rebollo as her legal name. In a key political act, bringing together her transgender self and her political identity, she announces out loud that she has voted for the Communist Party. By fulfilling her "compromisos de ciudadana" ("citizen duty"), la Madelón engages in this most fundamental act of political citizenship. Recognizing that she has transcended biological sex, gender, and even the law, the astonished voting booth attendants allow her to exercise her fundamental right to vote.

La Madelón also joins in almost every leftist political demonstration. Her list is long, having demonstrated against nuclear power, on May Day, in feminist demonstrations, and on Gay Pride Day. Noteworthy as well is her attendance at the first celebration of Andalucía Day, on 4 December 1977. As an immigrant from southern Spain, and in a move that echoes Ocaña's performances in Barcelona, la Madelón and la Begum attend the demonstration wearing, despite the persistent rain, traditional Andalusian dresses with the colours of the Andalusian flag.[32] By wearing these costumes, la Madelón and la Begum embody southern Spanish regionalism and its most stereotypical symbols. Obviously, the episode is poking fun at formulaic performances of Andalusian nationalism. But nonetheless, the demonstration is fundamentally a political event. The characters remind the reader of the importance of participating in mass protest and the significance of occupying public space, in this case by a group of immigrants often despised as poor and uneducated. More important, la Madelón and la Begum claim ownership of the powerful symbols of southern culture. These superficial aspects of traditional popular culture had grown trite after Franco's appropriation of them as representative of Spanishness in his efforts to promote the country to international tourism. That la Madelón and la Begum make use of the traditional southern dress constitutes a major act of resignification, much like Pedro Almodóvar donning a bullfighter jacket in the front cover photo of his book *Patty Diphusa*.[33]

A final example illustrating this novel's contribution to envisioning a pluralistic political community is its last chapter. This chapter revolves around the demonstration of 27 February 1981, when Spanish people took to the streets to demonstrate in support of democracy. Amid the massive crowds, la Madelón notes both the plurality of singularities and the equality of them all: "Había gente de todos los colores, alguna con un pelaje rarísimo, y yo comprendo que de eso se trataba, de que fuéramos todas, sin distingos, España entera ... porque lo más importante era el espíritu y, sobre todo, la democracia y la libertad" ("There were people of all colours, even some with weird hair, and I understand that that was precisely the point, that we should all go, without distinction, all of Spain ... because the most important thing was the spirit and, above all, democracy and freedom") (151). So huge is the gathering that the demonstrators overflow the main street, making it impossible to locate either the beginning or the end of the demonstration (152). The mass of people overwhelms the public space of downtown Madrid. The people come together "allí, para defender la democracia y la libertad, todas iguales" ("there, to defend democracy and freedom, all equal") (152). Words such as "democracy," "freedom," and "equality" proliferate as the novel drives home its central claim: that political equality and the exercising of citizens' rights is the foundation of a pluralistic democratic community.

Nancy Fraser has argued in her description of democratic participatory parity that traditional patterns of cultural value have excluded LGBTQ people from being inter-subjectively recognized, and therefore from participating as equal partners in the political process (Fraser and Honneth 47). Democratic participation was not a topic overtly present in the movies we have analysed in this chapter. *Una mala noche* counteracts this lack by showing its transgender characters voting, occupying the street for political purposes, and, more generally, simply talking about politics. Fraser argues that those excluded may change cultural values regarding participatory parity simply by being part of the body politic (47). This novel, therefore, is not simply an amusing chronicle of the Transition or the campy personal story of a struggle to become.

Put in its wider cultural frame, *Una mala noche* is the next step in the representation of transgender bodies and lives, one that claims their political and democratic equality as co-citizens.

Plural Bodies, Plural Communities

Una mala noche is a novel that presents unapologetic transgender characters. It fits in the larger cultural evolution toward normalization of non-normative bodies and lives. Laying the groundwork for a cultural environment in which a first-person narrative about a transgender communist, such as *Una mala noche*, could receive recognition were cutting-edge magazine articles and books, LGBT and feminist activism, underground comics, and films. As taboo and controversial topics had become progressively democratized and commercialized throughout the seventies, *Una mala noche* illustrates the presence of a new discourse on sex and gender and their relation to politics. This discourse, as we have seen, developed progressively during the seventies and paved the way for new sensibilities and practices. Magazines such as *Cuadernos* brought women's rights to the fore; *Triunfo* discussed feminism, eroticism, and the latest transgender research; and movies such as *Mi querida señorita* and *Cambio de sexo* explored the personal and social complexity of sex reassignment. Other, deplorably vulgar, movies such as *No desearás* nevertheless contributed to opening the floodgates that allowed for the representations of alternative lifestyles and desires, leaving tradition stripped of any discursive exclusivity on sex and gender. Lampooning official norms of being, *No desearás* was just the first, even if unwilling, item in a long arc of cultural products that contributed to normalizing alternative sexual and gender modes of being. These alternative modes of being would become increasingly visible during the eighties in Madrid, and were essential for the scandalous antics of *la Movida*.

That sex and gender – and therefore bodies – became commodities clashed directly with the Franco regime's Catholic morality, which typically restricted representations that challenged the traditional patriarchal heteronormative family structure. Topics that for decades had been taboo, such as divorce, out-of-wedlock sexual relations, abortion, prostitution, same-sex desire, or any alternative form of sexual enjoyment, in the seventies became central elements in mass media narratives. This chapter has shown that what Robbins has aptly described as the "celebratory funeral for the outdated repressions of national Catholicism" that took place in the eighties had begun well before the regime's demise (*Cruising* 35). Even if we consider with Alberto Mira that *el morbo* (Spaniards' sexual curiosity), and not anti-regime sentiment or other ideas about freedom, justice, and equality, had driven public attitudes toward sex and gender during the seventies, the presence of these topics in the mass media made them increasingly acceptable, even among the most conservative elements (*De Sodoma* 435). The more acceptable they became, the more they were integrated into the push for modernity and democracy. Although they were on occasion exploited for financial profit, as seen in the *comedia sexy* and *el destape*, cultural and film critics, thanks to their political and ethical positioning influenced in part by feminism, anti-capitalism, and egalitarian democratic ideological models, tended to denounce such appropriation.

If *el destape* conflated sexual and women's liberation as part of the same cultural change, so too did the feminist and LGBT militants who consciously created new webs of political solidarity among emerging social actors. Camp and drag would soon become central elements of *la Movida* and would eventually become the very symbol of Spanish modernity and sexual liberation (A. Mira, *De Sodoma* 526; Epps 148). Pedro Almodóvar's alter ego, Patty Diphusa, wrote about her deviant, amoral, and purposely provocative sex- and drug-fuelled fictional life; Nazario drew comics in which his transgender character Anarcoma solved crimes in the underworld; and la Madelón offered a politically committed alternative as she mused about her ideals of equality and what to wear to the next demonstration. Aside from her eccentricities, la Madelón represents the culmination of a zeitgeist, or, as she would have it, "un sentir popular" ("a popular sentiment") of openness and inclusivity toward sex and gender, and a shared universal subjectivity with respect to democracy and plurality that would characterize Madrid's new sense of community in the eighties.

Chapter Three

Drugs: The Burden of Modernity

Many bottles of cava were opened in celebration the day Franco died. It was a day that would usher in the full transformation of Spain's social, cultural, and political landscape. Yet the post-dictatorial period would not be characterized by the massive consumption of bubbly wine. Instead, changes in recreational drug use and abuse made heroin, a drug rarely used up to that point, a destructive popular choice. Often ignored or mentioned in passing, the heroin outbreak that began in the late seventies decimated a generation of youth in some parts of Madrid, either through death, incarceration, or chronic incapacity.[1] This chapter will illuminate the perfect storm that allowed the (ab)use of heroin to became so prevalent, as well as the contradictory discourse on drugs that, from the mid-sixties on, underpinned the cultural mechanisms that justified their use. In what follows, I offer a brief cultural history of the representation of drugs in mass media. I show that, as a result of the cultural shifts of the seventies, using heroin became, for many, a status-seeking act of rebellion against a society that, while transitioning rapidly to a consumer culture, still bore the trappings of the old regime.

Paul Manning has argued for the importance of distinguishing between the actual practices of those consuming drugs and the representations of drug use by media and cultural institutions (2). Heeding Manning's advice, this chapter considers mass media and identity construction emanating from the politics, culture, and economics of both Francoist and Transitional Spain, one of the main particularities of this period being a certain overlap between actual practice and representation. To this extent, I will show the way in which drug use was depicted in the media during the early seventies, and examine works by Ángel Montoto and Eduardo Haro Ibars as unique mediators between real drug use and its representation in wider social and cultural discourse in the public sphere. Through their writings, Montoto and Haro Ibars participated in the often-contradictory mass media representation of drugs while, at the same time, being users themselves. In this double role, they tried to articulate a view of drugs that was influenced by international discourse in dialogue with social and cultural trends local to Madrid. Concurrently, a wealth of films dealing with social fears and fantasies involving sex, violence, and recreational drug use represent another strand of my discussion. As the "actors" in these films were often individuals playing out their real-life criminal cases, fact and fiction could not easily be separated. Some actors were delinquents who eventually became drug users, and their arrests, trials, incarcerations, and deaths by overdose or violent armed confrontation made it into the headlines. Others were professional actors who, in strange cases of fiction-turned-reality, re-enacted in their personal lives the fictional plots of their movies, ending up in jail or dead by overdose.

In his thorough and indispensable book *Drogas y cultura de masas* (1996), Juan Carlos Usó has noted how particular Spanish institutions (law enforcement, the health care system, and the media) used foreign conceptualizations of drug use to make sense of a new reality (330). The mass media routinely produced a contradictory discourse on drugs, offering both judicious commentary by professionals and hyped-up, alarmist articles by journalists and cultural commentators.[2] The mass media's incongruous positions on drugs incorporated both a misinformed moralistic response to drug use and, for reasons we will see, a fascination with it.

Heroin: From Pharmacy to Black Market

"Heroin" is the commercial name for a synthetic form of morphine (diacetylmorphine) obtained from the opium poppy.[3] Synthesized in 1874 by English chemist Alder Wright, heroin was first commercialized in 1895 by Bayer in Germany. With the trademark name "Heroin," it was initially sold over the counter as a cough suppressant. The drug was originally considered less addictive than morphine, but the opposite was soon discovered, together with its other negative side effects. By 1925, heroin was officially outlawed internationally, though enforcement of the ban was uneven. After the Second World War, international consensus on enforcement arose, and there were two significant agreements about the issue in Vienna: the Single Convention on Narcotic Drugs (1961) and the Convention on Psychotropic Drugs (1971), both of which produced international agreements on controlling substances and enforcement. Signatory nations had to commit to limiting access to controlled substances and to setting up legal instruments to combat drug trafficking. Franco authorized Spain's signing the 1971 Vienna Convention in February 1973, but the Spanish state did not ratify it until 1976.[4]

This convention year of 1971 turned out to be an important one in opioid-related news. US president Richard Nixon declared his "War on Drugs," and Jim Morrison and Coco Chanel died of complications related to opiate use after Janis Joplin and Jimi Hendrix had died of overdoses the previous year.[5] It was also in 1971 that the Rolling Stones released their now classic album *Sticky Fingers*, which included the single "Sister Morphine."[6] The year is important as well because the pioneering film *The French Connection* was released.[7] Finally, in 1971 Alfred McCoy wrote the doctoral dissertation he would publish the following year as *The Politics of Heroin in South East Asia*, whose argument is now better known than the book itself. In it, McCoy suggested that the CIA turned a blind eye to, and even provided air transport for, the wholesale movement of heroin out of the "Golden Triangle" for the financing of anti-communist forces.[8] The magazine *Triunfo* promptly picked up this controversy from the US media by translating and republishing Frank Browning and Banning Garrett piece in *Ramparts Magazine*, "La CIA y la droga" ("The CIA and Drugs") in 1972.

This subject was not new for *Triunfo*. Since 1962, the magazine had been translating pieces published in the US media about drugs and drug enforcement, and it would continue to publish articles on the topic with regularity until its closure in 1982. For instance, the 1962 article "1500 millones en drogas" ("Millions in Drugs") related the New York Police Department's arrest of several members of a heroin-trafficking ring.[9] *Triunfo* afforded these articles a central position in the magazine, with explicit, full-page photos of users that, in one 1964 article, included close-ups of a subject injecting. In another 1967 article, the topic is illustrated with photos of a man shooting up in a bourgeois living room, and two photos of two men and a woman injecting in front of a British pharmacy.[10] These articles offered a cautionary tale about the use of heroin and other drugs by young, white, affluent, suburban kids, and they explained how, for these youth, the path to heroin had been paved by pharmaceuticals.[11] With the descriptions and photos of affluent co-eds replete with cars and all the other trappings of upper-middle-class privilege, *Triunfo*, throughout the sixties, established an image of the heroin user far removed from the gritty experiences that awaited users of the eighties.

From the early sixties into the late seventies, *Triunfo* coverage of drug use was extensive and varied. Some articles in the early sixties offered exposés of celebrity drug use in Italy.[12] Others naively provided lists of over-the-counter drugs (sedatives and amphetamines) and their effects.[13] A few articles attempted to demonstrate understanding of drug addiction, its causes, and cures, but most were seeded with misinformation.[14] The 1967 article "Drogas, un mundo dentro de otro" ("Drugs, a World into Another"), for instance, presented heroin as even more addictive than it really was, and furthermore claimed that it was very difficult to cure addicts, distorting public and personal expectations regarding addiction (26). In the seventies, many articles would support the idea that Western governments were actively and secretly encouraging drug use as a tool of social control. This conspiracy theory can be seen in articles like "El paraíso artificial" ("The Artificial Paradise") (Roy), "La CIA y la droga" (Browning and Garrett), "Juventud y drogas" ("Youth and Drugs") (Valtueña), "Una confusión interesada" ("An Interested Confusion") (Goicoechea), and many more from 1978 on.

Examining over two decades of articles in *Triunfo* reveals important shifts both in patterns of substance abuse and the social perceptions surrounding it. Earlier articles, many replete with photos, clearly associated controlled substances, including heroin, with Western, modern, wealthy, educated, and democratic countries that Spanish citizens in many ways aspired to imitate. The images accompanying these articles established an explicit link between drugs and the affluence and lifestyles of Western youth. Articles in the seventies presented drug use as a natural consequence of a consumerist society and as encouraged by governments and international corporations.[15] In making this argument, these articles were following the countercultural mantra that states were employing drugs as weapons of social control. What began as translations of English-language magazine pieces depicting drug use in the United States or the United Kingdom had, by the seventies, lost all sign of translation; emerging in their place were articles written by Spanish journalists grappling with domestic drug use and how to explain it. Despite their alarmist tone and the regular recurrence of the topic in the magazine, recreational drug use during the sixties and the early seventies in Spain was significantly more modest in scope than what *Triunfo*'s editorial line suggested.

According to Juan Carlos Usó, the records of the Ministry of Health indicate that in 1962 1,300 legal opiate addicts had documented permission to purchase opioids (*Drogas* 305). By 1970, the number had risen, but was still a relatively modest 1,500 (ibid.; Santo-Domingo, "Historia" 44). In a country of thirty million, as Spain was at that time, this number accounts for 0.005 per cent of the population, and thus did not represent a statewide problem. Most were morphine users, adults who were often well adapted to social, work, and family environments.

Many were employees of the health care system, which had, of course, provided them with access to the opioids. But by 1972, as we will see, the documentation attests to a growing consumption of psychotropic drugs in Spain.[16]

The approach taken by print media to drugs and drug use in the early seventies was not entirely sensationalist – it also on occasion appealed for reason and professional assessment. Félix Santos, for instance, in his article "Drogas y subversion" ("Drugs and Subversion"), published in *Cuadernos para el Diálogo*, related that during the debate in Congress about the *Ley de Peligrosidad y Rehabilitación Social* (Law of Dangerousness and Social Rehabilitation), a parliamentarian claimed that the reason behind the violent student revolts was that "dos traficantes extranjeros distribuían grifa gratis entre los alumnos" ("two foreign dealers distributed free hashish among the students") (52). Santos sarcastically concluded that students must surely have been high if they were pushing for a democratic, modern, and free university (ibid.). Speaking up publicly in support of the students to justify their revolts was a courageous act in Franco's Spain. More importantly for this chapter, in calling out the parliamentarian's fallacy, Santos was clearly separating drug use from the logical aspirations of students to a better university by challenging the concept that altered consciousness could be the only motivation behind an anti-government uprising. But Santos was not the only dissenting voice against the typical misinformed understanding of drug use. Just two years after Santos's article, a prominent scientist would sound a clarion call regarding the impending heroin epidemic he foresaw and offer his professional recommendations on how to avoid it.

Joaquín Santo-Domingo, then director of the national program for prevention of and attention to alcoholism and drug addiction, presented a professional assessment of drug abuse in 1972 in a lengthy article for *Cuadernos para el Diálogo*. In "Los drogadictos" ("Drug Addicts"), he reflected on substance abuse in Spain, warned of the public health and criminality problems that addiction causes, and recommended several actionable policy points. This research-driven article was far ahead of its time: already in 1972, it delineated what is today the medical, epidemiological, and criminological consensus regarding treatment of drug addiction.

Santo-Domingo began his article by characterizing the growing collective alarm as within "los límites desmesurados e ineficaces del histerismo colectivo" ("the disproportionate and ineffective limits of collective hysteria"), emerging from the belief that the use of some drugs fundamentally harms society while overlooking that other drugs are tolerated for cultural reasons (31). He warned his readers that the evolution of substance abuse and dependency was rooted in the larger global attitude toward drugs: the more "normal" users there were of a substance, the more "pathological" users of that same drug (32). He continued by clarifying the terminology and suggested that the term "drug addict," in his view, should be used only to refer to those who have biological dependency on a substance. The popular use of the term encouraged by the media had other ethical or moral connotations, and had been used to imply anti-social, criminal, or unproductive behaviour (33). This confusion was not useful for treating actual addicts, as it failed to differentiate between "normal" and "pathological" uses. Santo-Domingo proposed instead to conceptualize illegal drugs the same way society sees alcohol or pharmaceuticals – that is, with a distinction between "normal" social use, which has few personal or professional consequences, and "unreasonable" abuse, which has the potential to marginalize and criminalize the subject (33).

This approach is especially important because Santo-Domingo identified a type of drug use that was a "toxicomanía de moda" – trendy or modern drug addictions that youth use to rebel or to show their defiance of social norms (35). Society's stigmatization of this type of user, as well as the drugs used, only reinforced and encouraged the abuse, as it confirmed the rebellious nature of drug use by the very social reaction and alarm it sparked. Santo-Domingo explained how drugs could be a form of belonging in youth culture: "la droga da cohesión y subraya con sus ritos una normatividad creada y mantenida por el grupo propio" ("drugs give cohesion and underline, with their rites, a normativity created and maintained by the group") (35). Although the number of these "trendy" users was still low in Spain, Santo-Domingo called for the rapid medicalization of the problem.

Santo-Domingo issued yet another prescient warning: criminalizing access to or possession of substances only delays finding long-term solutions to the problem, concluding that "esto es sobre todo aplicable a la heroína, por fortuna poco o nada utilizada aun en España por el elemento indígena" ("this is especially applicable to heroin, which is luckily not used, or barely used, in Spain by the natives") (35). In 1972, Santo-Domingo considered real problem to be, instead, the numbers of alcoholics and users of legal pharmaceuticals. He concluded pessimistically that, given the minimal resources dedicated to assisting these people and the social attitude toward drug use in general, there was not much hope of effectively treating rising substance-abuse problems among youth (36).

Even though Santo-Domingo's biggest concern was alcohol and pharmaceuticals, in this article he presented the subcultural use of drugs as an identity and status maker, something that would be confirmed later when heroin use rose to epidemic proportions.[17] After reading Santo-Domingo, who was, after all, an influential professional in the health care system and who published in a widely circulated magazine, it is hard to argue that there was a lack of available information regarding drug use in Spain, its effects on society, and best practices for dealing with it.

Santo-Domingo's work did not go unheard, and by mid-1974 he was appointed to lead an inter-ministerial commission to address the consequences of drug trafficking and substance abuse. This was a multidisciplinary work group in which academics, professionals, and even civil society would be represented (Santo-Domingo, "Historia" 59). Members of the national health system, social workers, university researchers, police and Guardia Civil, as well as members of youth organizations, met to produce a study with actionable points.

The study, published in the *Revista de Sanidad e Higiene Pública* (*Magazine of Public Health and Hygiene*) (1975), exposed the lack of information across some professional sectors, and the need to improve health and law-enforcement systems with a special focus on prevention, treatment, and re-socialization. The study noted that "el amplio consumo de drogas" ("widespread drug consumption") was based in part on a collective attitude toward drugs that encouraged their use (Santo-Domingo, "Memoria" 511). Among the reasons for this were a curiosity for new sensations and a desire for instant gratification, but also "una situación consumista general que implica a los medios de comunicación" ("a general consumerism involving mass media") (511). The study noted that legal drugs (pharmaceuticals) were not restricted to one social class and were so widely available that Spanish society was witnessing "un consumo incluso masivo de alguna de estas sustancias" ("a consumption that was, in the case of some substances, even massive") (543). The report identified legal psychotropic substances as the most worrisome types of drugs, naming amphetamines, anxiolytics, and painkillers as the most popular among both youth and adult populations (543).

This study, in addition to being published in a professional journal, was submitted to Deputy Prime Minister Manuel Fraga, who ordered the implementation of its policy proposals in mid-1975 (Santo-Domingo, "Historia" 59).[18] Still under the dictatorship, professionals on the cutting edge of their practice managed both to produce sophisticated analyses, and to convince government officials to apply innovative plans to prevent and treat drug abuse. However, Franco's death in November 1975 postponed efforts to combat substance abuse, as Transition governments focused on seemingly more pressing issues, such the economy and terrorism. There would be no state-wide, coordinated, multidisciplinary approach to drug abuse until the creation of the *Plan Nacional Sobre las Drogas* (National Drug Plan) in 1985. We can safely conclude that the explosion of heroin use in the eighties can be traced directly to the seventies, with its powerful images of international use, the widespread availability of pharmaceuticals, and the frustrated attempts at prevention.

"A colocarse y al loro": *La Movida* and Drugs

The phrase "a colocarse y al loro" refers to Mayor Enrique Tierno Galván's famous encitement in 1984 that captured Madrid's collective party atmosphere of the moment.[19] As we have seen, the Spanish generation that dealt with the transition to democracy adapted to a new economic model and broke with the moral codes of Francoism. Most subsequent cultural criticism has taken a nostalgic, if not melancholic, view of the period. While giving an occasional cursory nod to the role of drugs at the time, such studies have rarely acknowledged the deeper cultural causes and consequences of drug use. Instead, they have simply lamented the detrimental effects of heroin, or eulogized a simpler, happy time, free of the spectre of AIDS. The most common line of analysis tends to consider heroin a mind-expanding drug whose use was inspired by foreign artistic heroes, and which was used in Spain by a countercultural few, almost always elites, for whom it liberated creative energies. When current criticism has accounted for wider heroin use, it has done so with reference to the same premise of the counterculture discourse of the seventies. In other words, it has interpreted non-elite drug use either as a way to escape local conditions (e.g., unemployment, lack of education and opportunities) or as a government plot to suppress a supposedly politically active generation of youth.[20]

The changes in attitudes toward drugs, as well as the ways in which they were used, occurred against the backdrop of a profound economic transformation characterized by a move from an agrarian, deeply Catholic, moralistic, vertically integrated authoritarian society to a liberal, post-industrial, increasingly secular, democratic consumer society. Despite the rapid improvement in the Spanish economy brought about by *desarrollismo* (development) policies during the sixties and seventies, the country experienced severe economic crises. A major crisis in 1977 caused inflation to run up to 40 per cent, while in the late eighties unemployment reached 20 per cent. The economy was not promising, and the old dictatorial regime, despite the Transition, was still ubiquitous in society. In addition, traditional models of identity formation – occupational stability and patriarchal family structures – reached a point of crisis with the new social, economic, and legal changes. While traditional norms and values receded, the market, through consumption, offered an alternative avenue for individuals to construct their identities.

Although the welfare state had long been established in the rest of Europe, Spain, in a breakneck race to catch up, fashioned a new society of spectacle and consumption, mediated, in part, by drugs. Aspirational images in the media of modern Europe and the United States, alongside neoliberal policies implemented in the sixties, generated a new sense of prosperity that liberated many previously repressed energies. Spaniards were looking for new ways to have fun, and most of them involved consumption. At the centre of contemporary Western societies, consumption is partly about pleasure and lifestyle: for example, commodities and vacations. But consumption is also about appearance and individuality. More to my point, the consumption of drugs, in addition to pleasurable sensations, provides an identity to the user. During the seventies and early eighties, drug use meant being modern and cutting edge, living dangerously in a continuous act of self-aggression and self-destruction. As Santo-Domingo had warned in his 1972 article in *Cuadernos para el Diálogo,* artists, intellectuals, and youth on the social and economic periphery found in drug consumption the path to a non-normative identity that would fill the void left by the social and political upheaval of the Transition.

José Luis Gallero in *Sólo se vive una vez: Esplendor y ruina de la Movida madrileña* (*You Only Live Once: Splendor and Ruin in la Movida Madrileña*) (1991) compiled interviews with participants in *la Movida.* These testimonies reveal that drugs were considered an element of urban culture, conspicuous consumption, and identity construction. One interviewee, Borja Casani, for instance, links the city to drugs and considers them a freeing personal adventure (19). Fabio McNamara, however, offers a useful framework for understanding the period: the best moment for him, he claims, lasted only from 1979 to 1983–84, years characterized by self-destructiveness, carelessness, lack of sleep, and partaking in as much sex and drugs as possible (318). Blanca Sánchez, in another interview, confirms McNamara's statements, explaining that, up to 1978 everyone had simply smoked joints. When, at the end of the seventies, new drugs appeared, everybody happily tried them. Drugs, she concludes, seemed divine and fantastic (295).

In hindsight, these perceptions of drug use seem simple, even naive: people wanted to feel free, to experiment, to cross social and personal limits, and to party hard. After decades of military dictatorship and being at the centre of power, Madrid became a site for wild revelry – and this quickly became central to its new identity. Drugs played a central role in this collective party, and using them, especially heroin, became the ultimate expression of being modern. José Manuel Lechado characterizes the time as marked by a new culture of intoxication – in this case, a collective one: "El que no se drogaba – o el que decía que no se drogaba – era un *pringao*: no estaba en el rollo ni en la Movida" ("Those who did not use drugs or did not say they used drugs were dupes; they were not in *la Movida*") (25). Drugs were central to the emerging cultural scene in Madrid. Collectively, they provided a cohesive element, and, for the individual, they served to project a personal image of daring and boundary crossing.

When restricted to artists, musicians, and creators, drugs were seen as part of a collective freedom experiment and an avenue to group belonging. However, the use of heroin outside the "creative class" has been given a classist explanation. Lechado, for example, attributes heroin use to unemployment and lack of progressive political outcomes for working-class youth: "Muchos jóvenes, habitantes de los suburbios industriales y las ciudades-dormitorio, comenzarán a experimentar de manera no tan festiva con el caballo" ("Many young inhabitants of the working-class boroughs begin to experiment in a not so festive way with junk") (21). Others, meanwhile, have linked drug use among working-class youth to disengagement from political or social problems and, in general, to the lack of any intellectual or spiritual interest (Escudero 149). In these top-down analyses, "youth" – almost always described in simplistically broad brushstrokes – are presented as powerless, soulless beings whose only act of agency is to insulate themselves from difficulty and pain by shooting heroin. The reality was much more complex than preconceived totalizing readings such as these would have us believe.

The contrasting reading of heroin – fun experimentation for artists and intellectuals, but sombre escapism for everyone else – contains, in my view, serious problems of conceptualization. First, it implies that working-class youth were driven only by basic needs and that they were fundamentally disconnected from the wider cultural environment and modern aesthetic concerns. Second, it class binds heroin use as a self-destructive, selfish way to escape personal or collective problems, and disallows the possibility of recreational, and therefore pleasurable, use of drugs. Third, it deems heroin use as a collective class weakness: a whole generation of working-class youth unable (morally, psychologically, or otherwise) to cope with circumstances. Typecasting working-class drug abuse as suicidal escapism fails to credibly explain

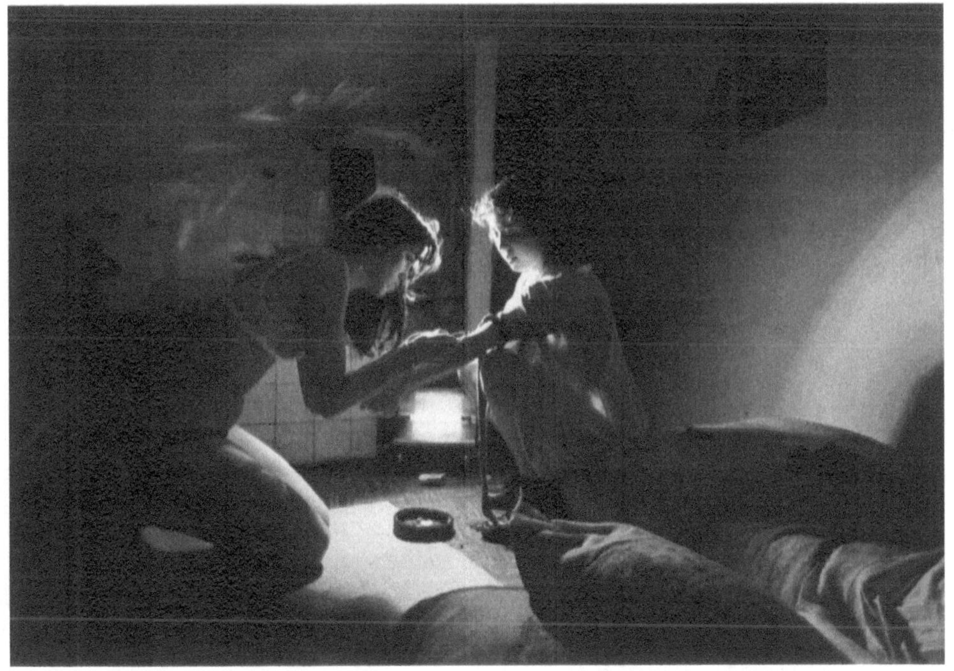

3.1 "Teresa y Carmen," 1978. Heroin's mystique, built up over decades in the mass media, contributed to encouraging its use and abuse.

why large numbers of youth would be out of sync with the culture of the period. Given the evidence, we cannot assume that working-class youth were immune to a public sphere steeped with images and texts that linked substance abuse to an attractive international youth culture. Many working-class youth, no differently than artists and intellectuals, perceived drug use as a vehicle for transgression, experimentation, and pleasure, as well as a marker of collective identity and status.

Bienvenida Mrs. Heroin

Although the real number of drug users in the mid-seventies was impossible to determine, the mass media had already, from the early sixties on, nursed the perception of massive, widespread, and uncontrollable drug use.[21] Until the late seventies, heroin use would be restricted to those elites who could travel and afford a drug rarely available on the streets. But their preferences, like those of most Spaniards, were for pharmaceuticals, readily available either over the counter or with a medical prescription.[22] The most popular substances enjoyed by all classes in this period were the traditional drugs: alcohol, coffee, and cigarettes. Hashish, originating in Morocco, enjoyed broad appeal in the sixties and remains today a very popular drug. From the sixties on, however, heroin made a noticeable entrance into Europe. Spain was one of its key entry points, and newspaper headlines informed readers of incessant confiscations and arrests for drug trafficking.[23] As print media created legendary associations between heroin and foreign rock musicians or the US counterculture, the drug burst onto Spanish streets in the late seventies, "democratizing" a practice that had so far been restricted to the upper classes.

Domingo Comas Arnau and Joaquín Santo-Domingo described the first heroin users in Spain as well-educated upper-class young men from permissive families (Comas 636–7; Santo-Domingo, "Los drogadictos" 36).[24] Eduardo Haro Ibars explained that the typical heroin user was "joven intelectual de la alta burguesía, homosexual y adicto al opio y a la morfina" ("a young intellectual from the high bourgeoisie, homosexual and addicted to opium and morphine") (*De qué* 74).[25] Photographer Alberto García-Alix's testimony is similar: "Los primeros yonquis que hubo en España eran gente con mucha clase" ("The first Spanish junkies were high-class people") (Gallero 156). Some travelled to Amsterdam to buy heroin, but "en el 78, había ya mucha gente en Madrid que antes de fumarse un porro se había chutado" ("in '78, there were already many people in Madrid who, before smoking hash, had already injected") (ibid.). By 1979, consumption had become "una seña de identidad para jóvenes miembros de grupos subculturalmente diferentes" ("an identity marker for young members of subculturally different groups" (Usó, *Drogas* 331). Soon, elite heroin use began to show its ugly side, with overdoses and arrests leading to jail terms.[26]

First restricted to the children of the upper class, heroin eventually hit all levels of Spanish society. It most deeply affected those poor areas suffering from an endemic lack of resources. These were the lower-middle-class and working-class districts whose urban planning, or lack thereof, we examined in chapter 1. Well into the eighties, these boroughs still suffered from a debilitating lack of infrastructure.[27] Although they were latecomers to heroin, youth from these boroughs would come to represent the quintessential heroin addicts. To know them better, we turn to Juan Gamella, who has conducted a detailed anthropological study of one of Madrid's mixed-class boroughs. His work serves as an illuminating map of the way heroin use spread.

Gamella shows that the typical heroin abuser during the eighties was male, with little formal education, born between 1956 and 1970 into a working-class or poor family, and living in a crowded flat, normally in the outskirts of Madrid ("The Spread" 138). These were not marginal populations so much as urban lower classes that were well-integrated in their community.[28] At the time of first heroin use, most subjects had peers that both regularly used other drugs (nicotine, cannabis, alcohol, amphetamines, hypnotics, sedatives) and had a positive image of intoxication (ibid. 139). The majority of first uses happened from 1978 into the early eighties, as heroin moved from the city centre to the *barrios* at extraordinary speed, spreading through networks of friendship or acquaintances. Nearly half of intravenous heroin users eventually contracted HIV/AIDS. For many users, heroin was perceived as heroic. The act of self-aggression necessary for shooting heroin differentiated them within their social group and reflected the courage, rebelliousness, and glamour that mass media and the entertainment industry had played up in biographies of pop icons such as Janis Joplin, Jimi Hendrix, and Sid Vicious. But heroin use was not only about relating to rock stars, as I shall argue later in this chapter – it also linked users to international literary figures and the Western cultural canon.

It is important to reiterate that heroin consumption normally comes in tandem with the use of alcohol, hashish, anxiolytics, and/or amphetamines. Gamella corroborates García-Alix's assertion that, prior to 1978, the heroin market was practically non-existent in Madrid. Before heroin arrived on the scene, needles were instead used to inject other drugs such as opiates, stimulants, and hypo-sedatives that could be purchased in pharmacies (Gamella, "The Spread" 140).[29] It is clear now that the heroin epidemic arose from specific cultural and historical circumstances and was not a product of covert governmental policies or actions.[30] Heroin became fashionable among working-class youth, just as it did among many artists and authors, its use spread principally among those who were already experimenting with, and who had a positive view of, drugs. In addition, heroin came to be perceived as an alternative to the traditional drugs (alcohol, coffee, or tobacco) identified with the old masculinity of Franco's regime. Heroin, by contrast, provided an identity associated with international rock stars, countercultural movements, and Western affluence. When we add the group ritual and the constant need to consume, it becomes clear that heroin had grown to be more than just a drug. It was, in the end, the consummate contemporary lifestyle. It is also the ultimate commodity, in that, due to its characteristics, it becomes the focal point of users' lives: they come to relate to themselves and to reality almost exclusively through buying, selling, and consuming it. Expensive, relatively hard to obtain, and necessarily gruesome in its application, heroin became the status-making commodity that Dr. Santo-Domingo, as far back as 1972, had anticipated.[31]

Building the Myth, Feeding the Habit

The mass media had been stoking concern in the public consciousness about drug use for so long that it is no surprise that there was an immediate reaction to the first news of overdoses. The result was increased social alarm and a widespread perception that the number of drug-related crimes was escalating. Newspapers and magazines put forth alarmist depictions, but based in Spain instead of suburban America; by contrast, comics and fanzines presented ludic representations of drug use. Another channel representing drug use was an avalanche of realistic movies that exploited Spanish society's fears and desires. These films contributed to the popular perception that rising crime and heroin use were linked, feeding an anxiety about public safety that was termed *inseguridad ciudadana* (citizen insecurity).

The effect of movies such as *Perros callejeros* (*Stray Dogs*) (José Antonio de la Loma, 1977) cannot be underestimated. Films such as these were taken as examples of a new reality, but, in many cases, it was a reality that the films were constructing. I am not referring to the experimental *Arrebato* (*Rapture*) (1979) by Ivan Zulueta, but rather to movies with provocative titles like *El último "viaje"* (*The Last "Trip"*) (1973), *Juventud drogada* (*Drugged Youth*) (1977), *Los placeres ocultos* (*Hidden Pleasures*) (1977), *¿Y ahora qué, señor fiscal?* (*And Now What, Mr. Prosecutor?*) (1977), *Las que empiezan a los quince años* (*The Girls Who Begin at Fifteen*) (1978), *Los violadores del amanecer* (*The Dawn Rapists*) (1978), and *Nunca en horas de clase* (*Never in Class Time*) (1978). I purposely provide this detailed, if onerous, list of films and their release dates to illustrate the frantic way in which this topic was exploited – too rapid for adequate quality and consideration of the subject. There were, among these, a few notable exceptions: *Perros callejeros* (José Antonio de la Loma, 1977), *Deprisa, deprisa* (*Fast, Fast*) (Carlos Saura, 1980), and *Navajeros* (*Muggers*) (Eloy de la Iglesia, 1980).[32] But despite the popular belief that the movies reflected urban street reality, there was little correlation between the new kind of working-class delinquency depicted in the movies and actual heroin use.[33]

In 1973, sociologist José Félix Tezanos documented and explained rising criminality under Francoism in an essay for *Cuadernos para el Diálogo*, noting that "parece obvio que una cierta psicosis de violencia empieza a extenderse en nuestra sociedad" ("it seems obvious that a psychosis of violence is beginning to spread in our society") (18). His essay directly contradicts the popular perception that the arrival of democracy and due process brought a concomitant rise in criminality. Juvenile delinquency films, what are now called *Cine Quinqui*, and their heroes *de barrio* (from the hood) depict heroin's early days in Madrid and Barcelona, yet strikingly, the early ones (those made prior to 1979) predate the actual popularization of heroine use among the working class. Those produced in 1979–80 or later parallel the drug's widespread use, and some delinquents would later claim that these early films provided the motivation and the education they needed to begin their criminal careers (M. Cuesta 100). Given Tezanos's research, it is safe to assume that these films were exploiting the "psychosis" that he had detected in a society that was still under the firm control of the regime.

The *Cine Quinqui* is generally characterized by poor production values, quick shooting schedules, and the use of non-professional actors. In a sadly ironic twist, the actors in these movies were often small-time criminals who vaulted to fame thanks to the movies that fictionalized their criminal exploits. Some of the actors who participated in these movies became addicted to heroin and died as a result of their drug abuse – José Luis Manzano, Antonio Flores, and Sonia Martínez are three of the most notable examples. The protagonists of the *Cine Quinqui* are youth from working-class families who embark on a criminal path in part due to their socio-economic situation.[34] They lack education and professional opportunities, and their crimes provide them with experiences that otherwise would have been off-limits: driving fast cars, using various drugs, and having expensive brand-name clothes, to name a few. In these movies, explicit drug use, sex, and extreme violence are central motifs. These are not presented like the titillating soft-core sex scenes from *el destape* movies, but instead, in scenes that were transgressive of bourgeois morals for their depictions of same-sex intercourse, genital mutilation, rape, and multiple forms of violent confrontation.[35] Thus, *Cine Quinqui* is a visual form of an accelerated and outlawed *bildungsroman* where spectators vicariously experience the young protagonists' progressive and intensive exposure to violence, sex, and drugs.

According to Mery Cuesta, two main schools of *Cine Quinqui* can be identified by the location of production and the approach to the subject: Madrid and Barcelona. They are represented, respectively, by directors such as Eloy de la Iglesia for the capital, and the more conservative José Antonio de la Loma for Barcelona (75–6). Trying to denounce moral corruption by showing the dangers of delinquency and drug use, de la Loma's films unwittingly glorified the petty criminals he hired as actors. Actors/delinquents such as *el Torete*, *el Vaquilla*, and *el Jaro* became urban legends and models for some working-class youth who interpreted these movies differently than the director intended.[36] Eloy de la Iglesia, on the other hand, presented a political and social critique. In his movies, disenfranchisement, need, and a culture of consumption propel working-class youth to engage in criminal behaviour. The genre was so compelling that even a director as distinguished as Carlos Saura would try his hand at it, with *Deprisa, deprisa* (1980).[37] The *Cine Quinqui* rendered drug use legitimate, despite its consequences, because the protagonists gained access, albeit short-lived, to fame, freedom, and a high-consumption lifestyle. As coming-of-age films, they justified drug use as another step in their protagonists' accelerated development. With these characters framed as modern rebels without a cause, their cautionary tale was missed by most younger viewers, who instead found in them a new category of urban hero.

Similar concerns about and contradictory discourses on drug abuse by the young are summed up in a 1978 *Noticieros y Documentales* (No-Do 1826, 23 January 1978).[38] A newsreel possibly shown in some theatres before the films discussed above, its voice-over presents the problem while images of intoxicated individuals flash across the screen. The viewer sees a young man and woman shooting heroin inside a bourgeois home. An interview with Pedro Rodríguez Nicolás, inspector of the Narcotics Brigade, follows. He declares that, in some geographical areas, abusive consumption of "hard" drugs has reached alarming levels. Professorial in demeanour and dress, Inspector Rodríguez continues that these drugs tend to be heroin and other opioids that, until recently, had been unknown in Spain. More images of drug use follow this interview, while the voice-over narrates the (now-discredited) escalation theory, which claims that addicts progress from "soft" drugs like cannabis to "hard" drugs like heroin, while explaining that rehabilitation is very difficult. Following this segment, Dr. Santo-Domingo is brought in, stating that treatment is relatively easy and that it would be profitable to society, as users would not end up in jail, incapacitated, or dead. The No-Do ends with the voice-over declaring how abandoning the "artificial paradises" of drugs is always a difficult fight. The narrative tension in this No-Do between the misinformed (although seemingly authoritative) narrator and the professional experts is clearly dominated by the voice-over, who has the last word. Like a societal alter ego, it frames and dominates the narration even though it displays an obsolete and factually incorrect understanding of drug use, even explicitly contradicting Santo-Domingo, one of the period's foremost experts. This No-Do illustrates the way that, throughout the seventies, the mass media continued feeding audiences the contradictory information about drugs they had already been pushing into the public sphere for well over a decade. It shows, too, the media's refusal to give full voice to the social and medical experts on drug addiction, whose prescriptions for treatment at the societal level would be woefully ignored.

A similar contradictory pattern can be detected in print media. What had started as articles on drug use in foreign locations had, by the end of the seventies, been all but replaced by local coverage of domestic drug use. At that time, there was a constant barrage of news involving drugs, arrests, and delinquency. In addition to these, more considered approaches appeared in op-ed articles and books, including reportage on junkies' lives or the kinds of medical attention they received. For instance, the Madrid newspaper *El País* ran headlines such as "El incremento de muertes por sobredosis es alarmante" ("The Increase of Deaths by Overdose is Alarming"), even though the article did not specify any number of deaths at all (16). In 1978, *El País* confirmed one death: "Muere un joven por sobredosis de heroína" ("Young Man Dies of Heroin Overdose," 12). In other publications, the trend is also noticeable, as in *Diario 16*'s "En Valladolid: nació heroinómana" ("In Valladolid: She Was Born a Junkie"), or in the fascist *El Alcazar*'s "La droga invade los colegios" ("Drugs Invade Primary Schools." These are but a few examples of the flood of headlines appearing in print media at the time. Alarmist and scandalous at times, like *El Alcazar*'s unproven declaration about drugs engulfing primary schools, these headlines replicated the alarm that the media had raised about drug issues in other countries, but now, this gritty urban depiction was local. The effect of the sensationalist coverage was nonetheless dissonant, since articles often espoused contradictory ideas. While sounding severe warnings against drug use, for example, they often simultaneously glamorized and exoticized it.

In February 1978, *Interviú* published an article on Ángel Montoto's trip to Southeast Asia to research opium and cocaine.[39] "*Interviú* por la ruta de las drogas 'duras': la muerte en polvo" ("*Interviú* on the Hard Drugs Road: Death by Powder") is the sensationalist title of the piece, which concludes with a subheading that spoke of the sordid world of cocaine and opioids.[40] In this article, Montoto recounted his experiences during 1976 and 1977 with cocaine, opium, and heroin in Thailand, London, and Barcelona. Mid-article, though, the reader finds an unexpected interview with Dr. Soler Insa from the psychiatric section of the Clinic Hospital in Barcelona. The article described the effects of cocaine, opium, and heroin, as well as their health risks and addictive potential. It also depicted the typical users of each drug. Finally, it declared the capitalist system responsible for the use of heroin and revealed the geopolitical culprit for its presence in Spain: US military bases.

The article could not be more contradictory in its messages. Despite wording in the title that associates drugs with death, the descriptions of drug use are beguiling and exotic. The author consumes cocaine after a fancy dinner in the flat of a "conocido fotógrafo londinense" ("a well-known London photographer") (23). It was Montoto's first use, and he details the effects as well as the patience of his host in response to his aggressive and hyperactive behaviour. Montoto also smoked opium in the "Golden Triangle" in northern Thailand, initiated by the wife of a tribal chieftain. The description of the pleasurable experience is again extremely enticing. Montoto says he tried heroin several times: once with only mild effects in Barcelona due to the adulteration of the dose, and another time in Chiang Mai in northern Thailand, where he snorted it. The effects of that experience he described in the following manner:

> El "flash." Algo muy difícil de explicar. Una especie de coz a todos los sentidos y a todos los puntos de un cuerpo que parecía insensible, una fabulosa coz de placer fabuloso. No sé. Es algo así como un tremendo orgasmo en el momento en que tu cuerpo levita. Luego, simples olas amables y llenas de sensualidad. Olas que te embaten y cuya intensidad disminuye con el tiempo para dar paso a una total dejadez. Nada importa. La misma euforia que sientes es egoísta, es para ti solo. (24)
>
> (The "flash" is something very difficult to explain. It's a kind of kick to the senses, a gigantic kick of fabulous pleasure. I don't know. It is like a tremendous orgasm in the moment that your body levitates. After that, there come nice waves of sensuality. Waves that hit you and with time leave you relaxed. Nothing matters. The euphoria that you feel is egoistic, because it is only for your enjoyment.)

The article illustrates a pervasive, contradictory discourse about heroin: it is glamorous, exotic, and pleasurable, and, at the same time, a forbidden substance used by the state as a destructive and sometimes lethal method of control. The implication is that artists, journalists, and professionals, apparently immune to heroin's addictive qualities, can use it, but unsuspecting others might well fall prey to the establishment's conspiracy to repress dissent.

Eduardo Haro Ibars was by 1978 becoming the cultural mediator of a generation, the interpreter of the birth and development of *la Movida*.[41] In the context of this discussion, two of his works are necessary to note: his article "Nos matan con heroína" ("They Kill Us With Heroin") and his popular book *De qué van las drogas* (*What Drugs Are All About*), both published in 1978. In "Nos matan con heroína," Haro Ibars declared that summer the end of the hippie movement and of the mystique of heroin: "la heroína ha dejado de ser una leyenda, relacionada con las canciones de Lou Reed, el flasheante y lejano New York, y los mitos de la decadencia neo-romántica que nos venden desde todos los medios de comunicación de masas" ("Heroin is no longer a legend related to Lou Reed's songs, the distant and flashy New York, and the myths of the Neo-Romantic decadence sold everywhere by the mass media") (8). He concluded his piece by listing heroin's nefarious characteristics and consequences, which, in his inventory, had little to do with health risks. Rather, the principal negative effect for Haro Ibars was the consequence of its adoption as a new weapon of state control, used to subdue university students in Paris in May '68 or the American hippies. Heroin thus "es utilizada para embrutecer, para violar el espíritu de quienes la consumen, para crear un nuevo conformismo: el usuario habitual de heroína es alguien que no plantea demasiados problemas, siempre que tenga resuelto el alimentar su hábito" ("is used to brutalize, to rape the spirit of those who consume it, to create a new conformism: the habitual user of heroin does not present too many problems, as long as he can feed the habit") (10). The only sacrifice required, in this scenario, is one typical of contemporary society: to submit oneself to the cycle of commodity consumption. From this perspective, and paraphrasing Marx, opioids become the opium of the people.

Haro Ibars's influential and best-selling book *De qué van las drogas*, published in an inexpensive paperback version by the anarchist publishing house Ediciones la Piqueta, illustrated drug use in Madrid. This very important book preceded Antonio Escohotado's monumental *Historia general de las drogas* (*General History of Drugs*) by four years,[42] and in it, Haro Ibars made many important points. The work's structure, organized by drug, its type of user, and the culture that it generated, was innovative. He acknowledged the contemporary economic model of consumer capitalism and observed that it had been able to assimilate something that in principle was negative and illegal (drug use) into a cultural event with an entire industry around it. He pointed out the contradiction of forbidding something that was continuously invoked by mass media and popular culture (17). In addition, he traced the construction of the "drug addict" type and noted how, just as Santo-Domingo had cautioned in 1972, it had become mixed with the concept of "dangerous delinquent."

The key contribution of *De qué van las drogas*, however, was its list of literary and artistic drug users who had produced renowned works while under the influence. Oddly enough, his semi-academic treatise directly influenced the way people on the street understood and justified drug use.

Recognizing how he had been affected by reading, at the age of thirteen, Théophile Gautier's descriptions of an implausible hashish trip, Haro Ibars described the drug habits of Charles Baudelaire, Honoré de Balzac, Walter Benjamin, Antonin Artaud, Milton Mezzrow, Thomas de Quincey, Samuel Taylor Coleridge, and Jean Cocteau. The pantheon of users extended to Louis Armstrong, Charlie Parker, Bob Dylan, the Beatles, David Bowie, Alice Cooper, Lou Reed, Jimi Hendrix, Diego Rivera, Errol Flynn, and members of bands such as the Grateful Dead, Pink Floyd, and Jefferson Airplane. The Beat generation figured prominently: Allen Ginsberg, Jack Kerouac, William Burroughs, and Michael McLure. In his work, Haro Ibars provided a genealogy of users and the veneer of respectability that high culture afforded to drug use. In other words, it was not just Lou Reed or Keith Richards using psychotropic substances, but myriad revered literary figures who had also experimented with drugs.

Haro Ibars's understanding of drug use could not be more highbrow and self-aware.[43] His description of his own hashish and opium trips were rooted in a literary culture both Romantic and Decadent, and mixed with later Surrealists and Beatniks, as De Quincey, Artaud, and Burroughs became key influences. While newspaper headlines registered mounting social problems resulting from drug abuse, and movies and magazines like *Interviú* cautioned against drug use while simultaneously making it alluring, Haro Ibars seemed more concerned with heroin's distinguished literary past and how this function was quickly vanishing. He was disturbed that heroin, no longer liberating the creative channels of an artistic generation, was becoming a product of mass consumption. He clearly intuited how the gathering European heroin crisis implied a new culture of drug use: once part of countercultural practices of the higher and educated classes, heroin had become depoliticized by its wide use or, similarly, by pleasure- and status-seeking consumerist youth. In a last-ditch attempt to save heroin's artistic status, Haro Ibars described addiction as a form of aesthetic living: "el adicto es, sobre todo, un artista de la enfermedad: la construye, la moldea a partir de su propia miseria" ("the addict is, above all, an artist of the disease: he constructs it and shapes it from his own misery") (74). His point was well taken. Those unable to attain fame through their artistic talents, discipline, luck, contacts, social class, or education could now garner cultural notoriety through addiction.

"La droga mata:" Lost Point

The mass media's reaction to heroin use during the late seventies and eighties was built on a platform it had been constructing for over twenty years: it was simultaneously exaggerated and moralistic, reinforcing and myth making. In many cases, this reaction caused an effect contrary to that which it theoretically sought, encouraging the use of heroin by making its consumption desirable. While the mass media reinforced what everybody already knew, that drugs could ultimately kill you, movie directors and journalists brought to light the existence of a drug subculture that was now both local and international. The images associated with drug use were almost always of middle- or upper- middle-class users. In some cases, journalists naively provided a list of pharmaceuticals and their effects. The drug culture they detailed was clearly not limited to northern Thailand, or to the rock and punk stars of Anglo-American pop culture. But, as Haro Ibars noted, this drug culture was also at the heart of the Western literary canon and widespread among the general population. Such an interpretation allowed the popular discourse on heroin and death, already present in the streets, to be even more seductive by giving it a highbrow gloss. It made getting high on heroin a form of symbolic upward mobility. Unable to travel to Thailand, the Spanish youth of the eighties would find no problem in bringing Thailand into their veins as a small form of sharing in the experience.

By the early eighties, the Spanish public had grown accustomed to witnessing visual representations of heroin use, if not the real thing in the streets. To scandalize such a public, Pedro Almodóvar in *Entre tinieblas* (*Dark Habits*, 1983) resorted to blasphemous heroin-shooting nuns. As we have seen, drug consumption in general, and heroin in particular, were part of larger shifts in Spanish culture. Politics and economics, as well as other cultural mores, were all in flux: sex, art, and a whole approach to life were affected as well. But to claim that Madrid's youth used drugs solely to escape their situation implies that they were powerless victims of social upheaval. They were not the carnivalesque lower class portrayed by Mikhail Bakhtin, Peter Stallybrass, or John Firske: an unruly, carnal, and transgressive group fundamentally opposed to bourgeois morals. Neither were Spanish youth the heroic, anti-Franco, organized classes, embodying the defeated ideals of the Second Spanish Republic. They were, instead, a complex group marked and shaped by migration, line of work, education, political identity, symbolic practices, hierarchies, and, increasingly, consumption and lifestyles. Working-class kids played their part in the evolving sense of freedom and the growing consumerism despite the economic crisis and thanks to a new-found modest wealth and an aspiring society. Among other reasons, such as pleasure or thrill seeking, youth used drugs because they offered them a cultural identity by way of an act that was both subservient to much-hyped international mores and a subversive local practice. In addition to maximizing the effect of expensive drugs, drug users shot heroin "to experience new sensations by engaging in practices that could grant them prestige and acceptance among groups of significant others" (Gamella, "The Spread" 152). This would explain why, despite the dire consequences of drug use depicted in the media, films, and comics, and clearly evident on Madrid's streets, hundreds of thousands would choose to abuse heroin intravenously.[44]

The start of the heroin epidemic in 1978 can be attributed to a perfect storm that took shape over the sixties and seventies: pre-existing experimentation with and availability of pharmaceuticals, new perceptions about intoxication influenced by discourses in the mass media, feelings of affluence and freedom, and immature institutions that were unable to respond effectively to the mounting crisis. Certainly, and especially among the working class, there was a lack of wider perspectives and opportunities, rooted in a disheartening labour market, lack of educational motivators, and ineffectual party politics. But these circumstances do not suffice to explain the growth in heroin use. Rather, the explosion of heroin use was due to many of the cultural transformations explored in this book, including a new sensibility toward intoxicating substances and consumption. The most common explanations for heroin use are, therefore, inadequate, based on class views and prejudices that stem from the discourses of the sixties and seventies that attribute to individuals and the working class either an essential inability to deal with reality or a total lack of agency, making them victims of the state's social control strategies. By contrast, this chapter has proposed that the "democratized" access to and abuse of heroin and other drugs facilitated by the availability of pharmaceuticals, discourses in the media, and wider cultural change during the seventies, were acts of rebellion. I conclude that Madrid's youth, in imitating discourses and tastes of the elite, impersonating international subcultures, emulating music and literary icons, and violating the class ethos of frugality, decency, and hard work, were acting out against the prevailing ideological order. Stepping out from under authoritarianism, youth identified heroin with modernity, both in the literary sense and for its relationship to international pop culture. If there was escapism, it was from the culture of the old regime into a world of media-driven, consumption-based status.[45] Unavoidably, the representation of international drug use in print media during the seventies directly linked it to the sense of modernity that Spanish citizens so badly craved. It suggested, to a generation lost in the Transition and the festive subversion of roles and traditional cultural values, that heroin use was nothing less than the burden of modernity.

Chapter Four

Fashion: Democracy Prêt-à-Porter

Fashion, not unlike heroin, became progressively more important from the mid-sixties onward as an identity maker and a central element of youth culture in Madrid. Aware of international trends and rebelling against the "official" dress options of the moment, youth in the seventies would embrace an array of contemporary styles. Moreover, young designers, and the lines they conceived, would come to be essential in shaping the new image of democratic Madrid during *la Movida*.

The emergence of these innovative designers, and their subsequent dominant presence in eighties' culture, can be attributed to a set of conditions that this chapter will explore. I will show how mass media, saturated for decades with images of haute couture, a population following the latest developments in international styles, and a progressively affluent middle class that no longer abided by the regime's postwar dogma of austerity, modesty, and conformity, created a fertile environment for the appearance and success of new fashion designers. Well before the eighties, however, fashion offered Spanish citizens the possibility of controlling their image, of sidestepping or challenging social norms, and of exercising a modicum of freedom in building a personal identity. In what follows, I present a brief cultural history of how Spanish *alta costura* (haute couture) gave way to a group of young designers who created a whole new way of dressing – which is to say, a new way of interacting with one's environment – one that kept pace with the collective changes in sensibility taking place throughout the seventies.

The emerging Spanish designers of the seventies – Francis Montesinos, Manuel Piña, Pedro del Hierro, Jesús del Pozo, Sybilla, and Ágatha Ruiz de la Prada, among others – were no doubt inspired by Cristóbal Balenciaga's formal aspects, by Japanese designers such as Issey Miyake who combined tradition and modernity, and by the radically innovative approach to fashion and retail modelled by Mary Quant, and later, by Vivienne Westwood and Malcolm McLaren. During the seventies, these young designers would occupy the space between the department store and the traditional tailor or dressmaker, a space that *alta costura* had never been able to capture, focused as it was on higher-class clientele. Spanish *alta costura*, unlike its Euro-American counterparts, never fully committed to designing for and marketing to a younger mass market and its new sensibilities and tastes.

In late Franco Spain and during the Transition, adopting international styles was a way to feel rebellious and modern – a visual way, even if superficial, of resisting the regime and embodying modernity.[1] Certainly, like much of the clothing many Spaniards were wearing in the seventies, it was a homemade modernity, or at the very least, a modernity that needed some alterations to fit. Nevertheless, in the suffocating official atmosphere of the later years of the Franco regime, people adopted and adapted international styles to build their images and identities, rejecting the stale models offered by the regime.[2] The strict ideals of *alta costura* and the class hierarchies that it sustained were no longer justifiable in a country with democratic aspirations. The growing middle class embraced "democratizing" lifestyle practices that included large-scale consumption and vacations while a youth generation sought to be like its Western peers. *Alta costura*'s progressive decline was not mourned for long, as new local stylists emerged by the mid-seventies to propose designs that bore no trace of class conflict or relation to the dictatorial regime. For a moment, fashion became a vehicle for new affects, like a sense of cosmopolitan modernity, or a new way to engage with Spanish cultural traditions (Robbins, "An Introduction" 40). While it cannot be denied that the desire to differentiate or distinguish the wearer continued to drive the new styles emerging during the seventies, this emerging fashion was not rooted in the prescribed mores of the old bourgeoisie, and instead operated from new structures of taste and meaning.

Leading this change in Spanish fashion were a number of journalists such as Margarita Rivière and José Eduardo Mira who in *Triunfo* documented and analysed international and local trends in the fashion industry. Rivière's 1977 book *La moda, ¿comunicación o incomunicación?* (*Fashion: Communication or Isolation?*), an early example of fashion studies in Spain, is fundamental for this chapter. No one today would seriously reject the idea that fashion – despite its apparent banality and frivolity – reflects economic, political, and social practices. No mere frivolous exterior, fashion is an indicator of societal transformations. Baudelaire, Simmel, Bejamin, Ortega, Barthes, and Lefevbre, among many other notable scholars, have contributed to the recognition that fashion is a legitimate area of study that reveals a lot more about systems of meaning and material culture than might be assumed. Rivière and others made this case in the seventies, analysing fashion as a representative cultural event, plotting the directions the industry might go, suggesting solutions for its problems, and laying the theoretical foundations for the emergence of Spanish fashion in the eighties. As historical events developed, so fashion adapted to and challenged the shifting ideas of what was beautiful, acceptable, or tasteful. That fashion as material culture serves as a representation of society was something that Franco's government capitalized upon in the sixties.

Franco's Fashion: International Image, Industry, and Identity

After the utter economic and social disaster of the autarkic model, the 1959 *Plan de Estabilización* (Stabilization Plan) completely liberalized the fashion industry from the strict controls that the government had imposed on every sector of the economy.[3] Although the use of the term "fashion industry" may seem an exaggeration, given the limitations of the sector in Spain at the time, I use it to refer to the textile industry, garment manufacturing, and *alta costura* in the Spanish state. Since the French king Louis XIV first put state support behind fashion, it has been evident that this industry has a role in modelling national identity and contributing to the national economy. Fashion, being one of the first forms of soft power, was yet another way to reflect national supremacy and international influence. Franco's government became aware of the power of fashion to change Spain's image abroad in order to attract tourism and foreign capital that would bolster the Spanish economy and, by extension, the regime. As a result, Spanish fashion and *alta costura* would in the sixties become another political prisoner of Franco's regime.[4] This made *alta costura* vulnerable to the status quo, poor state planning, and unfulfilled industrial integration, all of which ultimately precipitated its demise.[5]

To promote Spanish textile and garment manufacturing, the government placed Spanish *alta costura* designers in international trade shows, specifically those in Paris, and tried to break into the US market. Fashion featured prominently in the Spanish pavilion of the 1964 World's Fair in New York. The pavilion became the hit of the fair, with millions of visitors and great reviews in the media.[6] The custom-designed building cost seven million dollars and featured a mini-museum with masterpieces by Velázquez, El Greco, Picasso, and Miró, among other artists. It also boasted three restaurants, as well as an auditorium for performances of traditional dances and la Tuna.[7] In this auditorium, fashion shows by leading designers Asunción Bastida, Manuel Pertegaz, and Pedro Rodríguez promoted Spanish *alta costura* to American audiences. Pertegaz and Herrera y Ollero would eventually sell their lines in US department stores such as Lord and Taylor (Pasalodos 30).[8]

A contradictory message projected by the Spanish pavilion, in Neal Rosendorf's assessment, was that Spain was simultaneously an ancient and a modern country (81). While the pavilion displayed traditional trades and customs, it also placed a premium on conveying the message that Spain was aesthetically *au courant*, home to world-class architecture and design. Finally, the pavilion gave the impression, specifically through haute couture, that Spain was a glamorous gathering place for celebrities and other VIPs (81). Pieces like Richard Avedon's "In the Blaze of Spain," published in *Harper's Bazaar* (1965), would go a long way toward reinforcing this international image of Spain.[9] Thanks to a promotional campaign that both played with and challenged international stereotypes of Spain, Franco's government was partially successful at whitewashing its authoritarian and conservative nature.

Alta costura and tourism were mainstays of the government's larger economic plan, which invested heavily in promoting Spain abroad. To demonstrate this point, a No-Do in 1965 shows Manuel Fraga, minister of information and tourism, presenting a plaque to designers Asunción Bastida and Pedro Rodríguez for their contributions to attracting tourism to Spain during the New York World's Fair (No-Do 1177, 26 July 1965).[10] From this moment forward, No-Dos began to document Spanish fashion shows, textile and garment trade shows, the professional training of tailors and dressmakers, and new local trends such as *moda del sol* (beach fashion). No-Dos also continued reporting on international fashion and festivals, including the recognizable futurist models of Courrèges or Rabanne (No-Do 1205, 7 February 1966), the Spanish passion for the Beatles (No-Do 1233, 22 August 1966), and the Woodstock festival (No-Do 1410, 12 January 1970).[11] Thanks to No-Dos, we can confidently state that the fashion industry had clearly become a strategic sector for the Spanish economy.

Fashion, however, was yet another device utilized by the Franco regime in its attempt to appear sophisticated and in tune with international styles. But if we pay closer attention, we realize that the regime's approach to fashion revealed foundational classist ideals and a limited understanding of the contemporary state of the industry. At the same time that Balenciaga was closing his haute couture house in 1968 due to the onslaught of the youth prêt-à-porter market and the loss of clients who were no longer invested in the same class markers of the past, Franco was authorizing loans to the Ministry of Commerce to promote

Spanish *alta costura* abroad. In 1968 and 1969, the ministry authorized sums of twelve and twenty million pesetas.[12] The trends forcing Balenciaga's closure were no secret, and articles in Spanish mass media explained how youth culture, the acceleration of fashion trends, and middle-class-driven "democratization" of consumption were signalling the demise of high fashion as a driver of national status and industry – not to speak of its expiration as a sustainable business. Focused on the continued creation of status markers and superficial displays of technical prowess, the Franco government missed the opportunity to develop locally designed and produced prêt-à-porter styles for the growing Spanish middle class. Revealing its foundational biases, the regime could envision fashion only as a static elitist practice for displaying status. Yet fashion had already become a dynamic form of modern mass production and consumption. Skirting class differences, fashion responded to both the real and perceived aesthetic needs of large segments of the population, something abhorrent to the regime.

Even if the government could not fully comprehend the new world of fashion, there were many who saw the opportunities it presented for a modern Spain. Margarita Rivière, for example, called in a 1972 article for a "genuino diseño de moda español independiente" ("genuine design of independent Spanish fashion") that would not be based on the exploitation of "tipismo y del 'different' [*sic*]" ("archetypes and stereotypes") ("Una escuela" 51).[13] Rivière's push for authentically independent Spanish fashion is necessarily framed by a controversy surrounding Spain's entry into the Eurovision Song Festival in 1968. In a controversial decision, pop singer Massiel was selected over songwriter Joan Manuel Serrat to represent Spain in the festival because Serrat intended to sing the song "La, la, la" either totally or partially in Catalan.[14] What is less well-known, is that Massiel, after being named Spain's representative in the contest, rushed to Paris to get a dress made by Courrèges. This was no evening gown but, rather, a miniskirt designed by one of the most avant-garde couturiers of the moment.[15] Massiel's choice of dress is a clear indication of the tensions within Spanish culture at the time: the government was centralist enough that it would not allow the Catalan language to represent Spain in Eurovision, but not nationalist enough to stop Massiel from choosing a French designer at a moment in which Franco was releasing millions of pesetas to promote Spanish fashion abroad. Spanish leaders wanted the country to appear modern, but when it came to fashion, pretentiousness and self-importance, conveyed through a prestigious French brand, trumped patriotism.

Paris was the referent but not the model. While Parisian trends were adopted and replicated, French "democratization" of fashion was not.

4.1 Massiel sings the winning song of the 1968 Eurovision Contest in a shift dress by French designer Courrèges.

At an industrial level, democratization meant that the coordination and integration of design, textile production, manufacture, marketing, and sale systems, including mass media coverage of new trends, allowed widespread access to fashion. It also meant that haute couture designers took seriously and participated in the production of successful prêt-à-porter lines to be sold to a mass market of consumers. The backward state of the Spanish fashion industry of the time vis-à-vis its international counterparts did not go unnoticed. As we will see in the next section, *Triunfo*, from the early sixties to the mid-seventies, included a series of essays analysing fashion phenomena and uncovering international industrial strategies and trends, including reports of academic roundtables on fashion by the likes of Henri Lefebvre, Roland Barthes, and Jean Duvignaud.[16] *Triunfo* would be the magazine that tracked and analysed fashion as a cultural and economic phenomenon.

Bourdieu argued in *Distinction* (1984) that taste in culture (and its material representations) functions as an indication of class. Changes in taste and material culture may therefore signify changes in class structure. This was the case in Spain during this period, when mass upward social mobility appeared for the first time. The emerging and rapidly growing Spanish middle class would engage in pluralistic cultural behaviours and appearances to represent their status by both adopting international practices and partially breaking with old customs. International tourism and media-driven images provided models for dressing down and informal behaviour that coincided with the sense of affluence many Spaniards felt during the seventies (Rivière, *La moda* 41). Especially for youth, these changes in taste, driven by foreign models and democratic aspirations, would be mediated through both fashion and the advent of new practices of consumption for a growing middle class.

The Path to Consumption: Department Stores, Boutiques, and Prêt-à-porter

In the sixties, and then even more so in the seventies, Spanish citizens were offered a wide selection of possibilities for their shopping: traditional commerce, *mercadillos* (street markets), *almacenes populares* (warehouses), bazaars, franchises, supermarkets, department stores such as El Corte Inglés, Galerías Preciados, Sears, and also discount stores such as SEPU and SIMAGO.[17] For the poor and the working class, there were also *tiendas de confección* – bazaars that sold cheap, mass-produced clothes that fulfilled the functional needs of workers or farmers. *Tiendas de confección* sold mostly knits, including socks, underwear, working clothes, and wool garments. For special occasions, tailors and dressmakers made what, for most, was their only piece of formal attire – a garment that often lasted a lifetime.

Fashionable youth in the sixties, known as *yé-yés*, resorted to making their own clothes or had them made by a trusted tailor.[18] An interview with a young man in "Madrid Yé-yé," a two-part reportage by Jesús de Dueñas in *Triunfo* (1965), documented this practice: "Me fastidia llevar esas chaquetas que se venden por ahí. Mi ropa me la hago yo" ("It bothers me to wear those jackets that are sold all around. I make my own clothes") (31). This anonymous youth described how he would buy fabric in department stores and take it to a tailor, giving specific instructions on how to make the jackets, shirts, and pants. The young man displayed full awareness of current international fashion (it is noted that he was wearing a copy of a Pierre Cardin design) and knowledge of subcultures such as mods, rockers, and Teddy-boys (31–2). Dueñas confirmed, however, that no stores in Madrid catered to the needs of this population. For the most part, the author tells us, men were more concerned than women with their image, and most preferred clean-cut, modern clothes. These young males represented for the journalist a "fashion avant-garde," especially when compared to the lack of interest, on the national level, in men's clothing (37). Their clothes and attitudes, Dueñas argued, projected a sense of rupture with previous generations and with the environment in general, suggesting that a new time had arrived: "España, su juventud, cierta parte de su juventud, ha puesto el reloj en la hora yé-yé" ("Spain, its youth, a part of its youth, has set the clock in *yé-yé* time") (37). With this metaphor, Dueñas concluded that youth culture, generally alienated from the regime, was already marching to its own beat and had its own frames of reference.

If young *yé-yés* could not find trendy clothes, it was because, among other reasons, prêt-à-porter did not yet exist as a commercial category in Spain, even though the early expansion of ready-to-wear fashion was covered and encouraged by mass media. We can find the concept introduced as early as 1962 in a *Triunfo* article by someone writing under the pseudonym "Suzanne" in the context of a wider discussion of French fall fashion ("Bessart" 66).[19] In another article, Suzanne tied together the emergence of two new phenomena: prêt-à-porter and the untapped youth market. "La moda de 1962 adivina lo que sueñan las muchachas" ("1962 Fashion Predicts Girls' Dreams") mapped the critical situation of French haute couture and its designers' efforts to expand to new clients and markets. Since youth were defining their own fashion and no longer following the norms dictated by Parisian designers, Suzanne explained how fashion houses were trying to catch up and capitalize on this youth market and its aesthetics (92).[20] She offered Pierre Cardin as one successful example of how a couturier could profit through offering prêt-à-porter design at a moderate price through boutiques and department stores.

While Franco's government was promoting Spanish *alta costura*, magazines such as *Triunfo* celebrated the emergence of the youth market, the changes in trend setting, and the path toward integrating modern design and the production of ready-to-wear garments for a mass market. As we will see, prêt-à-porter was considered another stride toward democracy and equality. While today we may give little thought to the availability of ready-to-wear garments at every price point, the emergence of this model was considered a major social transformation. In Spain, this concept had more than just stylistic significance. For the aspirational Spanish middle class, ready-to-wear design was a way to erase or reduce the gap between social classes. This point was made clearly in 1963 by an unattributed article in *Triunfo* entitled "Prêt-à-porter."

Although Dior or Balmain were out of reach, the article confided, prêt-à-porter was the way to have clothes designed by top couturiers and produced with attention to detail. Reflecting the ideals of haute couture, prêt-à-porter was not "la moda de los pobres" ("the fashion of the poor") but rather "una conquista social, como la jornada de ocho horas o el seguro de enfermedad" ("a social triumph, such as the eight-hour work day or health insurance") (67). Now, the article continued, many could have ready access to well-fitting clothes at a moderate price point. Although contemporary readers may struggle with the idea that fashion is a right or a social conquest, the article presented the same point of view that Rivière would argue years later in her book *La moda*: that access to decent clothing that does not reinforce social class has, since the Middle Ages, been a fight against the exclusivity of elites (*La moda* 16, 44).[21] Prêt-à-porter, for Rivière, became a tool of equality and liberation, as one could no longer be automatically associated with a particular social class by the clothes one wore. Paradoxically, the emergence of prêt-à-porter fashion constituted a victory for capitalism in that it transformed the "irrational" act of buying unnecessary garments into an act of freedom that further erased the visual markers of class struggle (*La moda* 25). Fashion practices such as the emergence of prêt-à-porter reveal many of the cultural, social, and political hopes and anxieties of seventies Spain.

So notable was the advent of ready-to-wear clothing that it worried conservative columnist Ignacio Agustí. In a 1964 article, he lamented the new world order that he saw emerging on account of this fashion trend – a society ruled by the speed of prêt-à-porter. The column is inflected from the start with upper-class bias, beginning with a nostalgic remembrance of the dressmakers who made almost daily visits to bourgeois houses. He lamented the evolution of a made-to-measure world that "se vestía despacio" ("got dressed slowly") into a world of urgency and standardization encouraged by illustrated magazines (42). Bewildering to Augustí was that a dress could be purchased and worn short moments after its acquisition. Deeply nostalgic about class privilege, Agustí understood that the arrival of affordable prêt-à-porter was one more blow against traditional markers of status and an almost extinct lifestyle. Yet his article was thin on ideas about how to deal with mass society and an expanding middle class rushing through morning commutes to white-collar jobs. He appeared sincerely perplexed as to why the new middle class was not carrying on the venerable – and expensive – traditions of the high bourgeoisie (42). Agustí is yet another example of the limited and privileged outlook of a regime unable to conceive of the depth of change already underway.

Prêt-à-porter clothing was an outcome of modernizing practices of consumption at department stores and, more importantly, at boutiques. *Triunfo* introduced the boutique as a commercial model in the article "Mujer 66: La nueva frontera" ("Woman 66: The New Frontier"). Apparently a report on 1966 French collections illustrated with pictures of models wearing Féraud, Courrèges, Ungaro, Cardin, Rabanne, and Saint Laurent, the article was in reality a paean to the boutique. The anonymous author confirmed that fashion was no longer dictated by haute couture and the bourgeoisie. Freedom of style had come: young women could show some skin or combine different textiles or colours as expressions of their own personal taste (36). These fashion trends for young people called for new shops that fell between haute couture and department stores (36). This kind of boutique was unlike those that Carmen Martín Gaite identifies as run by "niñas bien" ("well-off girls") in her *Usos amorosos de la posguerra española* (*Love Practices of Postwar Spain*).[22] It was also unlike María Rosa Salvador's Dafnis, a boutique opened in 1965 that licensed Dior's patterns to be produced in her workshop in Madrid.[23] Rather, the boutique clearly referred to a type of shop that catered to a new category of customer: youth.

Boutiques, curated stores selling garments from different brands including, on occasion, their own, responded to the need for businesses catering to young *yé-yés*. Boutiques also allowed new fashion designers to test and market their concepts without the investment necessary to go commercially big. Copied from Mary Quant's model store, boutiques had been adopted by haute couture brands in other western European countries as a survival strategy: boutiques allowed brands to open additional commercial channels and to diversify product lines. Since Spain lacked fashionable department stores, boutiques were the most viable model for introducing and expanding prêt-à-porter fashion. "Bazaar," which Mary Quant and her husband opened in 1955 in London's Chelsea neighbourhood, targeted young middle-class women. In doing so, it abandoned wealthy, middle-aged buyers in favour of a larger young audience. The budget of these shoppers was limited, but there was a desire among these youth to follow changing fashion trends. Significantly, Quant's boutique offered its young clientele the experience of personal attention and intimate surroundings, in stark contrast to the physical disorientation and anonymity of the large department store.

In Spain, where department stores were in their infancy, boutiques represented a bridge, a way of accessing modernity without abandoning the customary shopping practices of the past. That is how young Barcelona designer Toni Miró saw it when in 1967 he opened Groc, one of Spain's first modern boutiques for men.[24] Within just a few years, fashionable young men had moved away from traditional tailors (see Dueñas), shifting instead to tailor-designers, such as Miró, who offered ready-to-wear garments with a contemporary sensibility. Many intellectuals in the orbit of the *gauche divine* would come to be dressed at Groc, to exchange gossip or simply to browse the novelties. Miró offered tailored but unstructured clothes in soft fabrics with a diverse colour palette, something that, at that time, no other store offered. Shopping at a boutique like Groc and wearing Miro's clothes signified being part of modernity, a public declaration of one's ideals and approach to life.

Finkelstein has noted that "clothes are regarded as the visible manifestation of entire systems of value" (16). With department stores expanding but still following the stodgy dictates of *alta costura,* and with *sastrerías* (tailors) and *modistas* (dressmakers) still the dominant shopping experience for many, the boutique became the shopping option for modern clothes. Perfect for style-conscious Spanish consumers, the prêt-à-porter revolution facilitated the emergence of new designers. But in the rapidly modernizing Spanish society of the seventies, several value systems continued to coexist. As middle-class consumers grew both in income and in their appreciation for dressing in quality clothing, they began to shop in part at department stores. Youth and the intelligentsia, on the other hand, found in boutique clothing a symbol of their opposition to the status quo and of their allegiance to a specific urban culture in touch with international trends. Paraphrasing a poem by Gabriel Celaya, fashion was a weapon loaded with future and also, evidently, political connotations.[25]

The Fashionable Is the Political

Fashion was a recurring topic in the public sphere for reasons other than style. For No-Dos, fashion was entertainment, the bolstering of upper-class values, and an opportunity to fan national pride. In *Triunfo*'s pages, meanwhile, fashion was used obliquely to critique the regime. For instance, the magazine was an early defender of the miniskirt. One 1966 article illustrated with photos of Brigitte Bardot declared, only one year after the launch of the first miniskirt, that the garment had passed its summer test and that England had been conquered by it. Apparently, France and Spain were the mighty little garment's next conquests. The wearing of the miniskirt was presented not as a moral issue, but rather as a social one, the piece being not merely fashion but rather a measure of modernity ("La minifalda" 24). Although the article vastly overstated the relationship between miniskirts and gender parity, it claimed that, for the miniskirt to flourish, society must have reached a minimum of economic and intellectual development. Only after this point, it claimed, were women able to become active agents in society and fully incorporate into public life (ibid.). The adoption of an international trend like the miniskirt was yet another benchmark in the process toward a culture alternative to that of the regime, one in which clothes were separate from the morality of the wearer. But, more importantly, in discussing the miniskirt, *Triunfo* also presented readers with a whole new value system: to be modern meant accepting not only the miniskirt but also gender equality and contemporary ideas about conspicuous consumption.

Beyond the miniskirt, *Triunfo* used essays on fashion and international topics to critically contrast Francoist Spain with other developed nations. These essays presented models of pluralistic democracies so that readers might imagine a future without Franco. For instance, in 1966, the anonymously written "Los sábados de King's Road" ("King's Road Saturdays") described a Saturday morning in London. The description suggested an idyllic society in which people of all classes socialize on weekends on King's Road. No longer Victorian, we read, London has outgrown prejudice and stands at the avant-garde of fashion (19). While the article emphasized the orderly way in which people conducted themselves, it also clearly linked democracy, plurality, and fashion. Dissenting groups of fashionably dressed youngsters expressed their rejection of tradition in ways that did not question the political or economic system (19).[26] This article provided an image that many Spaniards aspired to: a prosperous, peaceful, democratic society where class struggle did not monopolize or impede the development of new forms of being, and where dissent was expressed in many creative ways, one of which was fashion.

César Santos Fontela's 1966 reportage "Swinging London: Carnaby Street centro mundial de la moda joven" ("Swinging London: Carnaby Street, Center of World Youth Fashion") is another good example of travel journalism with a focus on how fashion is used for political purposes. Santos Fontela depicted London not only as a – indeed, the – fashion centre, but also as the capital of a new way of life. He noted its youth, who grouped in ways not bound by class, but rather by age and by habits of consumption. He noted with amazement the copious amounts of money spent on fashion, music, and movies (34). Santos Fontela concluded that traditional political parties misunderstood this new cultural trend because it was a type of political disagreement expressed through fashion and the consumption of culture: "El vestir es una forma –fundamental en mucho casos— de marcar una actitud de rebeldía, de exteriorizar una protesta" ("Dressing is a fundamental form – in many cases – of demonstrating a rebellious attitude, of exteriorizing a protest") (37). Within a decade, this description and analysis would be applicable to Madrid.

London, not Paris. Prêt-à-porter, not haute couture. Plurality, not exclusivity. These were the models and routes toward a new way of life characterized by non-conformist personal expressions against the traditions of the high bourgeoisie, but not, notably, against the capital ist system that, through the complex processes of producing and marketing fashion, allows protest to be expressed through consumption. Similar words could describe what would happen during *la Movida*: In Madrid during the eighties, lifestyle and fashion choices – free associative expressions that skirted class as a binding and organizing element and that avoided traditional party politics and aesthetics – became avenues for expressing political and social positioning.

Spanish Fashion in Theory

In the sixties and seventies, fashion was an avenue for criticizing, however subtly, the Franco regime. The fashion of that period, and the contemporary cultural criticism of it, remains a prism through which we may more clearly view changes in Spanish society. José Eduardo Mira, for instance, analysed fashion related industrial processes as they related to existing social structures. In his 1970 essay "El sistema de la moda en España" ("The Fashion System in Spain"), Mira presented the Spanish fashion industry in a devastating light. He framed the issue in the following way: fashion in England had been conceptualized as a mass phenomenon and produced at affordable prices. In Spain, however, high-end design remained out of reach for most, not yet a commodity of mass consumption. Mira also identified the sociological and technical issues affecting the fashion industry. Spain, he argued, was a patriarchal society in which families were dependent on the income of fathers and where limited or no income was dedicated to youth. He also held the fashion industry accountable, arguing that its fragmented composition of myriad small companies hindered coordination between designers and garment makers, and that its poor quality-control systems made Spanish products undesirable (29). With Zara still years off in the future, Mira illustrates how the seventies were a transitional moment. Critical of the traditional model of Spanish fashion, Mira saw mass-produced, affordable, and class-erasing prêt-à-porter as positive developments.

Two years later, Mira would show how countercultural fashion was absorbed and used by the regime. His essay "Ibiza, moda y anti-moda" ("Ibiza, fashion and anti-fashion") reported on a show of *Adlib* fashion, the supposedly liberating style of the Mediterranean island promoted by the Yugoslavian princess Smilja Mihailovitch.[27] The essay, reflecting on the concepts of fashion and anti-fashion, contrasted the authenticity of local farmers and hippies against the artificiality of the fashion show attended by intellectuals, politicians, aristocrats, and public administrators in dark suits. Citing Kimball Young and Roland Barthes, Mira argued that farmers and hippies represented the only true counterculture and anti-fashion force on the island, existing as they did at the edge of capitalism and the economy of status. He understood that to label something seen on the catwalk as "anti-fashion" meant little more than selling the counterculture through the capitalist retail system. Mira predicted the emergence of a Spanish hippie fashion that, sold in boutiques, would imitate countercultural aesthetics but avoid its ethics and praxis. Mira, critical of using fashion simply as an exterior performance unrelated to identity and experience, imagined a Spanish hippie fashion that would not bother or contradict the regime (35). He concluded that the only anti-fashion possible was one that comes from below, from the daily lived experience of the streets. In emphasizing street style over industry-promoted fashions, he caught hold of a trend soon to emerge in Madrid with the rise of urban youth subcultures.

Youth were also the focus of Margarita Rivière's approach to fashion. Her excellent 1971 essay "Las monas vestidas de seda" ("Monkeys in Silk") formed the basis of her 1977 book *La moda: ¿comunicación o incomunicación?*, in which she discussed many theoretical aspects of fashion. For the first time, Rivière argued, youth had collectively realized the scale of their numbers and the relative scarcity of products designed to fit their needs. Their demand generated an industry designed to create a world of commodities targeted to their taste. Responding directly to Susan Sontag's "Notes on Camp," Rivière continued that, although it may be said that pop fashion and culture was anti-academic, arbitrary, and freed from established taste, they were nevertheless controlled ("Las monas" 17). Young consumers created neither youth fashion nor democratic fashion. It was rather "un enorme tinglado económico sujeto a los imperativos del sistema económico que la sostiene y la promociona, un juego de 'mayores,' en que los jóvenes intervienen para promocionar nuevas y consumibles ideas" ("an enormous organization that is tied economically to the rules of the economic system that sustains it and promotes it, a game of 'grown-ups,' in which youngsters intervene to promote new ideas for consumption") (17). Sontag's idealization of subcultural trend-making gave way to Rivière's cold assessment of profit-driven fashion for a mass market always in search of new ideas.

Fashions may have originally appeared, as Sontag argued, out of the random, anti-establishment creativity of younth. At the same time, the mass production, distribution, and adoption of such fashions, Rivière concluded, was a result of capitalism. But fashion went beyond business, of course. It was a marker of integration in society, an indication of group belonging, and a way to express and recognize status. Above all else, Rivière argued in one of her most remarkable points, fashion offered both the security of being accepted in a group and, paradoxically, the guarantee of originality and individual singularity. In other words, fashion represented the affirmation of individuality in the illusion of differentiation (17–18). In this system, young people were passive consumers left to create individual identities by modifying the latest mass trend.

Beyond a theoretical reflection on fashion, Rivière's article also offers valuable information about the style of the moment. She reported that "the street" in Spain – and especially youth – had adopted a modern international style. This was achieved in spite of Spanish fashion publications, low-quality magazines that were still promoting a classic look and the antiquated values of the conservative bourgeoisie (18). She was presenting two overlapping, if contrasting, spaces: first, that of the fashion magazines focused on *alta costura* and the preservation of class differentiation and, second, that of the trend-chasing reality on the streets highly influenced by other mass media channels such as television and general information magazines such as *Triunfo*. Street style in Spain, she argued, contained a broad spectrum in which no fashion was rejected. In other words, longer or shorter skirts were acceptable as long as *el gusto* – taste embodied in the traditional ideals of femininity and class respectability – was not disturbed (19). "Good taste" in dressing, I would add, was generated at the dynamic intersection of age, body shape, and location, alongside the intangibles of appropriateness and personality. These factors, and not a general social moral condemnation, determined who could wear a garment such as the miniskirt, as well as where and when they could wear it.

Similar to its coverage of drug use, *Triunfo*'s fashion coverage started out with a focus on international developments. But as the Spanish fashion industry grew, the magazine shifted increasingly to domestic analysis. Just as media coverage of heroin abuse declined as use of the drug soared, by the late seventies – a period witnessing a burgeoning of new trends and designers – fashion disappeared from *Triunfo*'s pages. A mere handful of articles would constitute the magazine's sole mentions of fashion in those years.[28] Eduardo Haro Ibars's "La moda de la basura, un viejo estilo de vida" ("Garbage Fashion, an Old Life Style") (1977), a condescending essay theorizing punk, would be the last article on fashion that the magazine would publish, appropriately signalling that, in *Triunfo*, fashion had no future. After years of double entendre and subtle political critique, overtly political pieces progressively took over as the magazine struggled for survival during the Transition. From 1962 to 1974, however, *Triunfo* was a public platform for a sophisticated and theoretically up-to-date approach to fashion. In that period, it provided Spanish readers with a largely modern view of the fashion phenomenon, one in which fundamental concepts such as the democratizing effect of prêt-à-porter were extensively considered.

Alta Costura Is Dead, Long Live Design

Despite its progressive decline, *alta costura* had continued to bear its institutional role, appearing full force in a No-Do in 1971. The voice-over of this newsreel explained that Spanish fashion was conquering world markets, and it identified Berhanyer, Herrera y Ollero, Mir, Pertegaz, Santa Eulalia, Rodríguez, and Rovira as the couturiers participating in a Madrid fashion show (No-Do 1465A, 1 February 1971). The *alta costura* lineups in this No-Do, showing little evidence of having joined the seventies, held fast to rules of classic sobriety and elegance and displayed a decisive lack of interest in innovation and experimentation. And yet, as documented by other No-Dos, an undeniable transition was underfoot in the Spanish fashion world.

This transition began in 1971 with a new species of fashion show that exuded happiness and energy. A remarkable example can be seen in a 1972 No-Do that documented a fashion show by Juanjo Rocafort at the Cerebro discotheque in Madrid (No-Do 1561A, 4 December 1972). The opening images are perplexing, as they show a bouncer at the door dressed in the uniform of a Nazi SS officer, but they soon reveal that the fashion show is mixed with scenes from the film *Cabaret*. A Liza Minelli impersonator and dancers are props supporting Rocafort's models, all of whom sport the retro style that Yves Saint Laurent had launched the year before in his "Forties" collection (No-Do 1561A, 4 December 1972).[29] Rocafort's show represented nothing less than a new way of understanding fashion and how to sell it.

Newsreels are invaluable tools when it comes to tracking the fashion world. No-Dos would continue to report both on stodgy *alta costura* and on national and international shows exhibiting a radical change in the approach to fashion happening at the time. The voice-over of a 1973 No-Do described a fashion show of informal clothes "al son de modernos ritmos en una discoteca de Barcelona" ("to the beat of modern rhythms in a Barcelona discotheque") (No-Do 1572A, 19 February 1973). Instead of the semi-private, stately runway presentations of *alta costura*, spectators could see, for the first time, tall, reed-thin models who exuded attitude and energy on the catwalk. In a late 1973 No-Do that covered "the biggest fashion show in Madrid," the voice-over explained that the old model line-ups had evolved into entertaining shows where fashion, music, and lights were coordinated to launch the season's new fads (No-Do 1606A, 15 October 1973). It was not until 1978, however, that a No-Do would officially proclaim the end of *alta costura*. The voice-over of that short, declaring prêt-à-porter king, celebrated the worldwide export of Spanish ready-to-wear clothing and optimistically likened the Spanish fashion industry to those of France and Italy (No-Do 1868, 13 November 1978). *Alta costura* had reigned in No-Dos for ten years but would come to be replaced as quickly as one might change into new clothes.

To say that the seventies represented a changing of the guard in Spanish fashion does not automatically imply a direct connection between the couturiers that emerged in the fifties and sixties and the young designers of the seventies and eighties. Unlike French or Italian firms, Spanish *alta costura* did not have successors to carry on older prestigious labels. No young designer who made a mark – as far as I have been able to verify – would emerge from apprenticeship or *stages* at the established brands. For reasons that would be interesting to explore elsewhere, nobody took over and continued these *alta costura* houses.[30]

Although by 1970 most *alta costura* houses were producing prêt-à-porter lines, their efforts were to no avail. Asunción Bastida closed in 1970, Dique Flotante shifted that year to producing only prêt-à-porter, and Pertegaz closed his Madrid atelier in 1975 and the Barcelona branch in 1978. Elio Berhanyer, Pedro Rodríguez, and Pedro Rovira also closed in 1978. In fashion, as in other areas of Spanish culture, the Transition would see the end of companies and organizations that had been successful under Franco's regime but that came to struggle to find a sufficient client base to survive in democratic Spain.

Fashion Design: Identity and National Cohesion

The seventies, as this book illustrates, witnessed not only the political transition to democracy and the economic integration of Spain into European and American markets, but also the "democratization" of consumption and the emergence of an authentically Spanish fashion. Just after the middle of that decade, Rivière released a book that set out the theoretical basis for a modern, original, and locally produced fashion industry. Her first step, however, was to obliterate whatever ideas existed about Spanish fashion. To that end, she strongly argued that there was no real "Spanish" fashion, due to the foreign dependency of the designers, the taste of the clientele, the lackluster condition of the textile industry, and the non-existence of a specialized fashion print media. Instead, she labelled Spanish *alta costura*, which had always followed Paris, as a colonial branch of French fashion (*La moda* 50, 78, 138).

The success that Spanish designers met, as Rivière saw it, was directly related to how well they interpreted the new dictates from Paris, and not to their own originality or creativity (*La moda* 50). The rich in Spain were dressed by French couturiers, leaving the petite bourgeoisie and a decadent, bankrupted aristocracy as the only remaining clients for homegrown *alta costura* (50). From this assessment, it is easy to reckon that *alta costura*'s main problem was not talent but the social structure of prestige that valued foreign replicas over local originality. Spanish clientele wanted to look as if they had been outfitted in Paris – at Spanish prices, of course – and were uninterested in locally designed clothing, except perhaps for some "local accents." Spanish fashion, Rivière complained, was further hindered in its growth by celebrities, popular music idols, and even television anchors who imitated foreign models, leading the country, on account of pretentions, toward a state of fashion dependency justified as *aggiornamento* (78).[31] This was not an argument against modernization. She was rather pointing at how, in the race to look modern, the shortcuts taken were at the expense of local talent and industry.

Designers and clients were only one sliver in her shattering analysis of Spanish fashion. The textile industry was also partly to blame. There was little coordination, she argued, between the related industries of textile production, apparel design, and the manufacturing of clothing. In her assessment, and as Mira had argued in *Triunfo*, the Spanish textile industry lagged forty years behind European competitors both in terms of technology and in its understanding of fashion as an ever-changing mass commodity. Rivière's indictment is telling. The textile industry "decidía que tejidos iban a salir al mercado en función de una serie de criterios personales y económicos, pero nunca o casi nunca de moda" ("decided what fabrics were going to be marketed according to personal and financial criteria that were seldom based on fashion") (*La moda* 122). This system created a critical gap between textile producers and the designers dependent on their fabrics. It is easy to conclude that, without a guaranteed supply of desirable textiles, a sustainable Spanish fashion industry could hardly be successful in local or international markets.

Magazines, too, did little to support Spanish fashion. Rivière lamented the total absence of a proper fashion press in Spain (*La moda* 137). Magazines "directed at women," as Rivière described them, were unconcerned with fashion, despite reproducing the latest lines from both domestic and international haute couture houses. Rivière's analysis charged that the tone of magazines such as *Telva, Dunia,* and *¡Hola!* was conservative and brimming with old-fashioned clichés. These magazines reinforced petit bourgeois values but endowed them with a veneer of modernity by providing coverage of, while not quite endorsing, the novelties of French fashion. To fully validate international styles meant approving the social implications that new fashion conjured. And positioning their magazines against the regime's morals was something that very few editors were willing to do. Still, Spanish women's magazines presented the latest experimental lineups of Courrèges or Rabanne – as did No-Dos – but they were always offset by talk of "style" and "elegance." These key words stood for class and the moral attributes of traditional femininity: modesty, sacrifice, and compliance (138). These magazines "directed at women" were more concerned with shaping a classist discourse on femininity than in becoming a critical outlet for the fashion they ostensibly were meant to display.

Rivière found the non-existence of fashion media reflective of the lack of a genuine Spanish fashion, by which she meant fashion that was created, produced, and consumed in the country (*La moda* 138). Garments designed in France, but produced and bought in Spain, could not be called Spanish fashion. The same could be said of Spanish magazines that focused so much on French fashion that they asphyxiated local production with their lack of coverage. Rivière pointed at that, without an outlet for both promotion and critical reflection, no national fashion industry could fully develop. A specialized and mass-distributed press was fundamental for creating a profitable and sustainable national fashion industry. While Rivière did not explicitly contemplate that, for specialized media to exist, they first need a subject to cover, she did understand that having a synergetic textile industry or a solid fashion press means little if there are no ideas to sell.

Rivière then pivoted to focus on design as an overlooked form of art (*La moda* 108). The practice of creating comfortable and beautiful forms to accentuate the human body was, for her, not unlike creating beautiful living spaces, which is, of course, the work of the more socially appreciated architect (108–14). The focus on design had both practical and symbolic consequences. Local design, Rivière correctly argued, could provide a recognizable form of cultural and national cohesion filling the identity vacuum left by mass media's focus on *alta costura* and the lack of innovative design in Spanish fashion (175). She advocated that original fashion did not lie in up-cycling traditional folk culture but rather in promoting popular creativity and imagination, and in encouraging the mass media to celebrate notable achievements in domestic design (175). Following her recommendations, the seventies witnessed the emergence of fashion designers who creatively deconstructed traditional folk culture, making full use of the limited textiles available to create new identities that would reflect the sense of change and liberation occurring in Spain.

Modern Affects: *Enamorado de la Moda Juvenil*

The shift in the fashion world could be felt in cities, not only because people were better dressed but also because new boutiques were opening. Adolfo Domínguez and Francis Montesinos opened storefronts in 1972 in Orense and Valencia, respectively. Jesús del Pozo inaugurated his Madrid atelier on Almirante Street in 1974, the same year that Manuel Piña bought his knit factory in Carabanchel so he could produce and sell his designs. Zara would open its first store in 1975, launching the behemoth of fast fashion that today is the Inditex group. Many more designers would follow, such as Antonio Alvarado, Andrés Andrea, Paco Casado, Alfredo Carral, Domingo Córdoba, Gaspar Esteve, Luciano Pineda, Pepe Rubio, Juan Rufete, Nacho Ruiz, Ágatha Ruiz de la Prada, and Ignacio Sierra.[32] Later in the eighties, Devota y Lomba, Victorio y Lucchino, Purificación García, and Sybilla, among others, would emerge. Some of these designers would earn international recognition, occasionally catapulting their businesses into sizeable corporations, while others became victims of the ruthless economics of the industry and the excesses of *la Movida*.

If there were any doubt about the importance of fashion, Radio Futura's song "Enamorado de la moda juvenil" ("In Love with Youth Fashion") (1980) hinted at infatuation as one of the affects of the moment. To be enamoured with youth fashion, however, was not only about consumption, as the song suggested, but also about recognizing that fashion played an important social and cultural role. Youth subcultures such as mods, rockers, heavies, and punks had progressively appeared in Madrid as full-fledged urban tribes, and contributed greatly to the aesthetic renewal that would be consolidated during *la Movida* with the popularization of fashion design. Mass media contributed greatly, introducing urban subcultures to the public sphere as a *predominant* cultural trend in Western countries. For instance, 1964 articles in *Triunfo* dealing with pop and mod fashion illustrated, with photos of models by Courrèges, how youth street fashion was influencing haute couture.[33] It would be hard to overstate the normalizing effect of highly exclusive French designers appreciating, appropriating, and interpreting street style. By way of haute couture, yé-yés, mods, rockers, and eventually, punk rebelliousness would become *très chic*, adopted by the traditional haute couture trendsetters struggling to remain relevant in youth culture's blitzkrieg of street style and rebelliousness, with the ensuing collapse of the categories and hierarchies that had traditionally organized the fashion world.

During the seventies, young people could unambiguously adopt the aesthetics of these urban subcultures. For yé-yés, those early adopters of international fashion, this had been more difficult, if only on account of the lack of access to clothing that would identify them as part of this group, not to speak of social pressure and condemnation from both the right and the left.[34] By contrast, youth in the seventies could easily adopt these new aesthetics because the social sensibility toward urban subcultures had changed. Critical discussions, by the likes of Rivière, had done their part to frame and explain youth culture, markets, and the fashion industry. Through mass media, the public had become accustomed to seeing a broader catalogue of styles and possibilities for dress, radically expanding their options for expressing themselves through clothing. After being exposed to so many images of futuristic designs by Courrèges and Rabanne, seeing clean-cut mods in Madrid was no longer a shock. Even hippies and rockers could be immediately associated with American popular culture, providing the viewer with a reference for understanding the meaning behind their dress and attitude.

In thinking about these subcultures, we can come to the facile conclusion that Madrid's youth were late in embracing and imitating some styles that in Western countries were already passé. I would argue, however, in keeping with the main thrust of this book, that in adopting the looks and attitudes of foreign subcultures such as the Teddy-boys, mods, or rockers, Madrid's youngsters were freely experimenting with personal aesthetics and the affects related to those subcultures. They were also ascribing them new meaning in a Spanish context. They were not merely imitating but also searching for markers of collective identity, bonding, and experiences in a society that was shaking up the long-held, traditional forms of socialization of the dictatorship to find new ways of building communities.[35] Radio Futura's song articulated the meaning of youth fashion in Spain: the future had finally arrived. In other words, through fashion, the young had caught up to their Western peers.

In this cultural environment, it should not be surprising that new designers took a visual stand against everything pompous, conventional, and boring. Taking a page from old couturiers such as Chanel and Balenciaga, the emerging designers of the seventies and eighties created clothing that would provoke emotions and desires. Their designs reflected the kind of Madrid they wanted to see – free, fun, creative, cosmopolitan, and sophisticated. Their fashion followed Rivière's rules: it was designed, produced, and consumed in Spain, but not in any way that could be recognized by the old regime.

This is not to say that *alta costura* had not had original practitioners. Undeniably, from Balenciaga to Asunción Bastida and Elio Berhanyer, Spanish master couturiers had contributed original ideas and designs to world fashion. But what Spain had not produced, up to that point, was a group of designers uninterested in being mediators of status.[36] *Alta costura* might well have heeded architect Fernández Alba's warning to his colleagues discussed in chapter 1: that they would become superfluous if they continued to relegate themselves exclusively to being the mediators of the bourgeoisie's status and power ("De la arquitectura" 32). *Alta costura* struggled and ultimately failed to overcome its traditional role, production systems, and diminishing clientele and, most importantly, to connect with the changing collective sensibility.

Traditionally, the success of *alta costura* depended on the hierarchical separation between its designs and clothing for the masses. But in the changing social, cultural, and political environment of the seventies, *alta costura*'s efforts at creating viable prêt-à-porter lines did not resonate with a middle class that had been educated by mass media in the latest international trends, or with youngsters enamoured with international styles and fragmented into a multiplicity of subcultures. Furthermore, *alta costura*'s associations with the dictatorship, which had been solidified through mass media, were not easily erased in people's minds as they sought to feel and act differently in a rapidly modernizing country. By neither investing decisively in future clients' tastes nor recruiting young designers connected to the aesthetic needs of a younger clientele, *alta costura* quickly fell into obsolescence. Firms seemed to prefer instead half-measures focused on quality/price but not looks/affects. Mid-seventies magazine advertisements for *alta costura* prêt-à-porter labels clearly show how disconnected they were from youth taste and street fashion. The preppy clothes they sought to sell projected an ideal of wealthy youth.[37] This ideal, however, was no longer relevant in a cultural environment saturated with references to democratization, urban subcultures, and avant-garde fashion. Failing to transform themselves into "democratic" brands able to respond to changing mores, Spanish *alta costura* lost ground to new designers whose mission, in Manuel Piña's words, was to "crear emociones por medio del diseño" ("create emotions through design") (qtd. in Miguel). Putting their creativity and skills to use through the medium of clothing, and no longer interested in reinforcing social hierarchies, these emerging fashion designers, much like Fernández Alba had suggested for architects, sought to transform both environment and affects.[38]

For the new Spanish designers, who had no recourse to nostalgia, pastiche, or revisionism, everything was to be invented. To express Madrid's shifting affects, designers saw the whole world, and everything in it, as their own tradition. After so many years of being subjected to images of Parisian haute couture, including those of avant-garde designers such as Courrèges and Rabanne, the new designers, whose clientele was uninterested in anything passé, dull, or conservative, sought new models. Instead of France, Japan – and in particular Issey Miyake – served as a source of inspiration. Departing from traditional Japanese clothing, Miyake was able to extract its fundamental aesthetic to create garments that were modern, even futurist, and functional, with an air of easy sophistication and uncanny exoticism that made his clothes hard to locate nationally (Mendes and de le Haye 255). Miyake's garments were "democratic" in Rivière's sense since they did not automatically recall class structure, and yet they produced emotional associations typical of haute couture. The Japanese designer's Zen-inspired philosophy of simplicity and sobriety additionally resonated with Spanish designers who had grown up drilled by mass

4.2 Laura Ubago models a piece from Antonio Alvarado's *Baja costura* (low couture) made from overstocked tablecloths and hand-towels

media on the characteristics of Spanish *alta costura*: low-key style and classic elegance. Miyake provided them with a model for how to extract fashion from tradition. For many emerging Spanish designers, that was the road to follow, one in which the past could be exorcized through designs that did not recall class struggle and the dictatorship's rigid social order. For some, such as Sybilla, it took the shape of cocoons or flower-like organic silhouettes for dresses and coats, baggy pants, and blouses that transform into capes recalling calla lilies. Others, such as Ágatha Ruiz de la Prada, explored koan-like contradictory elements, juxtaposing saturated colours and odd combinations of shapes and silhouettes.[39]

Emerging designers Jesús del Pozo and Manuel Piña are further examples of this new aesthetic sensibility and were the result of the unorthodox zeitgeist of the time. Manuel Piña entered fashion through sales, later buying a Madrid knits factory that would produce his designs, while Jesús del Pozo opened a boutique to sell the clothes that he first asked tailors to make for him. Neither one, in other words, followed the standard training path for learning pattern making, cutting, and design. Neither had any experience in *alta costura* or an official apprenticeship in the business. Instead, they illustrate the spirit of the time, dominated by a can-do attitude, DIY, and a brazen willingness to put things together without long-term plans or technical knowledge. The historical Spanish *autoabastecimiento de la posguerra,* or need-based DIY, met punk ethics in Madrid to create fashion focused on creativity and the mobilization of affects. Many of these designers began by making one-off pieces with whatever fabrics they could find in Madrid's el Rastro flea market or the old-time specialized textile stores in the city's historic downtown.

Antonio Alvarado, for instance, reportedly used cotton hand-towel rolls, stolen from bar restrooms, and surplus linen tablecloths from Hotel Palace for his 1981 show "Baja costura" ("low couture") in Madrid's Rock-Ola.[40] Although it at first appeared to be a provocative performance typical of *la Movida,* the fashion lineups made it a true tour de force. Classic white linen tablecloths, forty centimeters wide with two red lines running along the edge, were expertly cut and sewn into a sophisticated high-waisted, form-fitting miniskirt, a short jacket knotted under the breast, and a round pillbox hat. In Madrid of the seventies, clothes were ready-made objects to be shared collectively. Just as Haro Ibars described junkies as artists of addiction, many *Madrileños/as* during the Long Transition had evolved into artists of the self, and fashion designers became their dealers of modernity.[41]

Conclusion

Legacies of the 1970s: The Origins of *la Movida*

This book has explored Madrid's public sphere and some ways in which its residents strived during the seventies to become modern. I am not referring to the type of modernity promoted by governmental *desarrollismo* policies, a Faustian bargain offering prosperity in exchange for democracy. Spanish citizens, exposed through mass media to optimized models of Western modernity based on the democratization of lifestyles, consumption, and sociopolitical pluralism, wanted more than what the regime was willing to offer. Faced with the apparent oxymoron of being a European country under military rule, citizens progressively changed their behaviours in ways that gave them a sense of modernity and freedom.

The Transition began long before Franco's death, with a sustained number of small but irreversible changes in the way people understood the way they lived their lives. Not a revolution per se, but transformational nevertheless, these changes left indelible traces in mass media. It was through the public sphere that people came to develop new narratives to make sense of their lives within larger historical and cultural trends, both local and international. Thanks to mass media, people accepted or adopted practices and behaviours that, framed by new discourses, rendered the regime's creed obsolete.

As Vázquez Montalbán illustrated in his "Crónica sentimental," the process of cultural change that this book has examined was full of contradictions. These cultural, social, and political inconsistencies have often been flattened into boilerplate readings of the period that do not reflect the multifaceted reality. Jordi Gracia and Miguel Ángel Ruiz Carnicer have detailed the myriad paradoxes of everyday life in late-Franco Spain. Significant among them were changes in the standing of women and their growing incorporation into the remunerated workforce, the redefinition of the role of religion in society promoted by the Second Vatican Council, migration to both national and international urban centres, improvements in the reach and quality of education, and the growth of the middle class (275–80). Numerous and far-reaching, these social changes did not always occur simultaneously and harmoniously, as people throughout the Spanish state lived with and grew accustomed to different levels of modernity.

New mentalities reached even the most entrenched rural landowners. Families pushed their children to pursue higher education, signalling a shift from the traditional trust placed in inherited lands to faith in other symbolic but moveable forms of capital (Gracia and Ruiz Carnicer 280). Thriving urban social movements, tourism, consumption, and a dissident avant-garde culture that filled the vacuum left by the regime's lack of a hegemonic intellectual project are other important areas that became "un semillero incontrolable de una nueva sensibilidad que prospera con intermitencias" ("an uncontrollable hotbed of a new intermittently thriving sensibility") (243). This modernizing sensibility, uneven and tentative as it might have been in some areas, illustrates how change during the seventies was ubiquitous.

Collective sensibility, a seemingly evanescent and elusive concept, can be identified through a number of practices. Some, such as fashion or substance abuse, this book has explored. The collective sensibility emerging in the seventies resulted in a kind of statewide cognitive dissonance produced, on the one hand, by Francoist ideology and on the other, by images widely available in mass media of advanced democracies, consumption, and the latest international trends. Even before Franco's death, rising numbers of citizens were already transitioning to democratic and pluralistic ways of thinking and living and were abandoning many of the fundamental principles of the old regime. To paraphrase Pavlovic, a society of postwar sacrifice became a society of leisure, a process that involved many steps, struggles, and mediations, some of which this book has shown (*The Mobile* 1, 15). Sculpted by mass media and international trends, the gradual transformation of life under the Franco regime was made possible by changes in the Spanish collective structure of feeling – or, restating Raymond Williams, in meanings and values as people actively lived them (132).

Madrid was central to this process because it was the capital of the state, and therefore an economic and cultural centre, as well as the location of major urban transformations. It was also the receiver of large numbers of immigrants who would settle in the city and help shape its culture, ethos, and physical space. Often presented as an entity separate from the real-life uses and emotional attachments of its inhabitants, Madrid is a character in the cultural history of this period. Historically,

Madrid has represented many things, but, thanks to the rearticulation of its identity during this period, it empowered citizens to do and to become. With a welcoming environment of urban anonymity and with a wider array of possibilities for modern lifestyle options, Madrid in the seventies offered a space of freedom to embody late twentieth-century styles and to display shifted attitudes toward, among other things, sex, substance abuse, and fashion.

It might be tempting to dismiss changes in collective sensibility as fleeting and immaterial. But these transformations of affects and mindsets taking place during the seventies had material consequences in the personal and collective spheres. To paraphrase Labanyi, rather than being merely states existing in the individual, these sentiments were also practices ("Doing" 223). And before Labanyi, Váquez Montalbán had explained other consequences of collective sensibilities, some of which materialized in popular culture. He made clear that music, fashion, and taste are driven by the collective sensibility of an era, as they, too, interact with its politics. Sensibilities, emotions, and affects are known to constitute an important element in forming political convictions (Snyder 45–6). They underlie networks of solidarity and social relations that, in turn, have consequences for the society, culture, politics, and even the physical landscape of the city.

Discernible from about 1970, this new collective sensibility would by the 1980s reach critical mass. Although the advent of constitutional democracy was a major event, far more was at play in the realm of culture. The alternative and innovative practices, ideologies, and behaviours that had incubated over the previous decade consolidated in the public sphere and became mainstream in what would be known as *la Movida*. In an unpublished manuscript from 1986 entitled *Madrid la tricolor* (*Tricolor Madrid*), Haro Ibars noted that "esto, que han dado en llamar 'movida,' en el slogan funcional del equipo de Tierno Galván ... Yo prefiero llamarle 'nueva sensibilidad'" ("This thing, called '*movida*' as a functional slogan by Tierno Galván's team ... I prefer to call it 'new sensibility'") (qtd in Labrador Méndez, *Culpables* 452). Haro Ibars's chosen term for denoting *la Movida* is no accident but rather the confirmation that one of the main cultural legacies of the seventies is the change in collective sensibility and its associated material consequences.

Susan Larson has defined *la Movida* as "a revolutionary political and aesthetic urban movement ... democratic and collective" (310–12). Jorge Marí compels us to think *la Movida* as "one of those spaces for cultural debate around which ideological positions, interests, desires and collective anxieties converge, are formulated and are managed" ("The *Movida*" 21). Tatjana Pavlovic has explained in detail *la Movida*'s practice of incongruous juxtapositions and the subversive redistribution of centre and margins (*Despotic* 92). The wilful erosion of categories and preference for apparent superficiality, she notes, was a subversive act on a city burdened by Franco's hierarchical society and his transcendental discourse of Spanish imperialistic destiny (93). In popular usage, however, *la Movida* refers to a period marked by collective affects of freedom and creativity, in which culture played a central role.

Not everyone, however, holds a positive assessment of *la Movida*. Critics have focused on its alleged lack of ethical and aesthetic commitment that, in their estimation, progressive and truly innovative art should have.[1] For Javier Escudero and José Carlos Mainer, *la Movida* represents the final blow to the idea of culture (high culture, that is), and the emergence of art that is narcissistic and lacking an agenda for progressive social and political change (Mainer 32). Teresa Vilarós has also written critically about *la Movida*, depicting it as a black hole or a cultural dead end: "Tenía más que ver con el exceso, con la ruina, con la alucinación y con la muerte, con el espasmo del éxtasis que con la alegría del reconocimiento" ("It had more to do with excess, ruin, hallucination, death and ecstasy than with the happiness of realization") (226). *La Movida* is, for Eduardo Subirats, a Trojan horse that, apparently banal and frivolous, "significó una verdadera y radical transformación de la cultura; neutralizó cualquier forma imaginable de crítica social y de reflexión histórica e introdujo la moral de un generalizado cinismo" ("signified a true and radical transformation of culture; it neutralized any imaginable form of social critique and historical reflection and introduced a morale of general cynicism") (21).

While I agree with these critics to some extent, we should note that their view of *la Movida* both confirms and condemns an alternative stance toward politics, society, and culture that they are hasty to dismiss as consequences of modern consumer capitalism and its simultaneous deactivation of political militancy. This conclusion is easy to reach if one is analysing *la Movida* as an *ex-nihilo* final product and considering it an existential threat to elitist culture. But to study *la Movida* should be to consider wider cultural processes by which citizens were crafting modern hybrid identities. They sought to be democratic, equalitarian, and creative while maintaining ambiguous relationships toward capitalism, consumption, and tradition. A wider view of this cultural phenomenon is therefore indispensable to offer a more nuanced reading of the period.

Criticism of *la Movida* should also consider Vázquez Montalbán's reflections on the Spanish cultural system.[2] In an analysis that echoes Adorno and Horkheimer's *Dialectic of Enlightenment* (1944), he argued that the problem of the Spanish cultural field, and the reason why "light" culture was so easily adopted, was not only consumption and the drive to be modern, but also the barriers between the cultural avant-garde and the public.[3] He focused his criticism on the role of the intellectual establishment in alienating the public from venues in which citizens could express their creativity. If, according to Adorno and Horkheimer, the industrial cultural complex's goal was integrative and unifying, compelling members of the public to see their lives fully submerged in consumer capitalism, for Vázquez Montalbán, Spanish establishment culture was divisive and exclusionary, "basada expresamente en el divorcio entre las élites y las masas. Ya no es tanto una ley del Mercado, como una medida superestructural perfectamente consciente." ("based precisely on the divorce between elites and the masses. This is not a law of the market so much as a perfectly conscious superstructural measure") (CSE III 32). One consequence of the cultural chasm between elites and the masses was that the public was alienated from highbrow culture while, the same time, struggling to have creative agency.

In 1970s Spain, youth had no other option but to create new forms of socialization and identity while a fading regime continued to push a socially and politically conservative ideology that its own government actively undermined. Spanish mass media kept tabs on international culture, disseminating information about the countercultural movements of the moment. As we have seen, this continuous flow of information allowed the public to imagine new, and democratic, ways of living. Furthermore, it made it possible for youth to imagine that they were part of a larger international movement as they adopted and adapted international fashion trends, increasing their moral, aesthetic, and political autonomy "respecto de los dispositivos que les habían sido previstos –familia, educación, trabajo, orden público" ("with respect to the social mechanisms that had been programmed for them – family, education, jobs, public order") (Labrador Méndez, *Culpables* 71). Inspired by the changing collective sensibility and influenced by international trends, Madrid youth did not wait for the cultural establishment to dictate what the new art, music, and literature should be. Instead, they created their own cultural space and became content producers themselves, even if – at first – that meant being poor copies of commercial Anglo-American popular culture. Sometimes they used the official channels available to them, as in the case of Televisión Española's (TVE) programs *Campo-Pop* or *Último grito*. In other cases, the only resources they had were their bodies, a principal creative asset that they transformed through drugs or fashion.

It is only by taking a long and wide view in interpreting the culture of the seventies and its development into the eighties that the quick popularization of what was first a set of underground cultural practices can be satisfactorily explained. Following Franco's death in 1975, the expansive desire for fresh modern culture devoid of any relation to the past, and speaking to the new collective sensibility, resulted in the demise of many cultural institutions. Magazines such as *Cuadernos para el Diálogo* and *Triunfo* did not survive the Transition, closing in 1978 and 1982, respectively, as readers and subscribers abandoned them in droves. Fundamentally alien to both the Franco regime and the orthodox left, there was something unapologetically modern, cosmopolitan, iconoclastic, and humorously liberating in the spirit of *la Movida*. It precisely materialized the *nueva sensibilidad* that Vázquez Montalbán and Haro Ibars had articulated, one that had been emerging over the course of the seventies throughout the public and private spheres.

The topics discussed in this book – namely, the development of a democratic understanding of urban space and its relation to the citizen, the subversion of gender roles, the public emergence of alternative sexual subjectivities, the evolution of substance-abuse culture, and the significance of fashion design in identity-building – were foundational elements for the popular culture that would emerge in 1980s Spain. For this reason, these were also foundational for *la Movida*. I concur with Labrador Méndez that *la Movida* "es continua en sus estructuras discursivas, en su imaginario, en sus horizontes de actuación respecto del mundo contracultural, alternativo, libertario que define la transición española en su cultural juvenil" ("is continuous in its discursive structures, imaginary, and objectives with the countercultural, alternative, libertarian world that defines Spanish youth culture of the Transition") (*Culpables* 580). The rapid success of *la Movida* and its significance in the collective imaginary is attributable, as Labrador Méndez points out, to its continuities with a dynamic alternative culture but also, I would suggest, to its capacity to respond to and reflect back the collective sensibility of the time. Throughout the long seventies, social, cultural, and political discourses and practices were changing so quickly that, by the time Franco died, citizens were already knee-deep into the process of acquiring a wholly different set of mentalities and values. This meant that, even if they did not altogether embrace them, the public was sufficiently familiar with international youth subcultures that they, at the every least, tolerated the affects and antics of *la Movida*.

Thanks to television and print media, countercultural practices spread throughout the peninsula, forming a parallel synergetic cultural environment: "La contracultura no era el trabajo marginal de unos pocos jóvenes, sino de un entero mundo alternativo, un completo espacio editorial, ciudad democrática alternativa" ("The counterculture was not the marginal work of a few youth, but rather a whole alternative world, a complete editorial space, an alternative democratic city") (Labrador Méndez, *Culpables* 480).[4] Labrador Méndez describes the existence of an active and ample alternative cultural sphere articulated through political and cultural languages that found their origin in the avant-garde theories of the sixties. This public, comprising content creators and consumers, concludes Labrador Méndez, produced a new sociocultural youth identity amalgamated through textual and cultural experiences (ibid.). But this was not limited to youth culture: the wider public, as we have seen, was also exposed to similar material in the mainstream mass media. Even if this alternative culture did not fundamentally change the public identity writ large, as it definitively did with youth culture, it facilitated the social, cultural, and political evolution of the Long Transition – changes all made possible by the dawning of a new sensibility.

Notes

Introduction

1 By 1964, eight out of ten households had a television set (Gracia and Ruiz Carnicer 296). For more on Spanish television, see Pavlovic's *The Mobile Nation*.
2 The date for this program in TVE's archive is 6 June 1968. But that date is clearly incorrect, since the groups perform songs such as "Venus" by Shocking Blue and "Whole Lotta Love" by Led Zeppelin that were not released in the United States and the United Kingdom until October and November 1969, respectively.
3 Tele-Clubs were part of a program initiated by the Ministerio de Información y Turismo to make television sets available in small towns. From 1964 to 1979, these small cultural centres were created to house a television and a small library. They were meant to be places for high culture to be shared, to support national cohesion, as well as, obviously, to push the agenda of the Franco regime. For more details, see Quaggio (72). For more on Fraga, see Crumbaugh.
4 Hosted by José María Íñigo and Judy Stephen, the program's first season was directed by Iván Zulueta and written by Pedro Olea. *Último grito* can be found in the Archivo Histórico de Televisión Española, http://www.rtve.es/alacarta/videos/programas-y-concursos-en-el-archivo-de-rtve/ultimo-grito-recopilacion/1829851/. For more on *Ultimo grito* and Ivan Zulueta, see Fernández Labayen. The conservative newspaper *ABC* published a number of surprisingly positive reviews of the program in 1968: *ABC*, 26 May, 23 June, and 24 November 1968, https://ivanzulueta.net/prensa/criticas/criticas-de-ultimo-grito-en-abc/, accessed 17 May 2018.
5 This program echoed *Cuadernos para el Diálogo*'s 1968 supplement "El apasionante mundo del tebeo" ("The Amazing World of Comics") (Lara). See also cartoonist Chumy Chumez's piece in *Triunfo* (1970), an illuminating

and didactic explanation of the US underground press written in and sent from San Francisco.

6 For a recent take on the sixties and seventies, see Labrador Méndez, *Culpables;* Costa; and Albarrán. For a comprehensive view of *la Movida,* see Nichols and Song.

7 In this book, "Transition" refers both to the political process of developing democratic institutions after Franco's death in 1975 and to the changes in collective sensibility and practices during the long seventies: "un cuerpos de experiencias, un paisaje de una época y una forma de habitarlo" ("a body of experiences, the landscape of an epoch and a way of inhabiting it") (Labrador Méndez, *Culpables* 75).

8 "Tourism became the linchpin of the Franco dictatorship's symbolic structure, not only facilitating the normalization of diplomatic relations with Western liberal democracies, but also affording the regime a previously unthinkable level of political stability at home" (Crumbaugh 4).

9 For more, see Martín Aceña and Martínez Ruiz; Tortella.

10 For more on the late Franco dictatorship, see Nigel Townson's introduction in *Spain Transformed.*

11 The *desarrollismo* plans were written and supported by the International Monetary Fund and the Organisation for Economic Cooperation and Development. It mainly opened Spain up to international investment, trade, and international markets. The regime, on the verge of bankruptcy and feeling the unrest of workers and student, had no choice but to implement these reforms.

12 Some scholars, pundits, and journalists have suggested the perplexing notion that Franco's regime acted intentionally to foster democracy and affluence. Yet all evidence points at how reluctant, vacillating, and dilatory the regime was in applying reforms to its economy. See Martín Aceña and Martínez Ruiz for a full discussion of this topic.

13 The numbers of televisions grew from 250,000 in 1960 to almost 6 million by 1970 (Sevillano, 112).

14 For views on the changing mentalities during the late Franco period, see Bernecker; Palomares.

15 By 1976, *Cuadernos* had a circulation of 58,146; *Triunfo* 87,795; *Cambio 16* 348,081; and *Interviú* 297,257, reaching 1 million two years later (Muñoz Soro, "Parlamentos" 455).

16 The concept of "structures of feeling" is partially explained by Williams:

> It is that we are concerned with meanings and values as they are actively lived and felt, and the relations between these and formal or systematic beliefs are in practice variable (including historically variable), over a range

> from formal assent with private dissent to the more nuanced interaction between selected and interpreted beliefs and acted and justified experiences. An alternative definition would be structures of experience ... We are talking about characteristic elements of impulse, restraint, and tone; specifically affective elements of consciousness and relationships: not feeling against thought, but thought as felt and feeling as thought: practical consciousness of a present kind, in a living and inter-relating continuity. (132)

17 See Labanyi, "Doing." See also the recent book co-edited by Delgado, Fernández, and Labanyi, *Engaging the Emotions in Spanish Culture and History*.

18 "The counter culture has its sacraments in sex, drugs and rock, its literature in hundreds of underground newspapers, its art in Day-Glow posters and in movie film [*sic*], its shifting pantheon of culture heroes in Zen gurus and rock groups, and, of course, its identifying costume, hair style, speech and signals of recognition" (Kern 77).

19 According to Haro Tecglen, Vázquez Montalbán's "Crónica" improved *Triunfo*'s sales. The essays were published in book format one year later with the same title, *Crónica sentimental de España*.

20 For more on this, see Colmeiro ("Mensaje"); Vernon; Salaün.

21 "Taste has no system and no proofs. But there is something like a logic of taste: the consistent sensibility which underlies and gives rise to a certain taste. A sensibility is almost, but not quite, ineffable" (Sontag, "Notes on Camp" 1).

22 Domingo Pérez Minik also reviewed *Contra la interpretación* in *Ínsula*. The title is indicative of the condescending tone of the review: "Susan Sontag nos cuenta una ordalía histórica" ("Susan Sontag Narrates for Us a Historical Trial"). While understanding that Sontag is suggesting that hermeneutics should be abandoned by an erotics of art in which the senses assume a major role in the analytical process, Pérez Minik concludes that "huyendo como liebre azorada de la escopeta del estructuralismo, ha caído pronto herida del primer tiro" ("running away like a frantic hare from the structuralists' guns, she fell injured at the first shot") (21).

23 Acording to Labrador Méndez, *Nueve novísimos* broke, at the same time, with the anti-Franco leftish concept of culture (that of committed art) and with the "official poetics" of the regime (*Culpables* 272).

24 "34. Camp taste turns its back on the good-bad axis of ordinary aesthetic judgment. Camp doesn't reverse things. It doesn't argue that the good is bad, or the bad is good. What it does is to offer for art (and life) a different – a supplementary – set of standards" (Sontag, "Notes on Camp").

1 Madrid: Planning the Democratic City

1 The Unión de Centro Democrático (UCD) and the Partido Socialista Obrero Español (PSOE) had equal numbers of city councillors elected. The Partido Comunista de España (PC) allied with the PSOE to form a municipal government. In order to consolidate the centre and right votes, Alianza Popular (today called Partido Popular) chose not to run a candidate. While then, like today, it could be argued that the party with the most votes should govern, a quick look at the distribution of votes brings another view. UCD, 632,329; PSOE, 619,772; PC, 230,651; Organización Revolucionaria de los Trabajadores, 37,396; Falange Española de las JONS, 25,038; PSOE histórico, 5,317; Unificación Comunista de España, 5,251; Partido Comunista Obrero Español 5,241. While the right got about 657,367 votes, the left received almost 1,000,000. The electoral history can be viewed at http://www.historiaelectoral.com/mmadrid.html.

2 For an excellent account about Tierno and the new democratic government of Madrid, see Stapell.

3 These were three examples of the few rationalist and art deco buildings in Madrid. In chronological order, with the names of the architects: Gesa Gas station, Casto Fernández Shaw (1927); Olavide market, Francisco Javier Ferrero (1934); Pelota Court in Recoletos (Frontón), Secundino Zuazo and Eduardo Torroja (1935).

4 See the following articles in *Triunfo*: Fernández Alba, "Una destrucción" and Márquez Reviriego "Manifiesto" and "El Madrid." See also Fernández Alba writing on this issue in *El País* in 1977: "La arquitectura."

5 Falange was the Spanish fascist party founded by José Antonio Primo de Rivera in 1933. For more, see López Díaz; also de Terán "Crecimiento," 155. See Santiáñez-Tió for a discussion of how social conflict is reflected in urban space by discussing Foxá, *Madrid de corte a checa*.

6 Tierno's speech specifically identifies children and the disabled as citizens of Madrid that need to be taken into special consideration.

7 *El derecho a la ciudad* was so popular that the 1969 Spanish translation was reprinted in two editions in 1973, a third one in 1975, and a fourth in 1978. *La revolución urbana*, translated and published in 1972, was similarly reissued in 1972, 1976, and 1980.

8 Tierno and Lefebvre read papers in the "Congreso sobre Ley Electoral y consecuencias políticas" organized in Madrid by Centro de Investigación y Técnicas Políticas (CITEP) in 1976. Lefebvre had close connections to Spain. Mario Gaviria and Lefebvre collaborated on an analysis of the transformation of Mediterranean beaches into commodified spaces for consumption by the northern-European middle classes. Three books emerged, in whole or in part, from their research: Gaviria's *España a go-go:*

turismo charter y neocolonialismo del espacio (*Plentiful Spain: Charter Tourism and the Neocolonialism of Space*) (1974) and Lefebvre's *The Production of Space* (1974) and *Toward an Architecture of Enjoyment* (2014). The unpublished manuscript of this last book sat for decades in Gaviria's personal library until Lukasz Stanek discovered it there on a research trip. See also Céline Vaz and Benjamin Fraser for an appraisal of Lefebvre's influence in Spain.

9 It is important to note that 1977 was the year that the government of Adolfo Suárez finally legalized the Communist Party in Spain. This marked one of the final steps of the Spanish Transition to Democracy.

10 The team included top-ranked professors and professionals such as Manuel Castells, Ramón Tamames, and architect Eduardo Leira, husband of the former mayor of Madrid, Manuela Carmena. It also included members of the neighbourhood association movement such as Ignacio Quintana.

11 For a thorough and illuminating history of Madrid's neighbourhood associations, see Radcliff. *Madrid para la democracia* followed influential books by Tomás Rodríguez Villasante and Jordi Borja. See Rodríguez Villasante's *Los vecinos en la calle: por una alternativa democrática a la ciudad de los monopolios* (*Neighbours in the Street: For a Democratic Alternative to the City of Monopoly*) (1976) and Borja's *¿Qué son las asociaciones de vecinos?* (*What Are Neighbourhood Associations?*) (1976).

12 See Fontana Líbano's 1974 article in *Telva*: "Madrid: 32.000 chabolas todavía" (Madrid: 32,000 Shanties and Counting).

13 See Antonio Capitel's blog, which offers an inside testimony of the changes and struggles happening during these years at Madrid's School of Architecture (Escuela Técnica Superior de Arquitectura de Madrid).

14 Malcolm Compitello, following David Harvey and discussing Madrid in the eighties and nineties, has put it this way: "Los arquitectos se convirtieron en héroes intelectuales y se les dio una posición no diferente a la de los artistas en la vanguardia de los movimientos de las primeras décadas del siglo XX" ("Architects became intellectual heroes, and they were given a position no different than that of the avant-garde artists of the first decades of the twentieth century") (330).

15 Issue no. 79 (1968). *Hogar y arquitectura* was published by La Obra Sindical del Hogar. La Obra Sindical del Hogar was part of the Sindicatos Verticales, the Franco regime's way of organizing labour relations and its agents under the same official structure. Obra Sindical was conceived as a way to help workers – in this case, as mediator between workers and the National Housing Institute. Obra Sindical promoted many housing projects in Spain, with the goal of providing comfortable and affordable housing for workers. It hoped to illustrate the ideology of the regime in its construction projects. These projects were not immune to speculation and fraud.

16 For more details on Spanish journals echoing international trends, see Alarcón Reyero.

17 *Arquitectura* (*Architecture*) (1918–), the journal of Madrid School of Architecture; *Hogar y Arquitectura* (*Home and Architecture*) (1954–74); *Nueva Forma* (*New Form*) (1966–75); *Informes de la Construcción* (*Construction Reports*) (1948–); *Ciudad y Territorio* (*City and Territory*) (1969–); and *Cercha* (*Truss*) (1967–). In Barcelona, *Quaderns* (*Notebooks*) (1944–) and *Arquitectura Bis* (*Architecture Bis*) (1974–85) would be two outstanding examples.

18 In the novel *Madrid de corte a checa* (*Madrid from Court to Jail*) (1938) by Agustín de Foxá, it is tellingly written: "Hervía de gente la Puerta del Sol. Todo el ambiente de la ciudad había cambiado ... Los obreros ya se atrevían a llegar al centro de la ciudad" ("Puerta del Sol was overflowing with people. The atmosphere in the city had changed ... Workers now dared to make it to the city centre") (88). For more on the fascist understanding of the city, see Nil Santiáñez-Tió.

19 Perhaps coincidentally, in this same issue of *Triunfo*, and preceding Márquez Reviriego's essay, was an interview of Henri Lefebvre interrogating him on multiple issues such as structuralism, socialism, sexual revolution, May '68, and his book *The Critique of Everyday Life*.

20 *Cuadernos* published a second special issue, entitled "La cuestión española" (number 22, October 1970), where urbanism was discussed along with other topics such as literature, art, medicine, and sociology. This second special cluster was the overflow of the first issue, presenting a roundtable and a study of Palomeras, one of the new working-class suburbs that had sprung up around Madrid.

21 This last essay foretells the citizen participation process that would be followed in crafting Madrid's 1985 *Plan General de Ordenamiento Urbano*.

22 The Athens Charter was a manifesto for urban planning published by Le Corbusier in 1943, a result of his work and that of the International Congress of Modern Architecture. This document and its proposals would wield immense influence in postwar urban development and architecture. It represented the ideal of the right to a healthy home for everyone. It identified mega-structures as the mechanisms that could solve the pressing problems of overpopulation and the saturation of city centres. Specifically, it proposed large apartment buildings set in parks with excellent infrastructure that would allow workers to commute efficiently to their jobs. The reality was, as critics have noted, that cost-driven design changes were made to the structures, reducing the apartments' space and light, not to mention the quality of the building materials. Many planned public spaces, amenities, schools, and offices were never constructed. Inhabitants of these buildings often found themselves in islands surrounded by little more than roads or parks and with long commutes into the city centre or

industrial zones. According to some defenders such as Ada Tolla, such projects did not represent "the failure of architecture and urban planning but rather of execution and management" (Lange 73). Even though this paternalistic, utopian, modernist model of zoning and high rises had already completely failed by the seventies, it continued until recently to serve as the model for urban development in Madrid.

23 Fernández Alba's "anti-city" differs from Lefebvre's in that, in the latter, the anti-city is the urbanizing of society to the point of collapse by its endless expansion ("Arquitectura" 23). See Lefevbre's *The Urban Revolution.*

24 Still fresh in everyone's mind was the 1969 collapse of the restaurant in Jesús Gil y Gil's development in Los Ángeles de San Rafael that killed fifty-seven people. The collapse was attributed to cost savings and shoddy construction practices facilitated by a lack of permits and a concomitant lack of project supervision. Jesús Gil's five-year jail sentence was annulled by Franco after two years and replaced by a fine of 5,000,000 pesetas.

25 A detailed account of this process can be found in Pamela Radcliff's *Making Democratic Citizens in Spain.*

26 For more, see Borja's "El movimiento"; Pérez Quintana and Sánchez León. Neighbourhood associations would also lead to the occupation of buildings. From 1978, with the occupation of an empty school building to create the Free Athenaeum of Tetuán, and the anarchist occupation of buildings that had historically belonged to the CNT-AIT in Villaverde, neighbourhood associations led occupations in Vallecas, La Elipa, and San Blas. In 1980, fifty families occupied a housing block in Carabanchel as an action against the shantytown.

27 Published in the original French in 1972; Spanish translation in 1974; English translation in 1976.

28 For a critique of Castells's key concepts, see McKeown.

29 By "collective consumption," Castells is referring to schools, hospitals, housing, markets, and leisure centres (culture or sports). All are units of collective consumption.

30 For more on this, see Abía de Tierra.

31 The plan would coincide with the 1980–81 European Council campaign to protect the architectural heritage of European cities and to revive their city centres. The motto was "Cities for Living."

32 For a detailed discussion, see de Terán's *Planeamiento urbano.*

33 For more on this, see Larson's "Architecture, Urbanism, and *la Movida madrileña.*"

34 The objectives of the 1985 *Plan General de Madrid* are quoted in Larson's "La Luna" (318–19) but can be summarized as follows: (1) To fight the gentrification of the city centre. (2) To protect historic buildings. (3) To maintain and protect industrial jobs in the city. (4) To stop the commercialization of

the city centre. (5) To limit access by car to the city centre and to promote public transport. (6) To protect open spaces in the city and develop environmental policy. (7) To avoid privatization of public spaces and buildings. (8) To fight pollution and to improve the image of the city. (9) To build resources accessible by public transportation. (10) To organize a balanced growth of the city.

35 In 1979, Tierno's government faced an US$81 million budget deficit. By 1983, the budget was balanced, and in 1984 a surplus of $1.9 million was reached without raising taxes (Stapell 65).

36 Larson ("Architecture") specifically discusses the *tertulias* in Buades, an art gallery on Claudio Coello Street that was founded in 1977 by Mercedes Buades.

37 See Larson's "*La Luna de Madrid*."

38 See Moral Ruiz for an illuminating explanation on the creation of the stereotypical Madrid character.

2 Sex: Building Plural Communities

1 For an explanation of this photo by Félix Lorrio and the circumstances in which it was taken, see Labrador Méndez in *Culpables* (304–6). Marisa Flórez took the photo of Tierno and Estrada.

2 Framed by the film industry, their nudity was accepted as part of a screenplay, while other "natural" forms of baring the body encountered the full force of the law. For more on the political role of these women, see Donapetry.

3 "Transgender" will be used as the umbrella term to refer both to people whose gender identity differs from the sex they were assigned at birth, regardless of their gender expression, sexual orientation, or physical anatomy, and to people that, through the use of hormones and/or surgery, transition from one binary gender to the other.

4 See Pérez Sánchez; Alberto Mira; Pérez.

5 Muñoz Soro also explains that "La mujer" generated significant tension among the male-dominated editorial board of *Cuadernos,* to such an extent that it contributed to a delay in inviting more women to the journal (*Cuaderno* 192).

6 This popular song was composed by Alfonso Jofre de Villegas and Carlos Castellano in 1939. Estrellita Castro first popularized this *pasodoble,* and Manolo Escobar rekindled its popularity in 1967.

7 Despite Marcelino's goal to win the 1964 European Cup final in Madrid, the Russians, staunch enemies of the regime, were the ones scoring now, by having their own sexual revolution. *Cuadernos para el Diálogo* had also printed articles entitled "Juventud y sexualidad" ("Youth and Sexuality")

by Federico Boix Junqueras (1971) and "Cambio social: Turismo-sex" ("Social Change: Sex-Tourism") by Vicente Verdú (1973).

8 Sex and eroticism had been important elements of some Spanish films since the silent period. For more, see the chapters by Fouz-Hernández, Gubern, Mercer, Peiró in the *Companion to Spanish Cinema* edited by Labanyi and Pavlovic.

9 The number of spectators (4,371,624) places this movie as eighth of the most-seen Spanish films. *La Celestina* (1969) had a respectable number of spectators: 2,845,300. By comparison, *Ocho apellidos vascos* (Martínez-Lázaro, 2014) is currently at number one, with 8,606,930 views; *Torrente 2* (Segura, 2001) is at number five with 5,321,969; and *Furtivos* (Borau, 1975) at number fourteen with 3,581,940. According to the Ministerio de Cultura de España film database, no movie by Almodóvar ranks in the top ten: http://www.mecd.gob.es/cultura-mecd/areas-cultura/cine/industria-cine/calificacion/base-datos-peliculas-calificadas.html

10 According to Martínez Expósito, the first unambiguous representation of gay characters in Spanish film was in the musical *Diferente* (1961). Due to censorship, however, the movie took pains to symbolize and allegorize the fact that the main character was a homosexual ("Visibility and Performance" 12).

11 For further discussion of the gay character in this and other movies, see Jordan; Melero.

12 Annabel Martín has explained the emotional "plus" in commercial melodramas from the 1940s and 1950s that allowed for potential ideological transgression. *No desearás* similarly has a plus of meaning.

13 For more on this, see chapter 4 of the present volume.

14 According to Fundación Triángulo's "Historia del movimiento lésbico y gai," the first clandestine gay liberation front was founded in Barcelona in 1970. See Alberto Mira for a cultural history of homosexuality in Spain. For an early account of the feminist movement in Spain, see Moreno's *Mujeres en lucha*. See Cornejo Parriego for a discussion about lesbians, the Transition, and the feminist magazine *Vindicación Feminista*.

15 *Mi querida señorita* would get about half the spectators of *No desearás*, about 1,789,977 (http://www.mecd.gob.es/cultura-mecd/areas-cultura/cine/industria-cine/calificacion/base-datos-peliculas-calificadas.html). The movie was nominated for an Oscar for best foreign movie, though Buñuel's *The Discreet Charm of the Bourgeoisie* eventually won that year.

16 For more, see Hontanilla, "Hermafroditismo y anomalía cultural en *Mi querida señorita*" ("Hermaphroditism and Cultural Anomaly in *My Dear Lady*").

17 For more on Bibi Ándersen and her role in the Transition, see Garlinger, "Sex Changes and Political Transitions."

18 This was a long-form feature entitled "The Transsexual Operation" by Tom Buckley (1967).

19 The hegemonic establishment of medical thought, processes, and categories in the description of transgender bodies is not without problems. This is a long process that Óscar Guasch and Jordi Mas have described as "techno-medical" (51–4). For more, see their essay "Bodily, Gender, and Identity Projects in Spain: From the Transvestite to the Transsexual."

20 *Me siento extraña* had 974,970 spectators; *Cambio de sexo* had 840,261; and *El transexual* had 419,400 (Ministerio de Cultura de España film database).

21 Chao noted the false sense of freedom that these movies conveyed about France, both because they were exploitative products for consumption and because movies about Algeria's war of liberation were still forbidden (46).

22 For more on Spanish celebrity culture, see "Stars, Modernity, and Celebrity Culture" by Pavlovic, Perriam, and Toribio.

23 Vicente Aranda, Carlos Durán, and Joaquín Jordá wrote a script first called "Una historia clínica," inspired by a note that Durán had read in *Le Nouvel Observateur* about the death of a transgender person in Belgium during reassignment surgery.

24 For more on the reception of the movies, see Feenstra (139–40).

25 Audience numbers for these movies are respectable. *Asignatura pendiente* had 2 million, *Los placeres ocultos* over 1 million, and *El diputado* 800,000 spectators.

26 The groups were FAGC (Front d'Alliberament Gai de Catalunya) (Gay Liberation Front of Catalonia), Coordinadora Feminista de Barcelona (Barcelona Feminist Coordinator), Colectivo Feminista de Barcelona (Barcelona Feminist Collective), and Dignitat (Dignity). This roundtable also illuminated the many strategic differences between the groups. According to the FAGC, for example, a united gay and feminist front should fight sexism, machismo, and heterosexism (Luzán 36). But the Colectivo Feminista's Marxist language made economic exploitation the centre of its agenda to free women (ibid.).

27 Narciso de la Torre-Velver, for instance, explains the Barcelona demonstration based on the theories of Guy Hocquenghem, Jean-Paul Sartre, and Jean Genet in "La homosexulidad masculina" ("Masculine Homosexuality") (39). Ricardo Lorenzo Sanz and Héctor Anabitarte in 1979 wrote a celebration of Gay Pride Day and pushed for an anti-religious and anti-capitalist position. Emancipation meant the elimination of private property and the idea of sin (13). Haro Ibars most noteworthy articles are "FLHOC: un combate" ("FLHOC: A Fight") (1978), "La homosexualidad: una herejía de nuestro tiempo" ("Homosexuality: The Heresy of Our Times") (1978), and "Los mariquitas" ("The Sissies") (1979).

28 This is not to dismiss Paul Julian Smith's argument about how important groups such as the Front d'Alliberament Gay de Catalunya were in organizing new political and social movements for homosexual emancipation during the Transition (34).

29 Eduardo Mendicutti, a non-professional author at the time, is an archetypical example of the expanded opportunities for new authors during the Transition. The novel he submitted to a literary contest in Barbastro (Aragón) received the contest's highest prize in 1982 and was published the same year by the regional UNALI Publishing House in Zaragoza. The novel would be re-issued in 1988 when Mendicutti signed with the publishing house Tusquets. Since then, *Una mala noche* has enjoyed several reprints.

30 Unlike today, hormonal treatment was not covered by the health care system during the eighties, and we can only assume that the doses were procured on the black market. Drug use will be further explored in chapter 3 of this book, but for now, suffice it to say that the novel reflects *la Movida*'s casual approach to drugs. For instance, early in the novel, la Madelón thinks about taking a Valium, a controlled substance available over the counter until 1984. Instead of using a benzodiazepine, or an antidepressant downer like Valium, la Madelón gets high on narrating her life.

31 For more on this aspect of the novel, see Alberto Mira.

32 A flamenco dress would be a good approximation of what they are wearing.

33 See Robbins, *Cruising through Chueca* for a discussion of drag performance and Andalucía (44). See also Chamorro's interview with Pedro Almodóvar and Fabio MacNamara in *La edad de oro* (*The Golden Age*).

3 Drugs: The Burden of Modernity

1 There is no mention of drugs in the pressbook for *la Movida*'s twenty-fifth anniversary. For some recent scholarship on the subject of drugs and Spanish culture, see Usó; Labrador Méndez's *Letras arrebatadas*. See also the documentary *Morir de día* (*To Die by Day*) (Manresa and Dies, 2011), which details heroin use in Barcelona. For other perspectives on drug use during the Transition see González del Pozo.

2 In addition, see Labrador Méndez's *Letras arrebatadas* for another cultural view on drug use among authors at this time.

3 Apart from physical dependency and other, more minor, symptoms, heroin can affect the liver and can produce acute depression of the respiratory system (sometimes leading to death), infections, and pneumonia. It also produces a rush of euphoria followed by a boundless relaxation.

4 See "Instrumento de adhesión de España al Convenio sobre sustancias sicotrópicas [*sic*]: Hecho en Viena el 21 de febrero de 1971," BOE-A-1976-17281, no. 218 (10 September 1976), amended in October, as the original had a surprisingly short list of controlled substances (BOE-A-1976-19744, no. 246, 13 October 1976).

5 Nixon's war on drugs resulted directly from the high number of US soldiers returning from Vietnam addicted to heroin. In 1971, the US Army administered a blood test to every discharged soldier. Those who tested positive had to stay in Vietnam to go through rehab.

6 The album's notorious Warhol cover was banned by Spanish censors, who substituted a disturbing image of female fingers emerging from a can of molasses, effectively moving from the suggestion of male sexual anatomy to the suggestion of amputated fingers. The album included songs such as "Brown Sugar," "Wild Horses," "Sister Morphine," and "Dead Flowers." Spanish censors banned "Sister Morphine" and the record label replaced it with a live version of "Let It Rock," automatically making this Spanish edition of the album a rare gem for collectors.

7 Directed by William Friedkin, the film featured Gene Hackman, Roy Scheider, and Fernando Rey. It was nominated for eight Oscars and won five: for best picture, actor, director, screenplay, and editing. The movie focused on the efforts of two New York City police detectives to block the Corsican mafia from trafficking heroin from the port of Marseille to the United States. For more on heroin routes and female mafia bosses, see Carey.

8 The "Golden Triangle" refers to the opium-producing area where the borders of Thailand, Laos, and Myanmar meet at the confluence of the Ruak and Mekong Rivers. It is important to note that McCoy does not subscribe to the conspiracy theory of 1970s heroin use and has explicitly said several times that he does not think that the CIA targeted Americans for drug use. His work demonstrates only that the CIA was allied with several characters who used the agency's name to deal drugs.

9 This raid was recounted in Robin Moore's non-fiction book *The French Connection: A True Account of Cops, Narcotics, and International Conspiracy* (1969). This book would be adapted into a screenplay for the movie *The French Connection* (1971).

10 Goldman, "Alarma en USA: Drogas 'a gogó'" ("Alarm in USA: Drugs Everywhere") and "Drogas: un mundo dentro de otro" ("Drugs: A World Inside Another," 1967). The subjects are white. The typically modern and sophisticated bourgeois interior of the pictures includes comfortable sofas, a desk, a full bookshelf, a contemporary painting on the wall, a coffee table with empty shot and wine glasses, an empty coffee cup and a bottle

of liquor, fancy ashtrays with cigarettes butts, and a small African bust sculpture.

11 Over the years, there has been a noticeable and progressive change in user profiles, from white middle-class youth in the sixties to inner-city blacks in the seventies. Later, the news about drug use in the United States was completely abandoned in favour of local news about drugs.

12 See Redi, "El camino de las drogas pasa por Vía Veneto" ("The Drug Road Goes by Via Veneto," 1963).

13 See Steen, "Un mundo de pesadilla" ("A Nightmarish World," 1963).

14 See Buchanan, "Drogas con naranjada" ("Drugs with Orange Soda," 1969) and Durand-Dassier, "El milagro de Daytop" ("The Miracle of Daytop," 1969).

15 See Valtueña, "La hipocresía de la lucha contra las drogas" ("The Hypocrisy of the Fight against Drugs," 1975).

16 Author's interview with Domingo Comas Arnau (technical director of Foundation Atenea) and Eusebio Megías Valenzuela (technical director of FAD, Fundación de Ayuda Contra la Drogadicción), June 2010. In "La hipocresía de la lucha contra las drogas," Dr. José Antonio Valtueña claims five deaths in September 1975 due to acute reactions to heroin (39). See also Dr. Santo-Domingo's "Los drogadictos" (35).

17 Although some may object to the medical terminology, I use the epidemiological terms "outbreak" and "epidemic" because both reflect the particularly rapid spread in use among Madrid's population, which created a public health crisis.

18 The report was published in *Revista de Sanidad e Higiene Pública* (1975).

19 "Rockeros: el que no esté colocado, que se coloque y ... al loro." Using slang, the mayor of Madrid encouraged concertgoers to get high (*colocarse*) and to pay attention (*al loro*). This populist statement probably echoed Baudelaire in *Le Spleen de Paris* and its enthusiastic appraisal of living in a modern city. In his poem "Get Drunk," Baudelaire says: "Always be drunk. / That's it! / The great imperative! / In order not to feel / Time's horrid weight / bruise your shoulders, / grinding you into the earth, / Get drunk and stay that way. / On what? / On wine, poetry, virtue, whatever. / But get drunk" (74).

20 Juan Gamella has argued in his "Heroína en España" ("Heroin in Spain") that the Spanish heroin crisis should be viewed from an European perspective, since countries such as England, Ireland, Switzerland, and Italy suffered similar epidemics at the same time. Obviously, each of these countries had specific socio-economic situations that should be taken into consideration. Nevertheless, they render the Spanish experience unexceptional.

21 Other documents reveal the extent of drug use at the time: "El consumo de drogas es ya masivo en España. Debido a que la marijuana [*sic*] y sus derivados son menos perjudiciales que el tabaco y el alcohol, y además tienen un mundo de experiencias mucho más constructivo que el de ellos, el tabú de la droga se ha derrumbado creándose un gran mercado en España, en donde la consume desde el ejecutivo para una juerga, pasando por el camionero que le gusta pegar un polvo estando muy ciego, el músico para componer, o el tío que escucha música, hasta llegar al escolar que la fuma en los lavabos del colegio." ("The consumption of drugs is already massive in Spain. Since marijuana and its derivatives are less harmful than tobacco or alcohol and offer a world of constructive experiences, the taboo surrounding drugs has come down, creating a market for drugs in Spain, where they are consumed by a businessman to party, a truck driver that likes to fuck while high, a musician to write songs, a dude that listens to music or a boy that smokes in the school bathroom.") (Sefer 10).

22 The list of controlled substances increased after Spain signed international agreements such as the Single Convention on Narcotic Drugs (1931) and subsequent supplementary treaties such as the Vienna Convention on Psychotropic Substances of 1971. But, as I explained earlier, the Vienna accord was not ratified until 1976, and many drugs continued to be sold over the counter without a prescription even after ratification. Amphetamines were available over the counter until 1980, when the Dirección General de Farmacia ordered them to be sold by prescription only (Santo-Domingo, "Historia de las addicciones" 57). In 1984, the Spanish attorney general advised his associates that Valium had been added to the list of controlled substances. Thereafter, those in possession of the drug without prescription could be prosecuted (Burón Barba).

23 By 1976–77, the national health care system was detecting a growing number of overdoses. But it is important to note again that, as yet, no retail market existed. For instance, the statistics on the quantities of heroin confiscated by police from petty dealers indicate that, in 1975 in the whole territory of the Spanish state, only 266 grams were confiscated; in 1976, only 151 grams were confiscated. The great majority of the drugs used in Spain at the time came from pharmacies. The office of the attorney general estimated that half of all drugs seized by the police in 1976 and 1977 originated in pharmacies. For a detailed account, see Usó, *Drogas y cultura*.

24 Santo-Domingo explained: "Aunque casi toda la información de que se dispone apunta hacia un grupo de población muy favorecido socioeconómicamente como víctima preferente de esta toxicomanía" ("Even though all the available information indicates that the victims of this drug addiction are a socio-economically highly privileged segment of the population") ("Los drogadictos" 36).

25 Haro Ibars is basically describing himself.

26 According to Domingo Comas Arnau, upper-class users received jail sentences and, by bringing opiate use to prison, helped spread the practice among marginal populations. Interview with the author, 15 June 2010.

27 Schools, which lacked sufficient seats for all school-age children in both primary and secondary education, were a notable example. As a result, in 1977, there were still hundreds of thousands of children in these neighborhoods without access to school. For more information, see Delgado Criado.

28 This is also confirmed by Usó (*Drogas y cultura* 330).

29 Amphetamines could be purchased over the counter in Spain until 1980.

30 See Juan Carlos Usó's recent book *¿Nos matan con heroína?* (*Do They Kill Us with Heroin?*) (2016) for more information and a thorough debunking of the conspiracy theory.

31 One haunting question that remains is why so many users continued to shoot heroin intravenously, even when they knew of the risk of contracting HIV. Gamella has a convincing argument about the parenteral use of heroin in Madrid. Users were able to have a more intense experience by injecting intravenously than by other means. Thus, by injecting, they were able to make more of the same amount of heroin (Gamella, "Spread" 152).

32 Later, Eloy de la Iglesia would contribute more movies, including *Colegas* (*Dudes*, 1982) and *El pico* (*The Shot*, 1983). Jose Antonio de la Loma would also produce popular movies like *Yo el Vaquilla* (*Me, the Young Bull*, 1985).

33 See works by Amanda Cuesta and Mery Cuesta for information on the *Quinqui* filmography. See works by Elzo Imaz and Otero López for detailed information on the relation between violence and drugs. See Usó, *Drogas y cultura*, for a detailed explanation of the relationship between drugs and delinquency (321). Finally, see *Fuera de la ley* (*Outside of the Law*) (Florido Berrocal et al.) for the best analysis of the phenomenon.

34 For a description of the *Quinqui* as a modern *Pícaro* character, see Fernández Porta. For an analysis of the *Quinqui* within the neoliberal policies of the Transition, see Torres.

35 "El destape" refers to the period after Franco's death and the end of official censorship during which Spanish media began portraying naked female bodies. For more discussion, see chapter 2 above.

36 These personal interpretations could be seen as a form of "disidentification." José Esteban Muñoz's concept, "disidentification" is the process by which minority identities and identifications are constructed by rejecting, appropriating, and resignifying normative models of social behaviour (4).

37 Saura won the top prize at the Berlin Film Festival with this movie.

38 "No-Dos" were produced between 1943 and 1981. It was mandatory by law to exhibit a No-Do before movie screenings until 1975. After that, they continued to be produced and sent to movie theatres on demand.

39 I select *Interviú* (1976–2018) as the most relevant of the new mixed-content magazines that began to populate Spanish kiosks during the Transition. In addition to *Interviú*, there were a healthy number of journals, fanzines, and comics: *Ajoblanco* (1974–80), *Star* (1974–80), *El Jueves* (1977–), *El Víbora* (1979–2005), and *Cairo* (1980–91). Despite their differences, they all represent the introduction to Spain of underground comics, pornography, and politics. Magazines and comics presented a new Spain in conflict with the old, granting public access to previously taboo topics such as political scandals, drugs, sex, crime, rock, and so on.

40 "*Interviú* experimenta en esta ocasión el sórdido mundo de la cocaína y de los opiáceos ... Matan y hacen matar ... Enfrentan a la sociedad a un problema que nadie sabe cómo solucionar" ("*Interviú* experiments with the sordid world of cocaine and narcotics. Drugs kill and make people kill. Drugs confront society with a problem that nobody knows how to solve") (Montoto 23).

41 For more on Eduardo Haro Ibars, see J. Benito Fernández's biography and Labrador Méndez's revelatory readings both of the time and of Haro Ibars's poetry in *Letras arrebatas*.

42 Escohotado's work would become the reference work on drugs. But up until 1983, Haro Ibars, with his privileged access to media, was one of the main voices interpreting drug use from a cultural history perspective.

43 See Vilarós (260–70) and Labrador Méndez (*Letras* 202) for a discussion of narcissistic consumption.

44 The idea of blaming the heroin epidemic on the "lack of information" in Spain has to be qualified. The problem, in my view, is not whether people knew that drugs were harmful or not. The issue is that that nobody thought that drugs would take so long to kill so many. The quick deaths of Janis Joplin or Jimi Hendrix would not be the destiny of tens of thousands of Spanish junkies, who would slowly fade away, consumed by multiple and concomitant infections into chronic incapacity and by particular afflictions such as AIDS, tuberculosis, and hepatitis, to name but three.

45 It should be noted that there were parallel currents of nihilist rejection of "media-driven consumption-based status" found among left-leaning punk or hard rock groups in addition to the already traditional hippie philosophy.

4 Fashion: Democracy Prêt-à-Porter

1 According to Bonnie English, popular music and its icons played a key role in establishing youth cultures in which clothes were central to "performing" one's identity (quoted in English 86).

2 For many, it meant "un tipo de ruptura biopolítica" ("a kind of biopolitical rupture") that allowed them to openly live new lives (Labrador Méndez, *Culpables* 309).

3 This liberalization would last only until 1965, when textile and garment production was subjected to new norms. These essentially protected the status quo of the industry: exaggerated government-mandated minimums on machinery and production, and therefore investment, made it almost impossible to expand or to open new factories. Five years of liberalization gave way to the stagnation of the sector. For more on this, see Buesa Blanco and Pires Jiménez's "Intervencionismo estatal durante el franquismo tardío" ("State Interventionism during the Late Franco Regime").

4 Despite the destruction of the Civil War, top Spanish couturiers organized the Cooperativa de alta costura (Haute Couture Cooperative) in Barcelona in 1940, the Catalan capital being the epicentre of Spanish fashion at the time, given its history of textile production, its proximity to France, and its ample bourgeoisie. The cooperative, clearly modelled after the French Chambre Syndicale de la Couture Parisienne, started with Pedro Rodríguez, Manuel Pertegaz, Asunción Bastida, Santa Eulalia, and Dique Flotante. It later included Pedro Rovira and Carmen Mir, and eventually Elio Berhanyer, among other couturiers. Early records of the *Cooperativa*'s work are few, as, until the fifties, the couturiers prohibited press coverage of their shows in order to protect their designs. The history of the *Cooperativa* has yet to be written, although exhibitions such as the Museo del Traje's "La edad de oro de la alta costura" ("The Golden Age of *Alta Costura*," July–November 2010), with eighty pieces donated by the Col·lecció Tèxtil Antoni de Montpalau in Sabadell, have begun to shed light on the period, the works, and the designers. For discussions of Berhanyer see Pena González; Mansilla.

5 Designer Miguel Dorian may help us understand the naive optimism of the time. He declared to the magazine *La moda en España* (*Fashion in Spain*) in 1955 that "once couture is noticed and is given the right facilities, Madrid can become one of the most important centers in the world as regards to fashion. Having great creators like Balenciaga and Castillo in Paris and Rodríguez, Pertegaz, Bastida, Marbel and Vargas Ochagavia in Madrid, this should not be difficult" (quoted in Pasalodos 32).

6 Extended archival content, including images, about the Spanish Pavilion at the New York World's Fair, collected by Bill Young, can be found at: http://nywf64.com/spain01.shtml

7 La Tuna is a musical group comprised of male university students who dress in sixteenth-century attire. They sing popular songs and play string and percussion instruments.

8 According to Pasalodos, these New York shows followed the massive promotion of Spanish *alta costura* at the 1958 World's Fair in Brussels. Asunción Bastida, Marbel, Pertegaz, Dique Flotante, Pedro Rodríguez,

Vargas Ochagabia, and Santa Eulalia had presented their designs there with uneven success in terms of orders (Pasalodos 30).

9 Neal Rosendorf, in *Franco Sells Spain to America*, has documented the many ways in which the US media represented Spain in uncritical ways that aligned with the Franco government's interests in whitewashing its history. *Seventeen*'s "Your Castle in Spain" (1963); *Cosmopolitan*'s "New Role for Spanish Women" (1964), *Ladies' Home Journal*'s "A Spanish Portfolio" (1965), and *National Geographic*'s "The Changing Face of Old Spain" (1965) are but a few examples of the interest in this "new" Spain in the US media (96–8).

10 As noted above, Noticiarios y Documentales (No-Do) were newsreels, produced between 1943 and 1981, that the Franco regime used as a propaganda tool. Until 1975, it was mandatory that they be played at the start of movie screenings. No-Dos are available at http://www.rtve.es/filmoteca/no-do/.

11 Even though the tone is often mocking, No-Dos presented the latest trends in segments like "La moda de los festivales hippies" (No-Do 1410, 12 January 1970). The condescending voice-over narration derides hippies for being susceptible to superficial images of a fun-loving international youth culture.

12 "Ley 39/1969, de 26 de abril, de concesión de un crédito extraordinario al Ministerio de Comercio de 12.000.000 de pesetas, con destino a satisfacer los gastos que origine la promoción de la moda española en el año 1968," Boletín Oficial del Estado, BOE A-1969-505, no. 101, 28 April 1969, 6364; "Ley 93/1969, de 30 de diciembre, sobre concesión de un crédito extraordinario al Ministerio de Comercio de 20.000.000 de pesetas, con destino a satisfacer los gastos que origine durante el corriente año la Promoción de la Moda Española," Boletín Oficial del Estado, BOE-A-1969-1551, no. 313, 31 December 1969, 20452. In 1968, a No-Do explaining the promotion of Spanish alta costura abroad featured a fashion show at the American Embassy. The voice-over states that "la moda de nuestro país a tono con la línea moderna internacional está siendo introducida poco a poco en los Estados Unidos donde tiene cada vez más aceptación" ("The fashion of our country, in keeping with modern international lines, is slowly being introduced in the United States, where it is meeting with progressively more acceptance") (No-Do 1398, 29 January 1968).

13 Rivière's use of "different" in English refers, of course, to Manuel Fraga's Ministerio de Información y Turismo slogan "Spain is different."

14 The song "La, la, la," written by Manuel de la Calva and Ramón Arcusa (Duo Dinámico) was recorded in several languages by Serrat (including in Catalan) and distributed around Europe for promotion. Easy to find on

YouTube are the video-clip versions of this song, in which Serrat sings in Castilian and Catalan. The promotional videos are taped in TVE's gardens of Prado del Rey, location of its main studio in Madrid. Serrat announced his intentions a week before the contest, whereupon the government, specifically Manuel Fraga, moved quickly to substitute Serrat with another performer.

15 The following year, Salomé would wear a set by Pertegaz that weighed fourteen kilograms (about thirty pounds). Hundreds of porcelain sequins were embroidered and tasseled onto a turquoise long-sleeved pajama, creating a mesmerizing effect with Salomé's every movement.

16 The unsigned article "La moda, estrategia del deseo" ("Fashion, Strategy of Desire") begins by reminding readers that fashion responds to social and political circumstances, and encourages them to take it seriously (58). The article covers the topics the three sociologists discussed at the roundtable: eroticism, desire, modernity, consumption, and fashion.

17 SEPU (Sociedad Española de Precios Únicos) opened a one-price store that evolved into a successful variety store in today's Primark building in Gran Vía. This building was designed to house Madrid's first department store, Almacenes Madrid-París, in 1923. Sears opened sixteen stores in Spain between 1967 and 1979. For more on the history of department stores in Spain, see the works by Arribas Macho and Toboso Sánchez. For a description of Madrid's commercial modernization, see Hernando Cuñado.

18 Coincidentally, it was also in 1965 that the song "La chica ye-yé," composed by Augusto Algueró and performed by Concha Velasco in the movie *Historias de la televisión* (José Luis Sáenz de Heredia, 1965), became a hit. The term *yé-yé*, also used in France, Portugal, and Italy to refer to sixties pop music and fashion, comes from the Beatles's chorus "She loves you, yeah, yeah, yeah." The term was so popular that it was used to refer to the Real Madrid soccer team when four players posed for *Marca* dressed as the Beatles after the team won its sixth European championship.

19 "Suzanne" is a pseudonym. I have not been able to verify the real name of the writer.

20 "Suzanne" offered other reasons for the crisis of French fashion: competition from countries such as England, Germany, and Italy; rising prices; a lack of interest on the part of US buyers; declining tourism; and the cut of a 250-million-franc subvention that the French government had given to support haute couture ("La moda" 92).

21 During the seventies, eighties, and nineties, some fashions such as punk and grunge similarly aimed at erasing class distinctions.

22 "Niñas bien" in Spanish vernacular refers to the privileged daughters of wealthy families.

23 For more on Salvador's important role in the development of fashion and couture in Madrid, see Lola Gavarrón's *La gran dama de la moda* (*The Great Dame of Fashion*).

24 Miró, the son of a tailor and also trained as one, opened his boutique in the centrally located Provença and Rambla de Cataluña. Allegedly, a *porrón* of cava, the traditional glass wine pitcher, was always at the ready. The store was remodeled in 1982 but closed in 2015 due to astronomical rents in the area.

25 I am referring to "La poesía es un arma cargada de futuro" ("Poetry Is a Weapon Loaded with Future," 1955).

26 To calm right-wing Spanish readers, the article claimed that the perceived anti-establishment position of youth urban subcultures was little more than a few upper-class youngsters interested in changing the social mores of society. It should be noted that *la Movida* is understood among some as precisely that: a group of privileged kids provocatively playing at being artists.

27 Created to promote Ibiza and attract tourism, *Moda Adlib* was inspired by the island's local dress and hippie fashion. The motto "Dress as you please, but with style" encouraged women to develop their own style while pushing flowing gowns in cool natural fabrics with traditional embroidery or crocheted garments.

28 See Dorfles's "Factores estéticos y sociológicos de la moda" ("Aesthetic and Sociological Factors of Fashion," 1973) and Barbén "Moda, democracia y fascismo" (Fashion, Democracy, and Fascism," 1972) and "La moda retro" ("Retro Fashion," 1974).

29 *Cabaret* was first a Broadway musical inspired by Christopher Isherwood's novel *Goodbye to Berlin* (1939). This novel was adapted into the play *I Am a Camera* (1951) by John Van Druten and later into a musical that debuted on Broadway in 1966. The movie, starring Liza Minnelli, was released in February 1972 and was directed by legendary choreographer Bob Fosse. It debuted in Spain in October 1972. Juanjo Rocafort's No-Do dates from December, barely two months after the movie was released in Spain. On a side note, *Cabaret* won eight Oscars the same year that Buñuel's *El discreto encanto de la burguesía* got the Oscar for best foreign movie.

30 This means that new designers had a steep learning curve, often starting from zero or, in some cases, after receiving training in pattern making and tailoring in the Escuelas de Artes y Oficios (Schools of Arts and Trades), which later became Formación Profesional (Professional Training). The reasons for which there was little intergenerational training are yet to be explored.

31 The term *aggiornamento*, or bringing up to date, refers to the spirit of open-mindedness after the Second Vatican Council (1962–65). This new position of the Catholic Church vis-à-vis the modern world influenced the changes occurring in Spain.

32 These are the names of those designers (in addition to Toni Miró, Francis Montesinos, Manuel Piña, and Jesús del Pozo) presenting lineups in "Vogue," a show of contemporary Spanish fashion that took place at the Museo Español de Arte Contemporáneo (MEAC) in spring 1981. Today's Museo del Traje is at the site of the former MEAC.

33 See the unsigned articles "La moda 'ye-yé'" and "La moda de los 'mods'."

34 Miguel Trillo documented urban subcultures in his 1980 fanzine *Rockocó*. See Javier Reguera for an interview with Trillo and images of Madrid subcultures. Many of Trillo's photos illustrate Hector Fouce's book *El futuro ya está aquí* (*The Future Is Already Here*).

35 For more on this, see Marcela Garcés's essay "Fashioning Transitions and Designing Identities in *El Calentito*."

36 By the mid-eighties, with renewed support from the Spanish state and the media in their efforts to refashion the country's international image, the aesthetic proposed by these designers would be adopted by both elites and the new socialist government. What had begun as DIY fashion had become central culturally. Fashion that departed radically from *alta costura* would succumb to the pressures of the market. Designer clothes became trophies for those who could afford them. Operating according to the dictates of the new symbolic order of high-consumption democratic Spain, design would be scaled down to the affordable prices of Zara's prêt-à-porter.

37 See, for instance, Pertegaz's six half-page advertisements in *Telva* no. 260 (June 1974).

38 While this sounds like the old modernist adage that good design can help people live a better life, it is only in the seventies that the emotional, financial, and social conditions were ripe for design to assume a primary role in Madrid culture.

39 In Zen Buddhism, a "koan" is a paradoxical riddle designed to short-circuit logical thinking and help facilitate enlightenment.

40 He would also design the clothes for Alaska in *La bola de cristal*, as well as for many movies by Almodóvar.

41 "The addict is, above all, an artist of the disease: he constructs it and shapes it from his own misery" (Haro Ibars, *De qué van las drogas*, 74).

Conclusion

1 That "la Movida" as a concept has until recently remained so vague reflects the difficulty of defining the term, which is generally thought to comprise multiple sets of intellectual projects and artistic practices; myriad processes of artistic, ethical, or political positioning; and, in general, distinctive new ways of being in the world.

2 Vázquez Montalbán's assessment resonates with the deep-seated hierarchies and biases that José María Rodríguez García has noted about Galicia, but which are also applicable to the rest of the Spanish state (Rodríguez García 551).

3 While Vázquez Montalbán generally agrees with Theodor Adorno and Max Horkheimer, whose *Dialectic of Enlightenment* portrayed popular culture as the product of industrial processes used to compel the public into passivity by offering them "easy" culture designed to be entertaining, pleasurable, and sentimental, he fundamentally departs from their view by giving the public a degree of agency (Vernon 30–1).

4 Teresa Vilarós noted the Barcelona–Madrid connection in terms of underground and avant-garde art in *El mono del desencanto* (188, 226).

Works Cited

Abellá, Rafael. *La vida cotidiana en España bajo el régimen de Franco.* Barcelona: Arcos Vergara, 1985.

– *La vida cotidiana en la España de los 40.* Madrid: Editorial del Pardo, 1990.

Abía de Tierra, Pilar. "Las aguas residuales y la infraestructura de saneamiento de Madrid." *Anales de geografía de la Universidad Complutense de Madrid* 3 (1983): 163–73.

Adamson, Glenn, and Jane Pavitt. *Postmodernism: Style and Subversion, 1970–1990.* London: Victoria and Albert Museum Publishing, 2011.

Adorno, Theodor, and Max Horkheimer. *Dialectic of Enlightenment.* 1944; London: Verso, 1986.

Afinoguénova, Eugenia. "El ciberántropo, la tecnocracia, y el desvío situacionista en la obra *subnormal* de Vázquez Montalbán." *Manuel Vázquez Montalbán: el compromiso con la memoria.* Edited by José Colmeiro, 53–74. London: Tamesis, 2007.

Agamben, Giorgo. *The Coming Community.* Translated by Michael Hardt. Minneapolis: University of Minnesota Press, 1990.

Agustí, Ignacio. "Las modas de ser." *Triunfo* 131 (1964): 42.

Alarcón Reyero, Candelaria. "La arquitectura en España a través de las revistas especializadas, 1950–1970: el caso de 'Hogar y arquitectura'." PhD dissertation, Escuela Superior Técnica de Arquitectura, 1999. Archivo Digital de la Universidad Politécnica de Madrid. http://oa.upm.es/9130/

Albarrán, Diego, (ed). *Arte y Transición.* Madrid: Brumaria, 2012.

Aldebarán, Juan. "El sexo y los ingleses." *Triunfo* 272 (1967): 12–15, 62.

Almodóvar, Pedro. *Patty Diphusa y otros textos.* Madrid: Anagrama, 1991.

"Almodovar y McNamara Entrevista+Satanasa 1983." *YouTube*, uploaded by Gustavo Febles. 1 November 2011. https://www.youtube.com/watch?v=DvBquNfDFR4

Amón, Santiago. "El mal ejemplo de la ciudad de Madrid." *El País* (Madrid), 28 August 1977.

Arendt, Hannah. *The Human Condition*. Garden City, NY: Doubleday, 1959.

Arribas Macho, José M. "Historia del consumo en España." *Politica y Sociedad* 16 (1994): 287–8.

Balfour, Sebastian. "Spain from 1931 to the Present." *Spain: A History*. Edited by Raymond Carr, 243–82. London: Oxford University Press, 2000.

Barbén, Pablo. "La moda retro." *Triunfo* 605 (1974): 38–9.

– "Moda, democracia y fascismo." *Triunfo* 514 (1972): 20–3.

Barthes, Roland. *The Fashion System*. New York: Hill and Wang, 1983.

Baudelaire, Charles. *Paris Spleen*. Translated by Louise Varèse. New York, NY: New Directions, 1970.

Beck, Haig. "The Madrid Guide." *International Architect* 2 (1983): 1–7.

Bermúdez, Silvia, (ed). "Spanish Popular Music Studies." *Journal of Spanish Cultural Studies* 10 (2009): 127–33.

Bernecker, Walter L. "The Change in Mentalities during the Late Franco Regime." *Spain Transformed: The Late Franco Dictatorship, 1959–75*. Edited by Nigel Townson, 67–84. New York: Palgrave, 2007.

Blanchot, Maurice. *The Unavowable Community*. Translated by Pierre Joris. New York: Station Hill, 1988.

Boix Junqueras, Federico. "Juventud y sexualidad." *Cuadernos para el Diálogo* 21 (1971): 11–20.

Borja, Jordi. "El movimiento ciudadano en busca de la ciudad futura (Frente a la ciudad disuelta y la izquierda errante)." *Memoria ciudadana y movimiento vecinal. Madrid, 1968–2008*. Edited by Vicente Pérez Quintana and Pablo Sánchez León, 319–35. Madrid: Los Libros de la Catarata, 2008.

– *¿Qué son las asociaciones de vecinos?* Barcelona: Ediciones de la Gaya Ciencia, 1976.

Bourdieu, Pierre. *Distinction: A Social Critique of the Judgment of Taste*. London: Routledge: 1986.

Browning, Frank, and Banning Garrett. "La CIA y la droga." *Triunfo* 494 (1972): 13–18.

Buchanan, Thomas. "Drogas con naranjada." *Triunfo* 386 (1969): 46–9.

Buchwald, Art. "La educación sexual: Pros y contras." *Triunfo* 362 (1969): 6.

– "La educación sexual en la televisión." *Triunfo* 387 (1969): 8.

Buckley III, Tom. "The Transsexual Operation." *Esquire* 401 (1967): 111–24.

Buesa Blanco, Mikel, and Luis Eduardo Pires Jiménez. "Intervencionismo estatal durante el franquismo tardío: un análisis del condicionamiento industrial." *Documentos de trabajo del Instituto de Análisis Industrial y Financiero* 22 (2001). https://eprints.ucm.es/23368/1/8816.pdf. Accessed 20 July 2019.

Burón Barba, Luis Antonio. "Circular 1/1984, de 4 de junio de 1984, sobre interpretación del artículo 344 del código penal." *Legislación española sobre drogas*. Vol. 4. *Circulares, Instrucciones, Resoluciones, Informes Parlamentarios*.

Plan Nacional Sobre Drogas. http://www.pnsd.mscbs.gob.es/pnsd/legislacion/pdfestatal/c13.pdf. Accessed 20 July 2019.

Calamandrei, Mauro. "Los transfugas del sexo." *Triunfo* 367 (1969): 39–42.

Calpena, Lluís F. "¿Mata la droga?" *Disco Expres* 485 (July 1978): 10.

Cambio de sexo. Directed by Vicente Aranda. Madrid: Sogepaq, 1977.

"Campo-Pop." *YouTube*, uploaded by Manu Guinarte, 11 October 2014, www.youtube.com/watch?v=Rn1DIdwZgcw

Capitel, Antón. "Mis memorias de la escuela de arquitectura." 7 May 2009. http://acapitel.Blogspot.com/2009/05/mis-memorias-de-la-escuela-de.html. Acessed 26 December 2015.

– "Un paseo por la Castellana: de Villanueva a *Nueva forma*." *Arquitecturas Bis* 23/24 (1978): 2–9.

Capmany, Maria Aurèlia. "Feminidad o el sexo como condición específica." *Triunfo* 434 (1970): 37–40.

Carandell, Luis. "Celtiberian sex." *Triunfo* 434 (1970): 47–8.

Carey, Elaine. *Women Drug Traffickers: Mules, Bosses, and Organized Crime*. Albuquerque, NM: University of New Mexico Press, 2015.

Carr, Raymond, and Juan Pablo Fusi. *Spain: Dictatorship to Democracy*. London: Allen & Unwin, 1981.

Castells, Manuel. *Ciudad, democracia y socialismo: la experiencia de las asociaciones de vecinos en Madrid*. Madrid: Siglo XXI, 1977.

– *Crisis urbana y cambio social*. Madrid: Siglo XXI, 1981.

– *La cuestión urbana*. Madrid: Siglo XXI, 1974.

– *Movimientos sociales urbanos*. Translated by Ignacio Romero. Madrid: Siglo XXI, 1974.

– *The City and the Grassroots: A Cross-Cultural Theory of Urban Social Movements*. Berkeley: University of California Press, 1983.

– *The Urban Question*. London: Edward Arnold, 1977.

– "Theoretical Propositions for an Experimental Study of Urban Social Movements." *Urban Sociology: Critical Essays*. Edited by Chris Pickvance, 147–73. London: Tavistock, 1976.

Celaya, Gabriel. *Cantos Íberos*. Madrid: Ediciones Turner, 1975.

Chamorro, Paloma. "Almodóvar y MacNamara: entrevista en *La edad de oro*." Archivo Histórico de Televisión Española, 26 July 1983. www.rtve.es/alacarta/videos/personajes-en-el-archivo-de-rtve/almodovar-mcnamara-entrevista-edad-oro-1983/349288/

Chao, Ramón. "En las pantallas francesas: erotismo a go-gó." *Triunfo* 626 (1974): 46–7.

Chumez, Chumy. "Prensa underground." *Triunfo* 434 (1970): 49–51.

Colmeiro, José. "Mensaje de náufragos contra el olvido." *Manuel Vázquez Montalbán: el compromiso con la memoria*. Edited by José Colmeiro, 1–18. Rochester, NY: Tamesis, 2007.

– "Plumas y pistolas: la crisis constitucional del 23-F y la memoria histérica de Eduardo Mendicutti." *Revista de estudios hispánicos* 44.3 (2010): 589–609.

Comas Arnau, Domingo. "Las drogas en la sociedad española." *España, sociedad y política*. Edited by Salvador Ginés Sanjulian, 633–53. Madrid: Espasa-Calpe, 1990.

Cornejo Parriego, Rosalía. "Lesbianismo de (la) Transición en *Vindicación Feminista*." *Revista Canadiense de Estudios Hispánicos* 35.1 (2010): 49–65.

Costa, Jordi. *Cómo acabar con la contracultura: una historia subterránea de España*. Madrid: Taurus, 2018.

Crumbaugh, Justin. *Destination Dictatorship: The Spectacle of Spain's Tourist Boom and the Reinvention of Difference*. Albany: State University of New York Press, 2010.

Cuesta, Amanda. "Els Quinquis del barri." *Quinquis dels 80: Cinema, Premsa I Carrer*. Edited by Amanda Cuesta, 14–47. Barcelona: Centre de Cultura Contemporània de Barcelona, 2009.

Cuesta, Mery. "Trenzar el mito: volteretas estéticas, cine de urgencia y prensa sensacionalista." *Quinquis dels 80: Cinema, Premsa I Carrer*. Edited by Amanda Cuesta, 64–103. Barcelona: Centre de Cultura Contemporània de Barcelona, 2009.

Delgado, Luisa Elena, Pura Fernández, and Jo Labanyi. *Engaging the Emotions in Spanish Culture and History*. Nashville, TN: Vanderbilt University Press, 2016.

Delgado Criado, Buenaventura. "La educación en la España contemporánea (1789–1975)." *Historia de la educación en España y América*. Edited by Buenaventura Delgado Criado, 916–25. Madrid: Fundación Santa María, 1994.

D'Lugo, Marvin. *Guide to the Cinema of Spain*. London: Greenwood Press, 1997.

Donapetry, Maria. *La otra mirada: la mujer y el cine en la cultura española*. New Orleans: University Press of the South, 1998.

Dorfles, Gillo. "Factores estéticos y sociológicos de la moda." *Triunfo* 566 (1973): 22–5.

"Drogas: Un mundo dentro de otro." *Triunfo* 258 (1967): 26–33.

Dueñas, Jesús de. "Madrid Yé-Yé." *Triunfo* 152 (1965): 30–7.

Durand-Dassier, Jacques. "El milagro de Daytop." *Triunfo* 395 (1969): 8–9.

"El erotismo y España." *Triunfo* 434 (1970): 23–48.

"El incremento de muertes por sobredosis es alarmante." *El País* (Madrid), 12 September 1978, 16.

Elzo Imaz, Javier. "Drogas y violencia juvenil." *Drogas y drogadicción: un enfoque social y preventivo*. Edited by Santiago Yubero Jiménez, 75–90. Cuenca: Ediciones de la Universidad de Castilla-La Mancha, 2001.

"En Valladolid: nació heroinómana." *Diario 16* (Madrid), 12 September 1978, 13.

English, Bonnie. *A Cultural History of Fashion in the 20th and 21st Centuries: From Catwalk to Sidewalk*. New York: Bloomsbury, 2013.

Epps, Brad. "The Queer Case of *Plumas de España*." *P/herversions: Critical Studies of Ana Rossetti*. Edited by Jill Robbins, 146–82. Lewisburg, PA: Bucknell University Press, 2004.

Escudero, Javier. "Rosa Montero y Pedro Almodóvar: misería y estilización de la Movida madrileña." *Arizona Journal of Hispanic Cultural Studies* 2 (1998): 147–61.

Ezquiaga, Jose María. "De la recuperación de la ciudad a la articulación del espacio metropolitano." *Alfoz* 62/63 (1989): 91–116.

Falcón, Lidia. *Los derechos civiles de la mujer*. Barcelona: Nereo, 1963.

– *Mujer y sociedad*. Barcelona: Fontanella, 1969.

Feenstra, Pietsie. *New Mythological Figures in Spanish Cinema: Dissident Bodies under Franco*. Amsterdam: Amsterdam University Press, 2014.

Fernández, J. Benito. *Eduardo Haro Ibars: los pasos del caído*. Barcelona: Anagrama, 2005.

Fernández Alba, Antonio. "Arquitectura y ciudad." *Triunfo* 476 (1971): 34–5.

– "De la arquitectura de la condescendencia a la arquitectura de la contestación." *Triunfo* 498 (1972): 32–3.

– "Enseñanza de la Arquitectura, y cambios políticos." *El País* (Madrid), 16 September 1976.

– "La arquitectura de Madrid." *El País* (Madrid), 27 March 1977.

– *La crisis de la arquitectura española 1939-1972*. Madrid: Edicusa, 1972.

– "Las flores silvestres del prado de San Sebastián: política urbana frente a cultura urbana." *Triunfo* 602 (1974): 38–9.

– "Los arquitectos en la sociedad industrial." *Triunfo* 691 (1976): 34–7.

– "Los destructores de la ciudad." *Triunfo* 766 (1977): 24–5.

– "Madrid: ¿Capital del desarrollo?" *Triunfo* 573 (1973): 25–9.

– "Una destrucción innecesaria" *Triunfo* 626 (1974): 18–19.

Fernández Labayen, Miguel. "The Televisual Practices of Iván Zulueta." *Cinema Comparat/ive Cinema* 3.7 (2015): 57–66. http://www.ocec.eu/cinemacomparativecinema/index.php/en/29-n-7-english/374-the-televisual-practices-of-ivan-zulueta#. Accessed 17 May 2018.

Fernández Porta, Eloy. "La picaresca negra de la Transició: la cultura quinqui i l'escola de la masculinitat." *Quinquis dels 80. Cinema, Premsa I Carrer*. Edited by Amanda Cuesta, 122–33. Barcelona: Centre de Cultura Contemporània de Barcelona, 2009.

Fernández Salgado, Carlos. "Democracia y participación: el plan general de Madrid de 1985." Special issue of *Cuadernos de Investigación urbanística* 79 (2011). http://polired.upm.es/index.php/ciur/article/view/1754/1767. Accessed 20 July 2019.

"Final del concurso Tele-Club Campo-pop." Archivo Histórico de Televisión Española, 1970. http://www.rtve.es/alacarta/videos/

programas-y-concursos-en-el-archivo-de-rtve/final-del-concurso-tele-club-campo-pop-1968/2481764/. Accessed 16 May 2018.

Finkelstein, Joanne. *After a Fashion*. Melbourne: Melbourne University Press, 1996.

Fiske, John. *Understanding Popular Culture*. New York: Routledge, 1990.

Florido Berrocal, Joaquín, Luis Martín-Cabrera, Eduardo Matos-Martín, and Roberto Robles Valencia. *Fuera de la ley: Asedios al fenómeno quinqui en la Transición española*. Granada: Editorial Comares, 2015.

Fontana Líbano, Nieves. "Madrid: 32.000 chabolas todavía." *Telva* 260 (1974): n.p.

Fouce, Héctor. *El futuro ya está aquí*. Madrid: Velecío Editores, 2006.

– "La cultura juvenil como fenómeno dialógico: reflexiones en torno a la Movida madrileña." *Cuadernos de Información y Comunicación* 5 (2000): 267–76.

Fouce, Héctor, and Silvia Martínez. *Made in Spain: Studies in Popular Music*. New York: Routledge, 2013.

Fouz-Hernandez, Santiago, and Alfredo Martínez-Expósito. *Live Flesh: The Male Body in Contemporary Spanish Cinema*. London: I.B. Tauris, 2007.

Foxá, Agustín de. *De corte a Checa*. San Sebastián: Librería Internacional, 1938.

Fraser, Benjamin. *Henri Lefebvre and the Spanish Urban Experience*. Lewisburg, PA: Bucknell University Press, 2011.

– *Towards an Urban Cultural Studies: Henri Lefebvre and the Humanities*. New York: Palgrave, 2015.

Fraser, Nancy, and Axel Honneth. *Redistribution or Recognition? A Political-Philosophical Exchange*. London: Verso, 2003.

Fundación Mapfre. "Análisis de la mortalidad por accidentes (II): España e Internacional." *Gerencia de Riesgos y Seguros* 105 (September/December 2009). http://www.mapfre.com/fundacion/html/revistas/gerencia/n105/estud_02.html. Accessed 17 May 2018.

Fusi, Juan Pablo. *Un siglo de España: la cultura*. Madrid: Marcial Pons, 1999.

Galán, Diego. "Me siento extraña y El transexual." *Triunfo* 772 (1977): 65–6.

Gallero, José Luis. *Sólo se vive una vez: esplendor y ruina de la Movida madrileña*. Madrid: Ardora, 1991.

Gamella, Juan F. "Heroína en España, 1977–1996: balance de una crisis de drogas." https://www.researchgate.net/publication/242485727_Heroina_en_Espana_1977-1996_Balance_de_una_crisis_de_drogas. Accessed 17 May 2018.

– "The Spread of Intravenous Drug Use and AIDS in a Neighborhood in Spain." *Medical Anthropology Quarterly* 8.2 (1994): 131–60.

Garcés, Marcela T. "Fashioning Transitions and Designing Identities in *El Calentito*." *Gender in Hispanic Literature and Visual Arts*. Edited by Patricia Bolaños-Fabres, Tania Gómez, and Christina Mougoyanni Hennessy, 155–70. Guilford CT, Lexington Books, 2015.

García de Dueñas, Jesús. "Un consumo erótico racionado." *Triunfo* 380 (1969): 10–11.
García Rico, Eduardo. "15 preguntas a Henry Lefebvre." *Triunfo* 341 (1968): 32–6.
Gardi, Henri. "El fin de los sexos." *Triunfo* 325 (1968): 46–51.
Garlinger, Patrick Paul. "Dragging Spain into the 'Post-Franco' Era: Transvestism and National Identity in *Una mala noche la tiene cualquiera*." *Revista Canadiense de Estudios Hispánicos* 24.2 (Winter 2000): 363–82.
– "Sex Changes and Political Transitions; or What Bibi Andersen Can Tell Us about Democracy in Spain." *Traces of Contamination: Unearthing the Francoist Legacy in Contemporary Spanish Discourse*. Edited by Eloy Merino and Rosi Song, 24–54. Cranbury, NJ: Rosemont, 2005.
Gavarrón, Lola. *La gran dama de la moda*. Madrid: Esfera, 2010.
Gaviria, Mario. *Turismo a go-go: turismo charter y neocolonialismo del espacio*. Madrid: Ediciones Turner, 1974.
Germain, Anne. "Prêt-à-porter: cuatro desconocidos confeccionan ropa para millones de mujeres." *Triunfo* 40 (1963): 54–7.
Giachetti, Romano. "La última ofensiva del feminismo." *Triunfo* 400 (1970): 12–13.
Goicoechea, Gonzalo. "Una confusión interesada." *Triunfo* 817 (1978): 19.
Goldman, Robert. "Alarma en USA: Drogas 'a gogó'." *Triunfo* 104 (1964): 8–15.
– "LSD 25: Un alucinógeno poderoso que puede conducir al suicidio." *Triunfo* 83 (1964): 26–37.
González del Pozo, Jorge. "*Báilame el agua*: la espiral de la heroína en el Madrid post-movida." *Hispanic Research Journal: Iberian and Latin American Studies* 11.2 (2012): 144–56.
– "*Madrid ha muerto* de Luis Antonio de Villena: la cronología de la cocaína en la urbe española de la democracia." *Bulletin of Hispanic Studies* 87.5 (2009): 571–83.
Gracia, Jordi, and Miguel Ángel Ruiz Carnicer. *La España de Franco (1939–1975): cultura y vida cotidiana*. Madrid: Síntesis, 2001.
Graham, Helen, and Jo Labanyi. "Introduction. Culture and Modernity: The Case of Spain." *Spanish Cultural Studies*. Edited by Helen Graham and Jo Labanyi, 1–19. Oxford: Oxford University Press, 1995.
Guasch, Oscar. *La sociedad rosa*. Barcelona: Anagrama, 1995.
Guasch, Óscar, and Jordi Mas. "Bodily, Gender, and Identity Projects in Spain: From the Transvestite to the Transsexual." *Hispanic (LGT) Masculinities in Transition*. Edited by Rafael M. Merida-Jimenez, 51–6. New York: Peter Lang, 2014.
Gubern, Román. "En defensa del erotismo." *Triunfo* 697 (1976): 50–1.
– "La industria del deseo." *Triunfo* 626 (1974): 45–7.

Hardt, Michael, and Antonio Negri. *Empire*. Cambridge, MA: Harvard University Press, 2000.
Haro Ibars, Eduardo. "Cultura a la contra: nueva ola." *Triunfo* 851 (1979): 60.
– *De qué van las drogas*. Madrid: Ediciones de la piqueta, 1978.
– "FLHOC: un combate." *Triunfo* 803 (1978): 40.
– "La homosexualidad: una herejía de nuestro tiempo." *Triunfo* 826 (1978): 59.
– "La moda de la basura, un viejo estilo de vida." *Triunfo* 763 (1977): 43–5.
– "Los mariquitas." *Triunfo* 882 (1979): 54.
– "Nos matan con heroína." *Ozono* 4.37 (1978): 7–10.
Haro Tecglen, Eduardo. "Como se hace una española." *Triunfo 434* (1970): 31–6.
Harvey, Jessamy. "Tropes of Freedom: Spectacular Eroticism and the Spanish New Woman On-Screen." *A Companion to Spanish Women's Studies*. Edited by Xon de Ros and Geraldine Hazbun, 317–28. Rochester, NY: Tamesis, 2011.
Held, Jean-Francis. "Sexo Über Alles." *Triunfo* 430 (1970): 14–15.
Hernández León, Juan Miguel. "The Impossibility of the School of Madrid: Between Rationalism and Eclecticism." *International Architect* 2 (1983): 9–15.
Hernando Cuñado, Jorge. "La modernización de la comercialización en la España del siglo XX: el caso de Madrid." PhD dissertation. Universidad Complutense de Madrid, 2015. http://eprints.ucm.es/28321/1/T35761.pdf. Accessed 16 May 2018.
"Historia del movimiento lésbico y gai." Fundación Triángulo. http://web.archive.org/web/20070927093649/ http://fundaciontriangulo.es/informes/e_Historia. Accessed 12 February 2016.
Hontanilla, Ana. "Hermafroditismo y anomalía cultural en *Mi querida señorita*." *Letras Hispanas* 3.1 (Spring 2006): 113–22.
Informe 2007 del Observatorio Español Sobre Drogas: Situación y tendencias de los problemas de drogas en España. Madrid: Ministerio de Sanidad y Consumo, 2007. http://www.pnsd.mscbs.gob.es/profesionales/sistemasInformacion/informesEstadisticas/pdf/2017OEDA-ESTADISTICAS.pdf. Accessed 23 July 2019.
Ingenschay, Dieter. "Identidad homosexual y procesamiento del franquismo en el discurso literario de España desde la transición." *Disremembering the Dictatorship: The Politics of Memory in the Spanish Transition to Democracy*. Edited by Joan Ramon Resina, 157–89. Amsterdam: Rodopi, 2000.
"Iván Zulueta: Último grito (José María Íñigo)." *YouTube*, uploaded by Manu Guinarte, 11 March 2009, https://www.youtube.com/watch?v=AbcCDHzPbu8.
Jordan, Barry. "Revisiting the 'Comedia Sexy Ibérica': *No desearás al vecino del quinto*." *International Journal of Iberian Studies* 15.3 (2003): 167–86.

Juste, María Victoria Bordonaba, Laura Lucía Palacios, and Yolanda Polo Redondo. "Evolución del sistema de franquicia en España: un estudio en los sectores de moda y hostelería." *Distribución y consumo* 19.105 (2009): 64–76.
Kern, Edward. "Can It Happen Here?" *Life Magazine* 67.16 (1969): 67–77.
Kinder, Marsha. "Sex Change and Cultural Transformation in Aranda and Abril's *Cambio de sexo* (1977)." *Spanish Cinema: The Auteurist Tradition*. Edited by Peter Williams Evans, 128–46. London: Oxford, 1999.
"La droga invade los colegios." *El Alcázar* (Madrid), 23 November 1978, 1.
La ley del deseo. Directed by Pedro Almodóvar. Madrid: El deseo and Laurenfilm, 1987.
"La minifalda." *Triunfo* 209 (1966): 22–5.
"La moda de los 'mods'" *Triunfo* 116 (1964): 58–9.
"La moda, estrategia del deseo" *Triunfo* 203 (1966): 58–61.
"La moda 'ye-yé.'" *Triunfo* 128 (1964): 78–9.
La Movida. Consejería de Cultura y Deportes. Madrid: Comunidad de Madrid, 2006.
Labanyi, Jo. "Doing Things: Emotion, Affect, and Materiality." *Journal of Spanish Cultural Studies* 11 (2010): 223–33.
– "Race, Gender, and Disavowal in Spanish Cinema of the Early Franco Period: The Missionary Film and the Folkloric Musical." *Screen* 38.3 (1997): 215–31.
Labanyi, Jo, and Tatjana Pavlovic (eds.). *A Companion to Spanish Cinema*. Oxford: Wiley, 2012.
Labrador Méndez, Germán. *Culpables por la literature: imaginación política y contracultura en la transición española (1968–1986)*. Madrid: Akal, 2017.
– *Letras arrebatadas: poesía y química en la Transición española*. Madrid: Devenir, 2009.
Lange, Alexandra. "Six Leading Architects Defend the World's Most Hated Buildings." *New York Times Style Magazine*, 14 June 2015, 70–80.
Lara, Antonio. *El apasionante mundo del tebeo*. Suplemento de *Cuadernos para el Diálogo*. Madrid: Edicusa, 1968.
Lara, Fernando. "Un triunfo en nombre del arte." *Triunfo* 543 (1973): 36–7.
– "Vallecas: Las víctimas del urbanismo oficial." *Triunfo* 625 (1974): 40–3.
Larson, Susan. "Architecture, Urbanism and *la Movida madrileña*." *Back to the Future: Toward a Cultural Archive of la Movida*. Edited by William J. Nichols and H. Rosi Song, 181–201. Madison, NJ: Fairleigh-Dickinson University Press, 2013.
– "*La Luna de Madrid* y la Movida madrileña. un experimento valioso en la creación de la cultura urbana revolucionaria." *Madrid de Fortunata a la M 40: un siglo de cultural urbana*. Edited by Edward Baker and Malcolm A. Compitello, 309–26. Madrid: Alianza editorial, 2003.
Lechado, José Manuel. *La movida: una crónica de los 80*. Madrid: Algaba, 2005.

Lefebvre, Henri. *El derecho a la ciudad*. Translated by Javier González Pueyo. Barcelona: Península, 1969.

– *La revolución urbana*. Translated by Mario Nolla. Madrid: Alianza Editorial, 1972.

– *The Production of Space*. 1974. Translated by D. Nicholson-Smith. Hoboken, NJ: Wiley-Blackwell, 1992.

– *Towards an Architecture of Enjoyment*. Minneapolis: University of Minnesota Press, 2014.

– *The Urban Revolution*. Translated by Robert Bononno. Minneapolis: University of Minnesota Press, 2003.

– *Writings on the City*. Translated and edited by Eleonore Kofman and Elizabeth Lebas. Oxford: Blackwell, 1996.

Llorens, Tomás, and Helio Piñón. "La arquitectura del franquismo a propósito de una nueva interpretación." *Arquitecturas Bis* 26 (1979): 12–19.

López Díaz, Jesús. "Vivienda social y falange: ideario y construcciones en la década de los 40." *Scripta Nova: Revista Electrónica de Geografía y Ciencias Sociales* 146 (2003). http://www.ub.es/geocrit/sn/sn-146(024).htm. Accessed 16 May 2018.

Lorenzo Sanz, Ricardo, and Héctor Anabitarte. "El orgullo gay." *Triunfo* 856 (1979): 13.

"Los sábados de King's Road." *Triunfo* 189 (1966): 18–21.

Luzán, Julia. "La homosexualidad quiere salir del 'ghetto'." *Triunfo* 759 (1977): 35–7.

Lynch, Kevin. *The Image of the City*. Cambridge, MA: Harvard-MIT Press, 1960.

Mainer, José Carlos. "1975–1985: The Powers of the Past." *Literature, the Arts, and Democracy: Spain in the Eighties*. Edited by Samuel Amell, translated by Alma Amell, 16–36. London: Associated University Press, 1990.

Mainer, José Carlos, and Santos Juliá. *El aprendizaje de la libertad, 1973–1986: la cultura de la transición*. Madrid: Alianza Editorial, 2000.

Manning, Paul. *Drugs and Popular Culture: Drugs, Media and Identity in Contemporary Society*. London: Willan, 2007.

Mansilla, Pedro. "Elio Berhanyer, retrato de una marca." *Elio Berhanyer: 50 años de moda*. Madrid: Museo del Traje. Subdirección General de Publicaciones. Ministerio de cultura de España, 2009. 15–35.

Marí, Jorge. "El umbral del destape." *Valoración de Francisco Umbral (Ensayos críticos entorno a su obra)*. Edited by Jorge Marí, 242–58. Gijón: Llibros del Pexe, 2003.

– "The *Movida* as a Debate." *Back to the Future: Toward a Cultural Archive of la Movida*. Edited by William Nichols and H. Rosi Song, 19–35. Lanham, MD: Farleigh Dickinson University Press, 2013.

Márquez Reviriego, Victor. "El Madrid que se va." *Triunfo* 749 (1977): 64.

– "La ciudad en el espacio." *Triunfo* 341 (1968): 39–51.

– "Manifiesto para la supervivencia." *Triunfo* 688 (1976): 42–3.

Marsh, Stephen, and Parvati Nair. *Gender and Spanish Cinema*. Oxford and New York: Berg, 2004.

Martín, Annabel. *La gramática de la felicidad: Relecturas franquistas y posmodernas del melodrama*. Madrid: Libertarias/Prodhufi, 2005.

Martín Aceña, Pablo, and Elena Martínez Ruiz. "The Golden Age of Spanish Capitalism: Economic Growth without Political Freedom." *Spain Transformed: The Late Franco Dictatorship, 1959–75*. Edited by Nigel Townson, 30–45. New York: Palgrave, 2007.

Martín Gaite, Carmen. *Usos amorosos de la posguerra española*. Barcelona: Anagrama, 1987.

Martín Villa, Rodolfo. *Al servicio del estado*. Barcelona: Planeta, 1984.

Martínez-Expósito, Alfredo. "The *Desarrollismo* Years: The Failure of Sexualized Nationhood in 1960s Spain." *Spanish Erotic Cinema*. Edited by Santiago Fouz-Hernández, 55–73. Edinburgh: Edinburgh University Press, 2017.

– "Visibility and Performance in the Anti-Gay Sexy Spanish Comedy: *No desearás al vecino del quinto* (1970)." *The Space of Culture: Critical Readings in Hispanic Studies*. Edited by Stewart King and Jeff Browitt, 12–28. Newark: University of Delaware Press, 2004.

Marx, Karl. *Capital*. London: Penguin, 1990.

Mayer, Margit. "Manuel Castells' *The City and the Grassroots*." *International Journal of Urban and Regional Research* 30.1 (2006): 202–6.

McKeown, Kieran. "The Urban Sociology of Manuel Castells: A Critical Examination of the Central Concepts." *Economics and Social Review* 4 (1980): 257–80.

Melero, Alejandro. "Hormones and Silk: Gay Men in the Spanish Film Comedies of the Transition to Democracy (1976–1981)." *Journal of Homosexuality* 60 (2013): 1450–74.

Mendes, Valerie and Amy de la Haye. *20th Century Fashion*. London: Thames & Hudson, 1999.

Mendicutti, Eduardo. *Una mala noche la tiene cualquiera*. 1982; Barcelona: Tusquets Editores, 1988.

Mestre, Carmen. "La emancipación de la mujer: ¿conquista o alienación?" *Cuadernos para el Diálogo* 95 (1971): 11.

Mi querida señorita. Directed by Jaime de Armiñán. Madrid: El Imán, 1972.

Miguel, Marina de. "El diseño español sigue vivo en la capital tras Cibeles." *La voz de Galicia*, 21 February 2003. https://www.lavozdegalicia.es/noticia/espana/2003/02/21/diseno-espanol-continua-vivo-capital-tras-cibeles/0003_1507370.htm. Accessed 23 July 2019.

Mira, Alberto. *De Sodoma a Chueca: una historia cultural de la homosexualidad en España en el siglo XX*. Madrid: Egales, 2004.

Mira, José Eduardo. "El sistema de la moda en España." *Triunfo* 440 (1970): 26–9.

– "Ibiza, moda y anti-moda." *Triunfo* 508 (1972): 34–5.

Miranda Mata, Antonio. "Arquitectura sin arquitectos" *Triunfo* 446 (1970): 36.

– "Fábula del urbanista." *Triunfo* 445 (1971): 40.

Moneo, Rafael. "Madrid '78. 28 arquitectos no numerarios." *Arquitecturas Bis* 23/24 (1978): 22–54.

Montoto, Ángel. "*Interviú* por la ruta de las drogas 'duras': la muerte en polvo." *Interviú* 97 (1978): 23–9.

Moore, Robin. *The French Connection: A True Account of Cops, Narcotics, and International Conspiracy*. Boston, MA: Little, Brown and Co.: 1969.

Moral Ruiz, Carmen del. "El género chico y la invención de Madrid: *La Gran Vía* (1886)." *Madrid: De Fortunata a la M-40: un siglo de cultural urbana.* Edited by Edward Baker and Malcolm Compitello, 27–57. Madrid: Alianza Editiorial, 2003.

Moreno, Amparo. *Mujeres en lucha: El movimiento feminista en España. Barcelona:* Anagrama, 1977.

"Muere un joven por sobredosis de heroína." *El País* (Madrid), 12 September 1978, 12.

"Mujer 66: la nueva frontera." *Triunfo* 196 (1966): 30–7.

Muñoz, José Esteban. *Disidentifications: Queers of Color and the Performance of Politics.* Minneapolis: University of Minnesota Press, 1999.

Muñoz Soro, Javier. *Cuadernos para el Diálogo (1963–1976): una historia cultural del segundo franquismo.* Madrid: Marcial Pons, 2005.

– "Parlamentos de papel: La prensa crítica en la crisis del franquismo." *Historia de la Transición en España: los inicios del proceso democratizador*. Edited by Rafael Quirosa-Cheyrouze y Muñoz, 449–62. Madrid: Biblioteca Nueva, 2007.

Nancy, Jean-Luc. *The Inoperative Community*. Translated by Peter Connor, Lisa Garbus, Michael Holland, and Simona Sawhney. Minneapolis: University of Minnesota Press, 1991.

Negri, Antonio. "Approximations towards an Ontological Definition of the Multitude." Translated by Arianna Bove. http://www.generation-online.org/t/approximations.htm. Accessed 16 May 2018.

Neuman, Michael. *The Imaginative Institution: Planning and Governance in Madrid*. New York: Ashgate, 2010.

Nichols, William J., and H. Rosi Song (eds.). *Toward a Cultural Archive of La Movida. Back to the Future*. Teaneck, NJ: Fairleigh Dickinson University Press, 2014.

No desearás al vecino del quinto. Directed by Ramón Fernández. Madrid: Atlántida Films and Fida Cinematográfica, 1970.

"No existen datos fiables sobre intoxicados por estupefacientes." *El País* (Madrid), 13 September 1978.

Nogués, Carmen. "Las españolas no somos diferentes." *Cuadernos para el Diálogo* 52 (1968): 31.

Ocaña, retrato intermitente. Directed by Ventura Pons. Barcelona: Prozesa and Teide P.C., 1978.

Otero López, J.M. *Delincuencia y droga: concepto, medida y estado actual del conocimiento.* Madrid: Eudema, 1994.

Palomares, Cristina. "New Political Mentalities in the *Tardofranquismo.*" *Spain Transformed: The Late Franco Dictatorship, 1959–75.* Edited by Nigel Townson, 118–39. New York: Palgrave, 2007.

Pasalodos, Mercedes. "Haute Couture: High Fashion in the 50's." *Indumenta: Revista del Museo del Traje* 1 (2008): 23–48.

Pavlovic, Tatjana. *Despotic Bodies and Transgressive Bodies: Spanish Culture from Francisco Franco to Jesús Franco.* Albany: SUNY Press, 2003.

– *The Mobile Nation: España Cambia de Piel (1954–1964).* Bristol, UK: Intellect, 2010.

Pavlovic, Tatjana, Chris Perriam, and Nuria Triana Toribio. "Stars, Modernity, and Celebrity Culture." *A Companion to Spanish Cinema.* Edited by Jo Labanyi and Tatjana Pavlovic, 332–45. Oxford: Wiley, 2012.

Pena González, Pablo. "Elio Berhanyer y el diseño moderno 1968." *Modelo del mes.* Museo del Traje (2008): 1–11. http://www.culturaydeporte.gob.es/mtraje/dam/jcr:b396dbfa-3f3c-487d-908a-8c77bf5e077e/11-2008.pdf. Accessed 23 July 2019.

Pérez, Jorge. "Undressing Opus Dei: Reframing the Political Currency of *Destape* Films." *Spanish Erotic Cinema.* Edited by Santiago Fouz-Hernández, 92–108. Edinburgh: Edinburgh University Press, 2017.

Pérez Minik, Domingo. "Susan Sontag nos cuenta una ordalía histórica." *Ínsula* 275.6 (1969): 21.

Pérez Quintana, Vicente, and Pablo Sánchez León. *Memoria ciudadana y movimiento vecinal: Madrid, 1968–2008.* Madrid: Los libros de la catarata, 2008.

Pérez Sánchez, Gema. *Queer Transitions in Contemporary Spanish Culture: From Franco to La Movida.* Albany: State University of New York Press, 2007.

Pero ... ¡en qué país vivimos! Directed by José Luis Sáenz de Heredia. Madrid: Arturo González Producciones Cinematográficas, 1967.

Platero, Raquel. "The Narratives of Transgender Rights Mobilization in Spain." *Sexualities* 14.5 (2011): 597–614.

"Prêt-à-porter." *Triunfo* 44 (1963): 66–9.

Prieto, Rafael. *La participación social y política de los jóvenes.* Madrid: Instituto de la juventud, 1985.

Quaggio, Giulia. *La cultura en transición: reconciliación y política cultural en España, 1976–1986.* Madrid: Alianza editorial, 2014.

Racionero, Luis. "La vivienda, función o rito: ¿Por qué se caen las casas?" *Triunfo* 442 (1970): 15.

– "Reencuentro: Arquitectura sin arquitectos y con arquitectos." *Triunfo* 449 (1971): 32–3.

"Racismo y antifeminismo." *Triunfo* 401 (1970): 7.

Radcliff, Pamela. *Making Democratic Citizens in Spain: Civil Society and the Popular Origins of the Transition, 1960–78*. New York: Palgrave Macmillan, 2011.

Recuperar Madrid. Madrid: Ayuntamiento de Madrid. Oficina municipal del Plan, 1982.

Redi, Ricardo. "El camino de las drogas pasa por vía Veneto." *Triunfo* 73 (1963): 8–17.

Reguera, Javier. "Miguel Trillo, identidades y miradas a la vuelta de la esquina." *Así se fundó Carbany Street*. 27 April 2010. https://carnabys.blogspot.com/2010/04/miguel-trillo-identidades-y-miradas-la.html. Accessed 23 July 2019.

Revista de Occidente 27–8 (1983).

Ribas, José. *Los 70 A destajo: Ajoblanco y libertad*. Barcelona: RBA, 2007.

Richardson, Nathan. *Constructing Spain: The Re-imagination of Space and Place in Fiction and Film, 1953–2003*. Lewisburg, PA: Bucknell University Press, 2011.

Rico, Eduardo. "Feminismo contra liberación." *Triunfo* 333 (1968): 7.

– "Susan Sontag revisionista." *Triunfo* 393 (1969): 54.

Ríos, Alfonso de los. "La ciudad Utópica." *Triunfo* 393 (1969): 54–5.

Rivière, Margarita. *La moda: ¿comunicación o incomunicación?* Barcelona: Gustavo Gili, 1977.

– "Las monas vestidas de seda." *Triunfo* 454 (1971): 16–21.

– "Una escuela de moda española." *ABC* (Madrid), 20 May 1972: 51.

Robbins, Jill. *Cruising Through Chueca. Lesbian Literary Culture in Queer Madrid*. Minneapolis: University of Minnesota Press, 2011.

– (ed.). "An Introduction, Postmodern by Design: Spectacle, Fashion, and Fashion Plates in Post-Franco Spain." *P/herversions: Critical Studies of Ana Rossetti*. Lewisburg, PA: Bucknell University Press, 2004.

Rodríguez García, José María. "Manuel María's Poetry." *Modern Language Quarterly* (2014): 541–75.

Rodríguez Villasante, Tomás. *Las democracias participativas: de la participación ciudadana a las alternativas de sociedad*. Madrid: HOAC, 1995.

– *Los vecinos en la calle: por una alternativa democrática a la ciudad de los monopolios*. Madrid: Ediciones de la Torre, 1976.

Rosendorf, Neal. *Franco Sells Spain to America: Hollywood, Tourism, and Public Relations as Postwar Spanish Soft Power*. New York: Palgrave, 2014.

Roy, Claude. "El paraíso artificial." *Triunfo* 385 (1969): 31–3.

Sáinz Gutiérrez, Victoriano. *El proyecto urbano en España: génesis y desarrollo de un urbanismo de los arquitectos*. Seville: Servicio de publicaciones de la Universidad de Sevilla, 2006.

Salas, Roger. "La ropa no es importante, lo que queda son las personas que hay detrás." *El País* (Madrid), 8 February 2004. https://elpais.com/diario/2004/02/08/espectaculos/1076194802_850215.html. Accessed 23 July 2019.

Salaün, Serge. "Defensa e ilustración de la canción popular según Vázquez Montalbán." *Manuel Vázquez Montalbán: el compromiso con la memoria*. Edited by José Colmeiro, 35–51. Rochester, NY: Tamesis, 2007.

Sambricio, Carlos. "A propósito de la arquitectura del franquismo, Carlos Sambricio responde a Tomás Llorens y Helio Piñón." *Arquitecturas Bis* 27 (1979): 25–9.

– *Madrid, vivienda y urbanismo, 1900–1960*. Madrid: Akal, 2004

Santiáñez-Tió, Nil. "El fascista y la ciudad." *Madrid: de Fortunata a la M-40. Un siglo de cultural urbana*. Edited by Edward Baker and Malcolm Compitello, 197–238. Madrid: Alianza Editiorial, 2003.

Santo-Domingo, Joaquín. "Historia de las adicciones y su abordaje en España." *Historia de las adicciones en la España contemporánea*. Edited by Miguel Ángel Torres, Joaquín Santo-Domingo, Francisco Pascual, Francesc Freixa and Carlos Álvarez, 37–82. Madrid: Ministerio de Sanidad y Consumo, 2008.

– "Los drogadictos." *Cuadernos para el Diálogo* 27 (1972): 31–8.

– "Memoria del grupo de trabajo para el estudio de los problemas derivados del alcoholismo y del tráfico y consumo de estupefacientes. *Revista de Sanidad e Higiene Pública* 49.5–6 (1975): 409–573.

Santos, Félix. "Drogas y subversion." *Cuadernos para el Diálogo* 81–2 (1970): 52.

Santos Fontenla, César. "Swinging London: Carnaby Street centro mundial de la moda joven." *Triunfo* 231 (1966): 34–44.

Sefer. "La droga no mata." *Disco Expres* 485.21 (July 1978): 10–11.

Sevillano Calero, Francisco. *Propaganda y medios de comunicación en el franquismo*. Alicante: Universidad de Alicante, 1998.

"Sexo salvaje o domesticado." *Triunfo* 371 (1969): 8.

"Sexo y U.R.S.S. I" *Triunfo* 365 (1969): 5.

"Sexo y U.R.S.S. II" *Triunfo* 369 (1969): 9.

Sieburth, Stephanie. *Survival Songs: Conchita Piquer's 'Coplas' and Franco's Regime of Terror*. Toronto: University of Toronto Press, 2014.

Smith, Paul Julian. *The Moderns: Time, Space, and Subjectivity in Contemporary Spanish Culture*. Oxford: Oxford University Press, 2000.

Snyder, Jonathan. *Poetics of Opposition in Contemporary Spain: Politics and the Work of Urban Culture*. New York: Palgrave Macmillan, 2015.

Sontag, Susan. *Contra la interpretación*. Translated by Javier González-Pueyo. Barcelona: Seix Barral, 1969.

– "Notes on Camp." http://faculty.georgetown.edu/irvinem/theory/Sontag-NotesOnCamp-1964.html. Accessed 6 December 2016.

Stallybrass, Peter, and Allon White. *The Politics and Poetics of Transgression.* Ithaca, NY: Cornell University Press, 1986.

Stapell, Hamilton. *Remaking Madrid: Culture, Politics and Identity after Franco.* New York: Palgrave, 2010.

Steen, Joan. "Un mundo de pesadilla." *Triunfo* 49 (1963): 12–15.

Subirats, Eduardo. "De la transición al espectáculo." *Quimera* 188–9 (2000): 21–6.

Suzanne. "Bessart, una moda para el sol del otoño." *Triunfo* 19 (1962): 66–9.

– "La moda de 1962 adivina lo que sueñan las muchachas." *Triunfo* 19 (1962): 92–5.

Tapia, Rosa. "Cuerpo, transición y nación en *Una mala noche la tiene cualquiera.*" *Una ética de la libertad: la narrativa de Eduardo Mendicutti.* Edited by José Jurado Morales, 83–96. Madrid: Visor Libros, 2012.

Terán, Fernando de. "Crecimiento urbano y planeamiento de Madrid." *La Revista de Occidente* 27–8 (1983): 151–67.

– *Madrid.* Madrid: Mapfre, 1992.

– *Planeamiento urbano en la España contemporánea (1900–1980).* Madrid: Alianza, 1978.

Tezanos, José Félix. "Delincuencia y desarrollo español: ¿Por qué crece la delincuencia juvenil?" *Cuadernos para el Diálogo* 31 (1973): 18–20.

Tierno Galván, Enrique. "Declaración de propósitos: el primer discurso del nuevo Alcalde." *Villa de Madrid* 63 (1979): 6–8.

Toboso Sánchez, Pilar. *Grandes almacenes y almacenes populares en España: una visión histórica.* Fundación SEPI. Documentos de trabajo 2002. ftp://ftp.fundacionsepi.es/phe/hdt2002_2.pdf. Accessed 16 May 2018.

– "Posguerra y ciudad, la memoria del comercio perdido." *Ería* 91 (2013): 111–28.

Torre-Velver, Narciso de la. "La homosexualidad masculina." *Triunfo* 770 (1977): 38–9.

Torrente Ballester, Gonzalo. "El erotismo en la calle y aledaños." *Triunfo* 434 (1979): 43–6.

Torres, Steven. "Las contradicciones del cine Quinqui en el seno de la reconfiguración del estado neoliberal." *Fuera de la ley: asedios al fenómeno quinqui en la Transición española.* Edited by Joaquín Florido Berrocal, Luis Martín-Cabrera, Eduardo Matos-Martín, and Roberto Robles Valencia, 67–90. Granada: Editorial Comares, 2015.

Tortella, Gabriel. *The Development of Modern Spain: An Economic History of the Nineteenth and Twentieth Centuries.* Cambridge, MA: Harvard University Press, 2000.

Townson, Nigel, (ed.). *Spain Transformed: The Late Franco Dictatorship, 1959–75.* New York: Palgrave, 2007.
United Press International. "1500 millones en drogas." *Triunfo* 26 (1962): 30–3.
"Urbanismo y sociedad en España." Special issue of *Cuadernos para el Diálogo* 19 (April 1970).
Uría, Leopoldo. "Los escasos ejemplos de la memoria urbana." *El País* (Madrid), 27 March 1977.
Usó, Juan Carlos. *Drogas y cultura de masas (España 1855–1995).* Madrid: Taurus, 1996.
– *¿Nos matan con heroína? Sobre la intoxicación farmacológica como arma de Estado.* Leioa: Libros Crudos, 2015.
Valtueña, José Antonio. "Juventud y drogas." *Triunfo* 525 (1973): 36–7.
– "La hipocresía de la lucha contra las drogas." *Triunfo* 663 (1975): 39.
Vanaclocha, José. "Entre la represión y el destape: cine 'erótico' español." *Triunfo* 637 (1975): 22–35.
Vaquero Argüelles, Isabel. "El reinado de la Alta Costura: la moda de la primera mitad del siglo XX." *Indumenta: Revista del Museo del Traje* 0 (2007): 123–34.
Vaz, Céline "'*Les Pyrénées séparent et relient la France et l'Espagne*': Henri Lefebvre et la question urbaine espagnole à la fin du franquisme." *L'homme et la société* 185–6 (2012): 83–103.
Vázquez Montalbán, Manuel. *Crónica sentimental de España.* Barcelona: Lumen, 1970.
– "Crónica sentimental de España I: los años cuarenta." *Triunfo* 380 (1969): 30–6.
– "Crónica sentimental de España II: casi todo en tecnicolor." *Triunfo* 381 (1969): 29–35.
– "Crónica sentimental de España III: cuando Di Stéfano y Kubala llenaban los estadios." *Triunfo* 382 (1969): 29–35.
– "Crónica sentimental de España IV: los felices sesenta." *Triunfo* 383 (1969): 35–40.
– "Crónica sentimental de España V: American way of life." *Triunfo* 384 (1969): 40–3.
– "El penúltimo tango en Perpignan." *Triunfo* 545 (1973): 46–7.
Verdú, Vicente. "Cambio social: turismo-sex." *Cuadernos para el Diálogo* 121 (1973): 69.
Vernon, Kathleen M. "Memoria histórica y cultura popular: Vázquez Montalbán y la resistencia española." *Manuel Vázquez Montalbán: El compromiso con la memoria.* Edited by José Colmeiro, 21–33. Rochester, NY: Tamesis, 2007.

Vilarós, Teresa. *El mono del desencanto: una crítica cultural a la transición española (1973–1993)*. Madrid: Siglo Veintiuno, 1998.
Villamandos, Alberto. *El discreto encanto de la subversión: una crítica cultural de la Gauche Divine*. Pamplona: Laetoli, 2011.
Walmsley, Roy. *World Prison Population List*. 8th ed. London: International Centre for Prison Studies at King's College, 2009.
Williams, Raymond. *Marxism and Literature*. London: Oxford University Press, 1977.
Young, Bill. "Spain at nywf64." 6 March 2012. http://nywf64.com/spain01.shtml. Accessed 16 May 2018.

Index

Adorno and Horkheimer, 119–20
affect, 9–11, 53, 92, 110–19
agency, 6, 90, 120
AIDS. *See* HIV/AIDS
alcohol, 73–4
Almodóvar, Pedro, 66, 68, 89
alta costura, 14, 15, 91–9, 105–15. *See also* fashion
alternative culture: 8, 15, 18, 42, 81, 122; gender roles and sexualities, 43, 57, 62, 121; lifestyles, 54, 67, 92, 119
Alvarado, Antonio, 110, 115
Anarcoma, 68
Ándersen, Bibi, 55, 60, 61. *See also* Fernández, Bibiana
architects: 12, 18–28, 37–40, 110–13; as cultural agents, 21, 24, 26
associations: athenaeum, 9; communes, 9; consumer organizations, 28; cooperatives, 8, 18; ecological organizations, 28; historical preservation societies, 28; housewives associations, 28, 44; neighbourhood, 8, 12, 17–21, 27–36, 40; parents, 8; pensioners clubs, 28; radio stations, 18; schools, 18; shopkeepers groups, 28; sports clubs, 28; women's groups, 28; youth groups, 28
Athens Charter, 25
autarky, 6, 93
avant-garde: culture, 117–22; fashion, 98, 102

Balenciaga, Cristóbal, 91, 94–5, 112
Barcelona: as urban model, 7, 22, 24; fashion, 101, 107, 108; gay and trans, 42, 61, 65; *Quinqui*, 83, 85, 86
Barthes, Roland, 92, 97, 104
Bastida, Asunción, 94, 107, 112
Berhanyer, Elio 106, 108, 112
body: commodification of, 13, 42, 43, 59, 60, 67; politic, 66; transgender, 55, 57, 61, 63, 66, 67; women's, 13, 42, 43, 52
Bourdieu, Pierre, 97
bourgeoisie, 26, 47, 92, 100–3, 105, 108–12
boutiques, 97, 100–4

Cambio de sexo, 55, 57, 60, 61, 67
camp, 11, 65–6, 68
capitalism, 9, 13, 20, 25–9, 47–52, 103–5; consumer capitalism,

7, 119. *See also* neo-capitalism; neoliberal
Capmany, Maria Aurèlia, 45, 47, 48, 49, 50, 52, 58
Cardin, Pierre, 98–100
Castells, Manuel, 12, 20, 28, 29
Catholic culture, 6, 43, 46, 67, 59, 76
censorship, 51, 53, 57–9
Cine Quinqui, 82–4
city: alternative, 29; centre, 22, 29, 30, 34–7, 81; civil society, 16, 18, 75; as experience, 24; as living organism, 22; problems and challenges, 22–3, 30; as utopia, 22, 25. *See also* associations
civil war. *See* Spanish Civil War
class struggle and conflict, 24, 28, 92, 99, 102, 113–15
cocaine, 85, 86
collective consciousness and imaginary, 41, 121. *See also* public consciousness
collective sensibility, 4, 8–13, 40–3, 59, 67, 91–2, 101, 111–21. *See also* sensibility
comedia sexy, 13, 44, 51–3, 59, 68
comics, 82
communist, 29, 32, 37, 67
Communist Party, 12, 18, 20, 30, 44, 65. *See also* Partido Comunista de España
community, 18, 31, 62, 112; pluralistic, 42, 44, 64–8
conspiracy theory, 72, 76, 81, 86
consumption: as bonding, 102, 111; culture of, 16, 46, 48, 49, 51, 59, 92; democratization of, 95, 108, 116, 120; of drugs, 75, 77, 80, 81, 84, 88–90; of fashion, 104, 108; as form of coercion, 48–9; new practices of, 97, 100, 105
Corte Inglés, El, 97. *See also* department stores
cosmopolitan modernity, 92, 112, 121
counterculture, 10, 40, 76, 80, 104, 120–1
Courrèges, André, 94, 95, 100, 109, 111, 113
couturiers, 95, 99, 106, 107, 108, 112. *See also* fashion
crime, 74, 82. *See also* delinquency
cross-dressing, 44, 64, 65
Crumbaugh, Justin, 51, 53
Cuadernos para el diálogo, 5, 8, 23, 27, 43–5, 67, 121
cultural imaginary, 18, 77, 92, 112, 116
cultural system, 119–20

delinquency, 82, 85, 87. *See also* crime
democracy: 3, 6, 23, 29, 36, 99, 116–21; institutions, 20, 30; participatory, 29, 47
democratization: of consumption, 95, 97; of fashion, 105–6; of lifestyles, 116; political, 8, 113
department stores, 15, 92, 94, 97–8, 100–1
desarrollismo, el, 6, 33, 52, 76, 116
design, 94, 104, 110, 111, 115. *See also* fashion
destape, el, 13, 42–4, 58, 60, 68, 83
development plans, 6. See also *desarrollismo*; *Plan de estabilización*
Domínguez, Adolfo, 110
drag, 64, 68
drugs: addiction, 72–4, 83, 87; consequences and health risk, 69, 70, 87; escapism, 76–8, 89; hard, 84, 85; over-the-counter, 72, 79; prevention, 75–6; recreational use, 69, 70, 72, 78; representation of, 70, 82, 84; social control, 72, 76, 86–8, 90; soft, 84; traffic, 71, 75, 80; treatment, 73–5, 84–85; use and abuse, 4, 9, 16, 50, 69, 73–5, 84–9, 106, 117–21

economy, the, 5, 6, 76
education: formal, 55, 76, 80, 83, 90, 117; sex, 47–50
elections: general 1977, 65; general 1982, 37; municipal 1978, 17, 32; municipal 1983, 37
equality, 65–8, 99, 119
erotic films and magazines, 57–63
eroticism, 48–50, 59

Falange, 19, 25, 32
fanzines, 82
fashion: 9, 10, 46, 91, 102, 111, 117–20; *alta costura*, 14, 15, 91–9, 105–15; as commodity, 104, 105, 109; design, 4, 15–16, 95, 97, 121; designers, 91, 92, 95, 98, 100–1, 106–15; fashion studies, 15, 92, 104; fast, 110; houses, 99, 100; as identity, 14, 91, 108–10; industry, 15, 92–9, 104–12; mass market, 97, 99, 105, 109; as politics, 102–3; shows, 94, 104–7; Spanish, 93, 95, 108–12
female desire, 54
feminism, 13, 42–50, 59–61, 68
Fernández Alba, Antonio, 12, 24–7, 29, 112–13
Fernández, Bibiana, 55, 60, 61
films: 13, 43, 51, 52, 57–60, 67, 70, 82–3, 88; commercial, 44, 45, 55; critics 13, 43
Fraga, Manuel, 3, 75, 94
Franco, Francisco, 3; death of, 6, 69, 75, 116, 121
Franco regime, 3–12, 26, 33–8, 93–5, 116, 120
free expression, 43, 59
freedom, 15, 42, 66, 89, 90–1, 99, 116–19
French fashion, 98, 107–11

Galerías Preciados, 97. *See also* department stores
gay liberation, 62
Gay Pride Day, 42, 61–2, 65
gender: bending, 44; bias, 55; equality, 46, 102; expression, 52; roles, 47, 48, 62, 116, 121; social construction of, 55, 57
gentrification, 37
Guardia Civil, 63, 75

Haro Ibars, Eduardo, 15, 80, 86–9, 106, 115, 118–21
hashish, 73, 80, 82
haute couture, 97, 98, 111, 113. See also *alta costura*
health care system, 70, 73, 75
heroin: 14, 69, 72–90, 106; as commodity, 81–82, 87; crisis, 88; epidemic, 73, 75, 81, 90
heteronormativity, 46, 54, 55, 60, 65
hippies, 87, 104, 111
HIV/AIDS, 76, 81
homoeroticism, 44
homophobia, 51–2, 61
homosexual characters in films, 14, 51, 52
homosexuality, 44, 50–1, 54, 80
housing, 22, 25–6, 30–1, 36, 40

identity: 16, 69, 75, 91, 108–12, 119–21; collective, 77–9, 93, 112, 122; cultural, 29, 31, 77, 89, 110; political, 65, 89
immigration, 22, 25, 41, 89, 117
industry: 34, 49, 87, 92, 93; fashion, 93–4, 97, 99, 103–12; garment manufacture, 93, 97, 109; textile, 93, 97, 108–10
inseguridad ciudadana, 82
intellectuals, 8, 77–9, 101
international styles, 91–4, 98, 102, 109–13, 120
international trends, 4–16, 90, 97, 102, 111–13, 116–20
Interviú, 60, 85, 88

journals, 5, 21–2, 37–8, 44. *See individual journals by title*
junkies, 80, 85
juvenile delinquency, 83. *See also* crime; delinquency

Labanyi, Jo, 9, 53, 118
Labrador Méndez, Germán, 7–10, 121–2
Larson, Susan, 37–8, 118
Lefebvre, Henri, 12, 19, 22–3, 92, 97
lesbian, 58, 60; organizations, 61
Ley de Peligrosidad y Rehabilitación Social, 73
Ley de prensa, 7
LGTBQ, 14, 42–4, 66–8
lifestyles, 5–6, 54, 67, 72, 89, 116
literature, 10, 47, 87, 88, 89
London, 85–6, 101–3
Luna de Madrid, La, 38–9

machismo, 45–6, 53, 60–1
macho ibérico, 51–3
Madrid: anti–city, 25, 29; architectural heritage, 18, 19, 26, 36, 37, 38; barrios, 18, 22–3, 28–36, 8081; as capital, 9, 30, 78, 117; centre, 22, 29–31, 34–9; countercultural hub, 7, 15, 68, 104; fashion, 103; living conditions, 21, 34; metropolitan area, 31, 32, 34; as modern city, 21, 54, 116; municipal government and services, 17, 19, 23–34, 41; public perception of, 12, 13, 28; reclaimed and appropriated, 12, 17, 23, 25, 39; reimagined, 18, 29–33, 36, 39, 118; School of Architecture, 21, 34
magazines, 8–14, 21, 43–5, 105, 109, 121
marketing, 49, 97, 103
Martínez–Expósito, Alfredo, 52, 60, 62
masculinity, 46, 51–4, 81
mass culture, 4
mass market fashion. *See* fashion
mass production, 97, 104–5, 109
mass society, 100
material culture, 50, 93
May '68, 87
media: 4–16, 40–4, 51–3, 62–70, 84–90, 110–22; fashion press, 105, 109–10; print, 17, 40–5, 73, 85, 90, 121; television, 3–10, 105, 108, 121. *See also* films
Mendicutti, Eduardo, 14, 44, 63
Mi querida señorita, 14, 54–7, 60, 67
middle class, 3–8, 80, 89, 91–109, 117
miniskirt, 95, 102, 106
Ministerio de Información y Turismo, 3
Miyake, Issey, 91, 113, 115
modern, 3–16, 108, 111–21
modernist, 19, 25–6, 33, 40
modernity, 3–15, 37, 46–9, 68, 90–2, 100–2, 116–17
mods, 98, 111, 112
Montesinos, Francis, 91, 110
morals, 43, 74, 88, 102, 106, 116. *See also* traditional values and morality
morphine, 70, 72, 80
Movida, la, 15–17, 44, 67–8, 78, 86, 91, 103, 111, 115–16, 118, 121
movies. *See* films

Nazario, 68
neo-capitalism, 48, 55. *See also* capitalism
neoliberalism, 6, 19. *See also* capitalism
No desearás al vecino del quinto, 14, 51–7, 67
No-Dos (*Noticieros y Documentales*), 84, 94, 102, 106, 107, 109
nudity, 42, 43, 59

objectification, 13, 60
Ocaña, 62, 65
opioids, 71–3, 81, 84, 87
opium, 70, 80, 85, 86, 88
opposition and resistance to Franco regime, 8, 23, 64, 73, 92, 117
Ortega y Gasset, José, 47, 92
overdose, 70, 82, 85

painkillers, 75
Partido Comunista de España (PCE), 12, 18, 20, 30. *See also* Communist Party
Partido Socialista Obrero Español (PSOE), 7, 18, 37. *See also* Socialist Party
patriarchy, 43–9, 52, 55, 104
Pavlovic, Tatjana, 5, 6, 8, 52, 117, 118
Pérez Sánchez, Gema, 63, 64
Pérez, Jorge, 42
Pero ... ¡en qué país vivimos!, 45, 48, 49
Pertegaz, Manuel, 94, 106, 108
pharmaceuticals, 14, 71–9, 89, 90
pharmacy, 70, 71, 81
Piña, Manuel, 91, 110, 113, 115
Plan de Estabilización, 93. *See also* development plans; *desarrollismo*
Plan General de Ordenación Urbana de Madrid, 32–7, 40
Plan Nacional Sobre las Drogas, 76
pluralism, 42–4, 64–9, 116–17. *See also* community
political parties, 29, 40, 64, 103. *See parties by name*
politicians, 25, 27, 104
politics, 5–12, 62–4, 118–19
pollution, 31–2, 34
popular culture, 6–11, 40, 66, 118–20
pornography, 43, 50, 58, 59
porros, 80
Pozo, Jesús del, 91, 110, 115
prêt-à-porter, 14, 91, 94–9, 100–08, 112–13
private property, 24, 25, 28, 30
private sphere, 9, 13
professionals, 4, 21, 24, 27–9, 41, 70, 75, 86
psychosis, 82–3
psychotropic drugs, 73, 75, 88
public consciousness, 82. *See also* collective consciousness and imaginary
public participation, 23, 29, 36
public space, 8, 13–16, 23–6, 31, 37, 39–42, 64–6
public sphere, 5–14, 18–24, 43–5, 55–6, 79, 102, 111, 116–21
public transport, 19, 24, 32, 36
publicity and promotion, 24, 36, 94, 113
punk, 106, 111, 115

Quant, Mary, 92, 100–1
queer characters in film, 63

Rabanne, Paco, 94, 100, 109, 111, 113
Radio Futura, 111–12
ready–to–wear. *See* prêt-à-porter
rebellious identities, 8, 14, 69
regional planning, 22
resettlements units, 22, 30, 33, 36
Right to the City, 12, 19, 22, 23, 35, 41
Rivière, Margarita, 92–3, 95, 99, 104–5, 108–12
Robbins, Jill, 63, 67
Rocafort, Juanjo, 107
rockers, 98, 111, 112
Rock-Ola, 115
Rodríguez, Pedro, 94, 106, 108
rollo, el, 78
Rovira, Pedro, 106, 108
Ruiz de la Prada, Ágatha, 91, 110, 115
rural, 3, 7, 10, 117

Saint Laurent, Yves, 100, 107
same-sex: desire, 54, 67, 83; relationships, 53, 54, 83
Santo-Domingo, Joaquín, 73, 75, 77, 80, 82, 84, 87
schools, 19, 48, 50, 85, 117. *See also* education
Second Vatican Council, 117
sedatives, 72, 81
sensibility, new, 4–15, 40, 90–2, 117–22
sex, 47, 54, 67, 83, 118; education, 47, 48, 50
sex and gender: desire, 42, 43, 54, 67, 83; identity, 4, 9, 56, 121; liberation, 13–14, 42–4, 48–51, 54–5, 59–61, 68; practices, 50; repression, 43, 48–9, 58; revolution, 43, 49
sex change, 55–6, 60; surgery, 56, 57, 60
shantytown. *See* slums
slums, 22, 30, 36, 41
social agent, 28, 37
social alarm, 82, 85
social control, 27, 90
Socialist Party, 7, 18, 37. *See also* Partido Socialista Obrero Español
Sontag, Susan, 9, 11, 12, 16, 105
Spanish Civil War, 19, 22
spectacle, 77
speculation, 21, 25–8, 30, 33
street fashion and styles, 104–5, 111, 113
style, 100–2, 104–5, 109–13, 118
subcultures, 4, 74, 89–90, 98, 111–13, 121
subversive, 53, 64–5, 89, 90, 119
Sybilla, 91, 110, 115

taboo, 51, 59, 62, 67
tailors and dressmakers, 92, 94, 98, 100–1, 115
taste, 11, 92, 97, 100, 105–13, 118
television: 3–10, 105, 108, 121; ownership, 6, 7; Televisión Española (TVE), 3, 4, 10, 16, 120
television programs: *Tele–Club Campo-Pop*, 3, 4, 7, 10, 11, 120; *Último grito*, 4, 120
Tierno Galván, Enrique, 17–19, 35–9, 76, 118
tourism, 5–6, 24, 66, 93–4, 97, 117
traditional values and morality, 13, 43–52, 66–7, 77, 90, 109, 116–20. *See also* morals
traffic, 24, 27, 29, 30, 31, 34, 37
transgender, 14, 44, 54–7, 60–1, 64–6, 68
transgression, 52, 53, 79, 89
Transition to Democracy, the, 4–9, 42–4, 61–6, 76, 108, 116
transition, 55, 57, 60–1, 62, 65
transvestite, 55, 63
Triunfo, 5, 8, 15, 21, 27; on drugs, 67, 71; on fashion, 97, 98–102, 106, 121; on sex and gender, 43, 44, 47–50

Una mala noche la tiene cualquiera, 14, 44, 63–7
underground culture, 4, 5, 7, 8, 10, 15, 44, 67, 121
unemployment, 76, 78
Unión de Centro Democrático (UCD), 35
upper class, 80, 88, 89, 92, 100, 102
upward mobility, 89, 97
urban planning, development, and theories, 4–13, 17–28, 32–41, 80
urban social movements, 7, 17–21, 27–30, 35–6, 40–1, 117. *See also* associations
Usó, Juan Carlos, 70, 72

value system, 4, 9, 13, 48, 66, 117, 121. *See also* traditional values and morality
Vázquez Montalbán, Manuel, 10, 11, 58, 116–21
violence, 82, 83

Western societies and culture, 4–13, 50–1, 111–12, 116
Williams, Raymond, 9, 117
women, 13–14, 28, 43, 44, 116. *See also* feminism
women's groups, 28, 44
women's liberation. *See* feminism
women's rights, 43, 44, 54
working class, 19, 78–9, 81–4, 89, 90
World's Fairs: Brussels, 139n8; New York, 93, 94

yé-yé, 98, 100, 111
yonqui. *See* junkies
youth: culture, 4–10, 98, 104–5, 120–2; groups and organizations, 28, 75; market, 94, 99–100, 104–5; rebelliousness, 42, 74, 81, 84, 90, 91, 103, 111; Spanish, 4–10
YouTube, 16

Zara, 104, 110
zeitgeist, 68, 115
Zulueta, Ivan, 82, 123n4

TORONTO IBERIC

1 Anthony J. Cascardi, *Cervantes, Literature, and the Discourse of Politics*
2 Jessica A. Boon, *The Mystical Science of the Soul: Medieval Cognition in Bernardino de Laredo's Recollection Method*
3 Susan Byrne, *Law and History in Cervantes'* Don Quixote
4 Mary E. Barnard and Frederick A. de Armas (eds), *Objects of Culture in the Literature of Imperial Spain*
5 Nil Santiáñez, *Topographies of Fascism: Habitus, Space, and Writing in Twentieth-Century Spain*
6 Nelson Orringer, *Lorca in Tune with Falla: Literary and Musical Interludes*
7 Ana M. Gómez-Bravo, *Textual Agency: Writing Culture and Social Networks in Fifteenth-Century Spain*
8 Javier Irigoyen-García, *The Spanish Arcadia: Sheep Herding, Pastoral Discourse, and Ethnicity in Early Modern Spain*
9 Stephanie Sieburth, *Survival Songs: Conchita Piquer's* Coplas *and Franco's Regime of Terror*
10 Christine Arkinstall, *Spanish Female Writers and the Freethinking Press, 1879–1926*
11 Margaret Boyle, *Unruly Women: Performance, Penitence, and Punishment in Early Modern Spain*
12 Evelina Gužauskytė, *Christopher Columbus's Naming in the* diarios *of the Four Voyages (1492–1504): A Discourse of Negotiation*
13 Mary E. Barnard, *Garcilaso de la Vega and the Material Culture of Renaissance Europe*
14 William Viestenz, *By the Grace of God: Francoist Spain and the Sacred Roots of Political Imagination*
15 Michael Scham, Lector Ludens*: The Representation of Games and Play in Cervantes*
16 Stephen Rupp, *Heroic Forms: Cervantes and the Literature of War*
17 Enrique Fernández, *Anxieties of Interiority and Dissection in Early Modern Spain*

18 Susan Byrne, *Ficino in Spain*
19 Patricia M. Keller, *Ghostly Landscapes: Film, Photography, and the Aesthetics of Haunting in Contemporary Spanish Culture*
20 Carolyn A. Nadeau, *Food Matters: Alonso Quijano's Diet and the Discourse of Food in Early Modern Spain*
21 Cristian Berco, *From Body to Community: Venereal Disease and Society in Baroque Spain*
22 Elizabeth R. Wright, *The Epic of Juan Latino: Dilemmas of Race and Religion in Renaissance Spain*
23 Ryan D. Giles, *Inscribed Power: Amulets and Magic in Early Spanish Literature*
24 Jorge Pérez, *Confessional Cinema: Religion, Film, and Modernity in Spain's Development Years (1960–1975)*
25 Joan Ramon Resina, *Josep Pla: Seeing the World in the Form of Articles*
26 Javier Irigoyen-García, *"Moors Dressed as Moors": Clothing, Social Distinction, and Ethnicity in Early Modern Iberia*
27 Jean Dangler, *Edging toward Iberia*
28 Ryan D. Giles and Steven Wagschal (eds), *Beyond Sight: Engaging the Senses in Iberian Literatures and Cultures, 1200–1750*
29 Silvia Bermúdez, *Rocking the Boat: Migration and Race in Contemporary Spanish Music*
30 Hilaire Kallendorf, *Ambiguous Antidotes: Virtue as Vaccine for Vice in Early Modern Spain*
31 Leslie Harkema, *Spanish Modernism and the Poetics of Youth: From Miguel de Unamuno to* La Joven Literatura
32 Benjamin Fraser, *Cognitive Disability Aesthetics: Visual Culture, Disability Representations, and the (In)Visibility of Cognitive Difference*
33 Robert Patrick Newcomb, *Iberianism and Crisis: Spain and Portugal at the Turn of the Twentieth Century*
34 Sara J. Brenneis, *Spaniards in Mauthausen: Representations of a Nazi Concentration Camp, 1940–2015*
35 Silvia Bermúdez and Roberta Johnson (eds), *A New History of Iberian Feminisms*
36 Steven Wagschal, *Minding Animals in the Old and New Worlds: A Cognitive Historical Analysis*
37 Heather Bamford, *Cultures of the Fragment: Uses of the Iberian Manuscript, 1100–1600*
38 Enrique García Santo-Tomás (ed), *Science on Stage in Early Modern Spain*
39 Marina Brownlee (ed), *Cervantes'* Persiles *and the Travails of Romance*
40 Sarah Thomas, *Inhabiting the In-Between: Childhood and Cinema in Spain's Long Transition*

41 David A. Wacks, *Medieval Iberian Crusade Fiction and the Mediterranean World*
42 Rosilie Hernández, *Immaculate Conceptions: The Power of the Religious Imagination in Early Modern Spain*
43 Mary Coffey and Margot Versteeg (eds), *Imagined Truths: Realism in Modern Spanish Literature and Culture*
44 Diana Aramburu, *Resisting Invisibility: Detecting the Female Body in Spanish Crime Fiction*
45 Samuel Amago and Matthew J. Marr (eds), *Consequential Art: Comics Culture in Contemporary Spain*
46 Richard P. Kinkade, *Dawn of a Dynasty: The Life and Times of Infante Manuel of Castile*
47 Jill Robbins, *Poetry and Crisis: Cultural Politics and Citizenship in the Wake of the Madrid Bombings*
48 Ana María Laguna and John Beusterien (eds), *Goodbye Eros: Recasting Forms and Norms of Love in the Age of Cervantes*
49 Sara J. Brenneis and Gina Herrmann (eds), *Spain, World War II, and the Holocaust: History and Representation*
50 Francisco Fernández de Alba, *Sex, Drugs, and Fashion in 1970s Madrid*

www.ingramcontent.com/pod-product-compliance
Lightning Source LLC
LaVergne TN
LVHW090200080826
844660LV00013B/886/J
9781487501488